IDENTITY CRISIS

Discover your purpose,
defeat the lies of the enemy,
and win the battle for your identity.

APRIL TELEE SYKES

For a free online study guide please visit:

AprilTeleeSykes.com

This study guide is designed to help readers analyze material,
stimulate dialogue, and facilitate application of knowledge.

Identity Crisis: Discover your purpose, defeat the lies of the enemy, and win the battle for your identity.
©2020 by April Telee Sykes

ISBN: 978-1-7923-3050-6

Arthur Biography Photograph| Davon Phillips
Cover image © Jasmine Raybon | Unsplash
Cover design by Shannon Williams | KLOG Designs
Executive Copyediting and interior design by Julie Vitto
Copyediting Vincent DeMasi

Scripture versions used include the Holy Bible, American Standard Version (ASV). King James Version (KJV). New King James Version (NKJV) ©1979, 1980, 1982 by Thomas Nelson. New International Version (NIV) ©1973, 1978, 1984, 2011 by Biblica. Amplified Bible (AMP) ©1954, 1958, 1962, 1964, 1965, 1987, 2015 by Zondervan. The Message (MSG) ©2002 by Eugene H. Peterson. English Standard Version (ESV) ©2001 by Crossway Bibles, a publishing ministry of Good News Publishers. Easy-to-Read Version (ERV) © World Bible Translation Center.

*I dedicate this book to my parents, Johnny Sykes and
Armintha Lewis-Williams, who provided both the spiritual and physical
framework of my identity.
I love you both.
Rest in peace, Daddy.*

CONTENTS

PREFACE

I remember being seventeen and living on the brink of endless possibilities. There were more years in front of me than behind me. At a distance, I perceived an uncharted world awaiting my arrival. Occasionally, I pondered my capacity and the type of life I would create for myself as an adult. I remember the limitations I put on that capacity. I just did not know if I had what it took to be really great. Outside of those occasional negative thoughts, I was a rather happy young woman. I remember enjoying the freedom of driving; earning money from my part-time job; hanging with friends; attending football games on Friday nights; preparing for prom; and endless practicing for drama and chorale performances. I remember my body shape and how I could easily wrap my hands around my waist so that my fingertips touched. I remember observing pregnant classmates temporarily lose their ability to do that and hoped that it wouldn't happen to me. Not then, at least, like it had for my older sister, cousins, aunts, and my mom. Getting pregnant before marriage was not going to be my future for sure, I thought.

I practically grew up in the church, but still experienced all the same temptations, fears, and insecurities that other teen girls did regarding sex, self-esteem, and acceptance. I had an amazing figure back then but was self-conscious about being flat-chested or too skinny. I was relatively smart but didn't know it because I only partially applied myself to school studies. Interestingly, some of those same insecurities would creep their way into my adulthood and stunt my personal growth. I was always slightly different, not much, but a smidge. I wondered if the kids at school thought I was odd or cool enough to hang with them. I didn't own all the fancy clothes, shoes, and nice hairdos the other kids had, but I dreamed of doing so when I got older. Michael Jordan brand shoes were even cooler when he played basketball. I watched him play, but my momma didn't have J's kind of money. I would never admit it then, but somewhere deep down inside, I envied the kids who had the means to wear nice shoes. I wished I could dress and look like the kids whose parents had money. My siblings and I wore clothes and shoes handed down or bought from Payless and Kmart. My younger brother had it the worst, since boys' clothes were more expensive. He didn't get many clothes at all, and they definitely were not name brand. Unfortunately, boys got picked on a lot for not having clothes and shoes with a recognizable label.

Today, he is considered by all means of the definition a "sneaker head!" He's not the only "sneaker head" I know, either. I know plenty of African-American men with similar upbringings who grew into self-proclaimed "sneaker heads" when they were old enough to earn money to buy the popular labels. It's funny how kids attach value and status to certain things and how this practice lasts well into adulthood. Labels are powerful and have a unique way of making us feel good or bad about our self-worth and identity.

Outside of us not having a lot of money growing up, I remember thinking to myself (maybe aloud in defiance) that we went to church too much! I am sure, if my seventeen-year-old self could see me now, she would laugh at how much I voluntarily attend church. Nevertheless, at seventeen, I recall my mom relaxing a bit, and I was finally able to enjoy some real freedom! Yes, freedom! I went to a few house parties, hung out with the fellas, drank some Cisco, smoked a little weed, and lost my virginity. Unfortunately, I was mistaken. My perceived freedom would eventually transform into mental bondage and chains I would eventually need to rid myself of later. More freedom to come, as I recall the excitement of knowing I am almost finished with high school. I was unsure of what I would do next, but I hoped I could go to college, like Denise from *The Cosby Show*. I remember wanting to be successful, but uncertain of how or if I had what it took to do it. I wondered about which major or career I would settle into. I wasn't sure what I'd be good at, but I was more than certain that I didn't want to work in a factory for the rest of my life. That was the line of work many adults in my community settled into. I imagined the type of spouse I would marry, and what our kids' names would be. I envisioned the kind of car I would drive and house I would live in. I thought about all those things. I am grateful for my desires, since they served as a source of motivation to move forward.

Fast-forward into today and you will find a more confident woman. My life journey has not been easy, but I've learned a lot along the way. I've made some good life choices, and even some bad ones, along the way. Some of those life choices I will share in the chapters to follow. However, one of the best decisions I ever made was reconnecting with the Christian faith introduced to me at an early age. The truth is we all make mistakes. Unfortunately, some mistakes can be devastating and life-altering to the point that you may struggle to ever find your way back. This is especially true when you are young and are trying to figure things out with minimal guidance from caregivers, or seeking to gain approval from your peers, parents, or love interest. Teens and young adults are faced with some serious decisions that they sometimes may not be ready for. Peer pressure, easy access to sex, drugs, and alcohol could lead you down a path that spirals out of control into a life of poverty, drug addiction, depression, and even death.

Regardless of your preparation, or lack of it, every person faces life challenges. These challenges have an uncanny way of helping us grow, stay stuck in place, or be defeated. Every challenge serves as an opportunity and a choice to pursue greatness. Our final outcomes in life are the result or consequence of both our good and poor choices. In spite of my flaws, mistakes, and mishaps along the way, I made it through, and so can you. This was truly by the grace of God. I am older and much wiser now than I was at seventeen and in my twenties. There were undoubtedly plenty of errors I would have avoided had I connected to my identity through the eyes of my heavenly Father sooner. I sometimes catch myself repeating the old adage, "If I only knew then what I know now."

Well, there are no time machines around here, so that's not going to happen. However, there is good news for you! You are privy to know what I didn't know back then, right now. Right there, sitting on your sofa, or listening through your earbuds, you can glean from what I've learned over the years and make the necessary changes to have the life God intended for you to experience. For those of you that may be a little older, there is good news for you as well. Rest assured that nothing about us is ever truly permanent, so you can always change yourself and the life situations around you for the better. Today marks the moment for allowing yourself to learn something new and perhaps shift into doing something different. We can always make improvements to our thinking and behaviors to get us in a better position. I've heard these sayings before: "This is just the way I am," and "I can't change!" If this is you, let's make this the first lie you get rid of on your identity journey. That way of thinking is unwise and potentially dangerous. It could prevent you from establishing a more intimate relationship with God and definitely limit you from being everything you can be. Everyone's story is different and is the reason we decide to move down a certain path.

Growing up in the 1980s and '90s was a lot different than it is growing up today. The challenges and obstacles we faced were quite different from what young adults face today. However, the questions I held back then about my identity are probably very similar to some of the ones you have now: "Who am I?" and "What is my purpose for being here?" Maybe you are older now and you are still searching for the answers to those same questions. If so, you are in the right place.

Identity has always been a topic of interest for humanity. Throughout history, mankind has experienced various influences affecting its identity within surrounding cultures and environments. Even Jesus Christ experienced such influences and nuisances within the culture He was born into. You and I are no different. Cultural influences have helped shape acceptable standards of behavior in society. Truthfully, it is expected and quite natural for this to happen. However, cultural influences, no matter the origin (family, friends, church, or television), have an uncanny way of drawing us closer or further away from God. This is why it is of extreme value to thoroughly understand the influences presented to you and their impact on your thinking. Why, you may wonder? We have to be careful not to fall into traps that lead us down paths that place us out of God's will and, subsequently, out of reach from the blessings He promises to give His children. Unfortunately, staying on the right path is not always easy when we are faced with so many options from society and culture. Following culture, in itself, is not bad, but it becomes dangerous when we detach ourselves from God the Creator and seek reliance and approval in things outside of Him, like money, government, and social media likes. If you're not careful, you could find yourself like the Israelites often found themselves. They were desolate, captured by their enemies, and severed from God and His protection as a result of their disobedience. We have an open invitation to being deceived by the enemy when we haphazardly do what is acceptable in society and never reflect on the consequences. Most importantly, we may miss the opportunity to participate in the purpose and blessings God has for us, which is truly a great loss. Many people walk around so depressed and unhappy with their jobs, family, finances, and lives because they are outside of God's will for their lives. Thankfully, God is merciful and seeks to get our attention to steer us back on track and onto a righteous path. A path that was designed especially for you. He does this best through His word and Holy Spirit.

If these words are new to you, I encourage you to keep reading. I intend to bring you into an awareness of yourself and God that will help you understand these terms better. God knows you better than you know yourself and is ready to show you your truest identity and purpose. Life can feel overwhelming at times and can leave us feeling lost and confused. If you are like me and have felt like you are stuck in place and can't seem to move forward then this may be the perfect opportunity for you to shake up the status quo, obtain some vision, and explore a journey full of excitement and self-discovery. How God sees you is the only thing that matters in this life. Your responsibility is to get in the know and discover what He sees in you. Once you are connected to the Creator of all things, He will begin whispering your identity to you. If you haven't heard, God knew you even before you were formed in your mother's belly and He's ordained you for such a time as this (Jeremiah 1:5).

God desires greatly for us to be in full connection with him. After enough time spent in the presence of our King, your identity and purpose will be so clear that you will speed race out of bed, ready to take on a new day. No more strolling through your friends' and classmates' live feeds on social media, wallowing in regret, self-pity, hopelessness, and defeat. You are victorious in Christ Jesus! It is time to get moving. You have a lot of work to do, and the kingdom of God needs you. Being too young or too old should not even be a thought. If He could use a fearless young David to slay a giant in front of his own army, then He can use you, too, young girl or man. If He could use a faithful, seasoned Abraham to be the father of all nations, then your older age will not stop God from using you, ma'am or sir. *All* have been commissioned to be fishers of men, to stand out as light in darkness, and minister the good news of salvation and access to the divinity that lives inside each of us. You are unique and uniquely chosen to make a difference in your lifetime. You have been promised kingdom living and have the weapons to succeed in every area of life that presents challenges. The sooner you are able to understand this message and apply it to your daily life, the better off you are. God is willing and ready. Allow Him to blow your mind with what He reveals. Let's go get it!

CHAPTER 1

IDENTITY

*"While I know myself as a creation of God, I am also obligated to realize
and remember that everyone else and everything else
are also God's creation."*
—**Maya Angelou**

I am God's creation. Just take a moment to mentally process that and then say it aloud: I AM GOD'S CREATION! Yes, you are! How wonderful is that? Have you ever just taken the time to stare up in the sky and admire the stars and the moon? Perhaps you've experienced a sunset during a stroll along the shoreline at the beach while listening to the sound of the waves beating against the sand. Maybe you've had the opportunity to peer down from a mountaintop and observe the beauty of water crashing against rocks, carving a work of art into the stone. If you haven't, I implore you to do this at some point in your life. There is so much beauty that surrounds us daily that, in the loudness of life, we often rush pass the evidence of His greatness without a second glance.

God's creation is filled with so much beauty, and each day that we are afforded the opportunity to breathe, we should pause for a moment to become enveloped by the smell of a sweet flower or sit under a tree and enjoy a cool breeze. I love to marvel at God's work. In fact, one of my favorite pastimes involves sitting alone on a blanket and sinking my toes into the sand at Jacksonville Beach. I relish hearing the sound of the waves as the blue-gray water crashes against the shore. I bask in the warmth of the Florida sun on my skin. I could stay there, staring up at the sky and listening to the ocean's orchestra for hours. Those silent moments in which I've stolen away have proved to be some of the most amazing and serene of my life. All of God's creation is glorious, but there is something about water that calms my soul. In my beach moments, my understanding of God gains depth, and I discover a peace in knowing my relationship to Him and His ginormous creation. I sometimes think to myself, "My God is so BIG."

I am from a small town in the south suburbs of Chicago called Kankakee. Kankakee is situated in the eastern part of the state of Illinois and is located about forty-five miles south of Chicago. Unlike the concrete jungle most people envision when they think of Chicago, my little city was surrounded by rows and rows of corn.

If you are older than thirty years and are at all familiar with horror films, I want you to think back to a movie from the 1980s called *Children of the Corn*. Yes, there was enough corn surrounding the city of Kankakee that our town could have been included in one of the sequels. Keeping that in mind, I'm sure you can understand how the change from cornfields to coastlines was a pleasant one for a young midwestern lady like myself. As I've grown older, I've been afforded a few opportunities to travel abroad and experience different terrains, and one thing remains certain: God's creation is varied, colorful, vivid, and spectacular! We get to experience His beautiful creation while alive on this earth. He is the author of it all and it all began with Him, the story of creation starts in Genesis and reads like this:

> In the beginning God created the heavens and earth. And the earth was without form and void; and darkness was upon the face of the deep. And the Spirit of God was hovering over the face of the waters. Then God said, "Let there be light"; and there was light. And God saw the light, that it was good. (Genesis 1:1–3, NKJV)

The verses thereafter go on to describe how God called light into being from darkness, water from land, grain and seed from the earth, creatures of the sea, fowl of the air, beasts, cattle, and creeping things and then blessed them to be fruitful and multiply (Genesis 1:4–25).

If you've read thus far and are thinking to yourself, "I thought this was a book about identity. Why is she talking about creation?" My rebuttal is simply this: I'm glad you asked! Having a deeper understanding of God's creation will give you the foundational components, or blueprint, to knowing who, what, and why you are to help you better understand your identity. The best way to understand the operation and functions of anything created is to go to the source of the creation. God is the manufacturer of mankind and has provided us all with the manual for effectively living here on the planet He created. He blessed us with the Holy Scripture, the word, the bible. I am notorious for getting a new device or product and skipping pass reading the instruction manual before using it. This is especially true for my new cell phones. I'm quick to pull it out the box and immediately start using it. I've been purchasing cellphones since the early 2000's so I understand the base functions enough to get the most basic use out of it without every looking at that small pamphlet placed inside of the box. I can make a phone call, send a text message, receive an email, and pull up the internet to search ideas on google. I even know enough to add an app or two to my home screen but I am fully aware of that I am not using my cell phone to its full capacity. There are many functions and features that Apple has placed in that small device that I never experience because I'm clueless of what they are or how to fully operate it. I was reminded of this very fact when I kept missing phone calls because my phone was unknowingly on silent mode. After months, okay years, of missing calls unless the phone was in close proximity, I finally was able to hear the phone when someone called me. It took another Apple user to show me there was a small switch at the upper left side of the phone that allows for the ringer and notifications to be silenced. My ringer was turned off, but I never questioned it because I could still use the phone when I desired. Unfortunately, many of us go through our lives with a similar approach to living as I have with my phone. We never question or seek to understand the full capacity of what God created in us and his full intentions for us. One of my favorite quotes from Myles Munroe says, "when purpose is unknown, abuse is inevitable". That is so powerful. We don't intend to abuse our bodies, our minds, or this planet but because we are not completely aware of its purpose—unfortunate things happen. Therefore, I want you to establish the groundwork for what I like to call your spiritual genetic makeup. If you know anything about biological science, then you are familiar with the term genetics. Just in case you aren't familiar with the term, I'll give you the quickest genetics lesson ever, so that you have a greater understanding but don't fall asleep before we begin.

According to Webster's dictionary, genetics is the science of heredity dealing with resemblances and differences of related organisms resulting from the integration of their genes and the environment. Our genes help to give life to individual characteristic traits, such as gender, eye color, race, predisposed health conditions, height, and so forth. Although our genetics are passed down and may be very similar to our parents, siblings, and post generations. There are not two people on the planet that are exactly alike. Not two! All and all, your genetics serve as the foundation for your unique physical identity at conception and, subsequently, birth. Every person inherits genetics from their earthly parents with any combination of personality, physical attributes, or certain behaviors. Christians experience a second birth by water called baptism, which represents being born again in the spirit. God then becomes our spiritual parent. Being in relationship with God is the foundation to understanding and developing your spiritual identity.

What is identity anyway? Identity is defined as a set of behavioral or personal characteristics by which an individual is recognizable as a member of a group or a distinct personality of an individual as persisting entity; individuality. I have come to learn that God is very much interested in His human creation understanding their spiritual identity. Don't believe me? Take a look at this Scripture from Genesis 1:26–28:

> And God said, Let us make man in our image, after our likeness: and let them have dominion over the fish of the sea, and over the fowl of the air, and over the cattle, and over all the earth, and over every creeping thing that creepeth upon the earth. So God created man in his own image, in the image of God created he him, male and female created he them. And God blessed them, and God said unto them, be fruitful, and multiply, and replenish the earth, and subdue it: and have dominion over the fish of the sea, and over the fowl of the air, and over every living thing that moveth upon the earth. (KJV)

I don't know about you, but the very idea that God created us in His image and after His likeness brings chills to my bones. I want you to take a moment to grasp the depth of that. You and I were created to be the likeness of God. Whoa! That's kind of mind-blowing.

I wonder if Adam, and especially Eve, really knew what that meant. Had they known, would things in the garden of Eden been different? Would they have been able to withstand the deceit of the enemy and not eaten the fruit from the forbidden tree? Could they have just been content with an existence of God as their chief leader? Unfortunately, they were not alone in the garden, and a dark force lurking was more aware of Adam and Eve's identity and God's plans for the earth than they were. That one, the adversary—the devil who is also referred to as the serpent—he knew (Genesis 3:1–5). And he devised a plan to confuse mankind through deceiving Adam and Eve to believe (think) what God told them was indeed a lie (Genesis 3:7). This introduction of deceit has remained the fundamental drawback for mankind, and he/she has wrestled with their identity ever since.

Mankind internalized guilt, fear, and shame which pushed them further and further away from the presence of God. This is not how it was initially, Adam and Eve enjoyed the presence of God daily and were obedient to His instruction. Maybe you've heard the story. Eve was minding her own business in the beautiful plush garden that God bestowed to her and her husband, Adam. The subtle serpent capitalized on an opportunity to place doubt in Eve's heart by questioning which fruit she could or could not eat in the garden. Eve's belief (which was instruction from God) essentially was that eating fruit from the tree in the midst would lead to death. The serpent advised that what God told her was untrue and eating the fruit from the tree of the knowledge of good and evil, which was in the middle of the garden, would not lead to an actual death, but wisdom to be like God. She listened to the enemy and then convinced Adam to partake of the tree as well. Essentially, the enemy presented options for reasoning and thinking independently and differently from their Creator. Their disobedience to God's initial instruction was the origin of Sin, and fear, guilt, and shame followed. The fall of mankind into a sinful nature began, and the rest is history. The enemy has been on his job ever since and has done a great work to deceive God's people—His most cherished creation.

Peter says that we are to be self-controlled and alert. Your enemy, the devil, prowls around like a roaring lion looking for someone to devour (I Peter 5:8). Satan (evil forces) is on the prowl, and if you are not watchful, he will cause you to live in fear, snatch your dreams, hopes, and earthly desires right from underneath you. The enemy's attack or deceit does not exclude you because of the color of your skin, gender, religious affiliation, or social status. He is not a respecter of person and is clever in using your weakness against you.

One of humanity's greatest weaknesses is not knowing or having true understanding. The Scripture in Hosea 4:6 says, "My people are destroyed for lack of knowledge" (KJV). The enemy is looking for ways to take the faith of God from your heart and ultimately confuse you about your identity. I pray that the information provided in each chapter empowers each of you to truly understand who you are, so you are equipped to strip the enemy of the power he thinks he has over you. There are certain tricks that the enemy has used overtime to get and get us off track. He plays games with our minds, often through things in our environment, families, words spoken over us, media, and our desires. As you embark on this discovery of understanding your personal identity, be encouraged, open, reflective, and courageous. Hopefully, you will begin to ponder what the connection to God's creation could mean for your future and begin to shape a peaceful existence void of fear, anger, anxiety, and confusion.

The purpose of this book is to outline God's original intent for you, His most precious creation, and identify mankind's obstacles to reconnect to that intent. The world in which we live is overwhelmingly sensual and sometimes it is difficult for us to secure our footing to walk out our intended purpose when we are bombarded with so much compounding noise and distraction. It is my firm belief that you must have a true understanding of what God's will has been for you and his creation from the foundations of the earth in order to truly grasp the full extent of your identity. One of my favorite Scriptures that confirms this is found in Jeremiah 29:11 and reads, "'For I know the plans I have for you,' declares the Lord, 'plans to prosper you and not to harm you, plans to give you hope and a future'" (NIV).

Let us always be reminded of this very fact, no matter what. I hope you are ready to explore how misconceptions learned through our culture and subculture lead us down a path of truths and untruths about your identity. God created everything in the universe, and He has great plans for us all. Whether you are a Christian or not, I urge you to be open to embarking on this journey of discovery in understanding your identity through the lens of your uniquely lived experiences, but most importantly through the eyes of your heavenly Father. I pray that God opens your heart and mind to eventually come to know the truth about God's intentions for your life so you may fight, win, and soar beyond this spiritual identity crisis.

CHAPTER 2

NATURE VERSUS NURTURE

"Our first impressions are generated by our experiences and our environment, which means that we can change our first impressions ... by changing the experiences that comprise the impressions."
—**Malcolm Gladwell**

I cannot begin to emphasize the value or the relevance of genetics and environment on a person's character and life choices. The environment into which we are born are beyond our control. Just the same, the people we are born to are as well. Nature versus nurture has been a controversial topic for decades in relation to which has greater influence over a person's identity and his/her subsequent behaviors. Scholars from all parts of the world have researched, analyzed, dissected, debated, and published tons of literature on the topic. Therefore, I want us to explore what all the hoopla is about. I'd first like to start by explaining what these two terms mean.

Let's look at the term "nature" first. When referring to someone's nature (intrinsic) you are speaking to the genetic or biological predisposition of a person. Nature is related to what's within us. As I stated in the previous chapter, our genes are inherited characteristics passed down to us by our parents. It is the argument that our behavior is reflected more from genetics, which are originated from our families. Genetics trickle down from generation to generation and are reproduced in a person's offspring. Those who argue the notion of nature's influence on behavior lean toward the idea that genes are why people behave the way they do. Genes are responsible for one's emotional, mental, and physical health. Dependent on the parent or ancestor producing that gene, this could be positive or negative for the person inheriting the gene. Genetics (nature) are beyond our control, sometimes more than the environments from which we come. Therefore, it can be deduced that if you have a parent who has displayed addictive behavior, you may be expected to develop addictive behaviors as well. I have actually seen this play out with family and friends.

One example is with a good friend of mine and her son (we'll call them "Denise" and "Jay"). Denise and her high school sweetheart conceived a child just after graduating high school. Unfortunately, soon after their son was born, her boyfriend was incarcerated for drug possession and distribution. He was locked away in prison for several years and, subsequently, had limited interaction with his son.

All the while, Denise worked hard by earning both undergraduate and graduate degrees and steadily climbing the corporate ladder at her company. Denise did all she could to raise her son in a nurturing home by taking him to church and providing him with positive male mentors throughout the years to facilitate him becoming a productive citizen. She was able to afford him more than just the bare necessities of food and shelter, and he always had the latest electronic gadgets and stylish clothes and shoes. All was going well until he became a teenager and his personality started shifting. The well-mannered and behaved young man she raised now stayed out late, acted bizarrely, and gravitated toward a negative crowd. He began to display many of the characteristics of his incarcerated father, which seemed unlikely since Jay really did not have a relationship with him nor was privy to spending time with him. Although the environment did not cause him to him act like his father, his genetics expressed themselves in such a way that everyone would tell him how much he reminded them of his father.

Nature says if one of your parents has blue eyes, then there is a chance that you or a sibling will inherit that trait. As I stated earlier, your genetics are any combination of personality, physical attributes, or behaviors that are inherited from a parent. I'm sure you have been told how much you act or resemble your mom or dad, aunt or uncle, grandparent, or sibling. When I consider my own family, I look at my mother and see that my eldest sister and only brother were blessed to inherit her beautiful hazel eye color. I, on the other hand, did not, but I did get her feet. (Thanks, Mother.)

Okay, for those of you who do not know me, there is a small knot at the base of my big toe that I refuse to call a bunion. I have had this knot on the side of my foot since I was a young girl, and it may very well be the reason I opt to wear thong sandals and flip-flops over closed-toe shoes. Open-toe shoes are just so much more comfortable. I'm not the only one blessed with this feature; a couple of my aunts and my sisters (Charlene and Darlene) have it as well. For all those who poked fun at my feet, blame it on my momma, not me!

I also inherited a love of music and writing from her, which was passed down from her mother. Our family gatherings quickly transform into mini concerts or talent shows when everyone gets together. I come from a long line of dramatically and musically inclined people. I have likewise observed several other families inside and outside the Church with genetic dispositions towards the arts. Maybe you have heard of some of these families, such as the Clark Sisters, the Winans, the Jacksons, and the DeBarges. Like myself, these families more than likely have a genetic expression of music in their DNA. They were able to form singing groups amongst their siblings since they all were musically gifted. It was just in their genes to sing, and present generations, and generations to come, are the benefactors.

There were some genetic (nature) traits that did not come from my mother. Remember, genetics is the combination of both parents. Over the years, all of my sisters, aunts, and nieces would marvel and comment on the size of my derriere, because none of them inherited that trait. Well, if you meet any of the women on my dad's side of the family, then it would become clear where all my "junk in the trunk" came from. My inherited traits from him did not end there. I also got his lips, nose, quirky sense of humor, a tamed taste for alcohol (managed well through my faith), and, at times, a quick temperament. I mentioned the alcohol because some things unchecked could manifest unknowingly if you are not careful. Just because you have a predisposition to certain habits does not mean you have to accept it as your truth. My dad has gone on to be with the Lord now, but fragments of his personality, work ethic, and behaviors live through me, his offspring. We all have these mixtures of genetic traits that were inherited from our family bloodlines. They are some of the most visible features of our identities.

On the other hand, nurture describes the stimulant, which affects personality and behavior, based on environmental factors. Nurture is outwardly influential and considered extrinsic. Nurture ruling is the idea that our context shapes our feelings and actions throughout life. There are several contextual or environmental influences, which may contribute to different attitudes or ways of behaving. A person could be influenced by their social, personal, temporal, and cultural contexts. I will go into more detail as to what these different contexts mean later, but I want you to take note that there are different levels of environment.

Now, the controversy lies within the dynamics of which term, nature (genetics) or nurture (environment), has more influence over a person's character, behavior, and subsequent actions than the other. There was a longitudinal study of twins over a span of fifty years published in *Nature Genetics* in 2015. The report's finding suggested that both genetics and environment have equally the same amount of influence on a person's behavior. The implications of this data will be utilized two-fold to grasp a deeper understanding of the environment and genetic influences on human behavior. Ultimately, this means that many of a person's decisions in life will be positively or negatively influenced by either nature or nurture as it relates to careers, spirituality, interests, food choices, and relationships. Having a full picture of what we were naturally born with and influences of things outside of us has great significance. We learned how genetics work and, ultimately, are the basis to human traits (eye color, hair texture, ear lobe attachment, temperament, talents, etc.) and spiritual essence. Now, let's explore the effects of context (environment) on what we do or don't do respectively.

As I stated earlier, there are different components to context (environment) within our social, virtual, physical, personal, cultural, and temporal backgrounds. These contexts are often interwoven to capture a larger picture. I am sure, at some point in your life, you have been either accused of taking someone's words out of context or have experienced someone taking what you said out of context. Without the contextual foundation, words or a story can be easily misinterpreted, and the initial meaning could be lost. The origin of the term "context" comes from the Latin word *contextus*, from *con*, meaning "together," and *texere*, meaning "to weave." Context defined means the whole situation, background, or environment that is relevant to a particular event or personality (Webster's New World Dictionary, 1994). Thus, in order to accurately understand an individual, idea, or an event, one must have a full understanding of the circumstances surrounding the person, thought, or situation. We are complex individuals and placing everyone into our small box of relativism diminishes the experience and existence of others outside what may be perceived as normal or adequate.

Recognizing the unique qualities of people requires you to view things objectively and act as a detective to gather as much insight or facts before you formulate an opinion about anyone or their situation. Often, this is done too infrequently and, ultimately, it is the primary reason why people lack empathy when dealing with other people of different social or cultural backgrounds. I believe this is how some people develop feelings of racism or bigotry. Also, this is where issues of classism and prejudices arise. I am sure I'm not the only person, at some point in life, who looked at a beggar on the street and thought to myself, "Why can't he/she stop being lazy and get a job?" or became impatient in the grocery store line when the person in front of me began a series of questions to the store clerk that I did not have time to listen to. It is my belief that the number of little and big things that frustrate us about other people would diminish if we started to think outside of ourselves more often. No one person is the same, and everyone is dealt a different deck of cards at the start of life. How people are raised and the contextual factors surrounding them will more than likely (at least 50 percent of the time) become reflected in how they respond and behave to life situations. Taking time to seek understanding about why people take or do not take a particular course of action requires patience and grace. Paul writes in Romans 12:3, "For I say, through the grace that was given me, to every man that is among you, not to think of himself more highly than he ought to think; but so to think as to think soberly, according as God hath dealt to each man a measure of faith" (ASV).

It is God's desire that we do this with friend or foe (enemy). Everyone is unique, and there are no two people alike. Not even identical twins. When you place your personal expectations onto someone else regarding who they should be and how they should behave, you have done a disservice to that individual and yourself. It is so unrealistic to expect others to react and handle life and its array of situations the same as we would. When a person does have these expectations, they are often disappointed at the outcomes because, if I know one thing, I know that people are unpredictable and hard to control. This is coming from a reformed control freak that learned this lesson the hard way. I may have a few close family and friends who would insert an "Amen" right there. I'd often ponder, "If only they would just listen to me and do things my way, things would be so much better for them." You would think that with all the training I obtained early on in business-to-business sales I would be persuading family, lovers, and friends to see and do things my way all the time. However, as the late comedian Charlie Murphy said on the Chappelle's Show sketch highlighting Rick James, "Wrong!" I was wrong and I very rarely got anyone to buy that my way of doing life was supreme.

Persuading people to buy into your ideals could be a daunting task. Truly, we can take a hint from our Creator. In all of His infinite wisdom and ability to be omnipresent, God, the Creator, graced us all with free will. We are blessed to exercise the utilization of that gift daily. We even get to choose to believe or not to believe in Him. If God doesn't control us like puppets into doing His will, then what gives you or me the right to attempt to control others in such a way? God has created everyone with a special purpose and varying gifts to operate in that purpose. We are individually unique and possess different approaches to managing people, circumstances, and events in life. He has great intentions for us all to function in this life simultaneously and operate in our special gifts for the greater good of humanity (Romans 12:4–8). This is when we choose to operate in those gifts for the edification of His glory. We should regard everyone we encounter as a viable entity of God's creation and let that motivate us all to learn the contextual background that shapes people's behaviors so that we can more effectively connect with them.

Again, here are the five essential contexts I would like you to be familiar with:

Social context consists of stable and dynamic factors, such as gender roles, friends, family, teachers, coworkers, and support resources or people in the community, such as neighbors or postal workers.

Personal context relates to a person's internal environment derived from age, sex, race, mood, and ethnic identity (ethnicity).

Temporal context refers to time's influence on shaping ideas, motives, and actions (for example: being born in the 1940s as a baby boomer following World War II, hippies born in the 1950s, or millennials raised at the turn of the twenty-first century).

Virtual context involves interactions experienced in real time or near real time but lack physical contact (i.e., video games, internet, websites, social media, etc.).

Cultural context includes the norms, values, and behavior patterns that serve as guidelines for people's interactions with others in their environment.

I defined cultural context last since it has such a significant impact on human behavior, so I will begin there. I believe Marcus Garvey stated it best when he said, "A people without knowledge of their past history, origin and culture is like a tree without roots." This is particularly true when examining spiritual roots, as well. We can be swayed into many beliefs without a deeper understanding or knowledge of who we are or, most importantly, who we are in God. Out of all the contexts we looked at, culture is the most varied and powerful influence on our behaviors and daily routines. This is primarily because the context of culture has been there since birth within the family and society you were born into. Society and your family represent the values you hold during your development that shape your identity in many ways.

Have you ever just sat back and considered the influence of culture on the activities you engage in daily? If you haven't, take a moment to close your eyes and think about your family and the country in which you were born. Reflect on the types of foods you eat with your family, the schools you attended, your religious affiliation, and the way you talk (language and accents). When I think of good food, I immediately think back to fried fish and spaghetti, Home Run Inn pizza, Garrett's cheese and caramel popcorn mix, Italian beef, and beef hot dogs garnished with tomato, celery salt, and pickles. I think about growing up in a small town surrounded by cornfields and going to public high school with kids I've known since kindergarten.

Some of us went to the same Seventh Day Adventist/Baptist church with my mom every week. I attended a pseudo–Seventh Day Adventist church, and the people I grew up with grabbed pop from the pop machine when we wanted something cold to drink with a little fizz. My friends and I wore gym shoes for footwear when playing sports and if you caught me in a playful mood, you just might hear me say something or someone is "bogus" if they did or said something I did not agree with. You may or may not relate to any of this, because you have a different culture in which you were raised. Pairing fish and spaghetti may sound absurd to you but for me it was delicious. If you are from the Chicago area, much of what I'm saying may resonate as a familiar memory. Whatever you thought of while reflecting, whether it was a Philly cheesesteak or an Indian curry over rice, that food is a part of your culture. There is not a person alive who has not been influenced positively or negatively by culture.

Culture surrounds us every day and is a strong factor in our daily habits, routines, and rituals. The phrases and language you speak are determined by culture. What you prefer or don't prefer to eat for a meal is culture. Whether you set out every morning to go to a job or if you awake at dawn prepared to hunt and gather your food for the day, it is your unique culture. It is your way of perceiving your world and how you essentially do life. It is fascinating how people all over the world can be similar in so many ways but so different based on what culture they were cultivated in. People rely heavily on culture to determine their language, symbolism, social norms, and values. These cultural identifiers are developed whenever two or more people are together. It is how mankind connects, socializes, and communicates. These are considered normal behaviors or what sociologists may call "norms." Norms are defined as the predictable behaviors expected from a person based on their distinct roles or situations within a group. Each group holds a set of values or norms within the roles they establish, and much of their daily routines are geared around these activities. The values we hold are equally driven by our religious choices as well, whether it is Buddhism, Hinduism, Islam, or Christianity.

Without social norms and/or religious customs, the world as we know it would be in chaos. Society would be able to behave as positively and negatively towards each other as it deemed fit without any sense of consequence, so I am thankful for religion and government. I think the atheist and humanist could set their differences aside for a moment to affirm that fact as well. People benefit from statutes and rules to govern groups of people. A lawless environment would be catastrophic to society, possibly apocalyptic (of relating to the end of world). I imagine we would be able to purchase and utilize illicit drugs without any boundaries; any person at any age may be able to drive a car on whichever side of the street they prefer; people may steal, kill, gender nonconform, and commit adultery without any outward social ramifications. This is what a world without parameters would be like.

Interestingly enough, this world without parameters is growing more and more prevalent today. In the 2013 film *The Purge*, the writers and producers of the movie entertained the notion that the aggression and crime of America would be at bay for a year with the exception of one night of lawless behavior—including murder. The people could be as violent and uncivil as they wanted without being reprimanded for a 12-hour period. In modern day some parts of the movie look similar to the United States and other parts of the world as humanity pushes toward the acceptance of a humanistic worldview to allow people to live freely without boundaries and rules.

Humanists share a stance of extreme value for human beings' natural reasoning and talents to obtain purpose. Humanists believe in mankind's innate ability to manage life separate from religion or supernatural (spiritual) influences. Humanists think that holding onto beliefs of an afterlife are fruitless and the focus should be on enjoying the here and now, while we are living on earth. Many Scriptures define this perspective as carnal thinking.

Dictionary.com gives the word "carnal" two definitions; one is characterized by the body or flesh, and the other as merely human and not spiritual. Carnal comes from the Greek word *sarkikos*, which relates to fleshly and earthly desires. A carnal person is concerned with what their senses perceive and are generally unspiritual. Those who follow a humanistic approach rely on proponents of carnality, which the Word of God warns the Body of Christ against. Scripture from Romans 8:5–8 offers Christians the best way to understand this type of mind-set:

> For they that are after the flesh do mind the things of the flesh, but they that are after the Spirit, the things of the Spirit. For to be carnally minded is death; but to be spiritually minded is life and peace. Because the carnal mind is enmity against God: for it is not subject to the law of God, neither indeed can be. So then they that are in the flesh cannot please God. (KJV)

It is impossible to please God when we desire after our flesh and build up our belief system on world systems, because God is a spirit. The flesh and spirit are contrary, and it is difficult for a person to truly submit to God (whom they cannot see) when their mind is set on believing on what is physically tangible in this world. Humanists are against making decisions related to supernatural phenomena or spirituality and are intentionally in direct conflict with God. Many of those behind the humanist worldview are atheists and do not believe in a spiritual God. If they cannot see it, smell it, or feel it, then it does not exist and, therefore, God does not exist. Furthermore, they believe it absurd to make social and global decisions which affect the populations based on a spiritual worldview, so they influence the decision makers of many established institutions like government, education, and media with propaganda to enlighten the rest of the world with this naturalistic mindset.

We live in interesting times, where many people are searching for truth and there are plenty of people offering their version of the truth to anyone who is listening. Unfortunately, the humanistic worldview has crept its way into our public schools, music, pop culture, television, movies, and even our churches are unknowingly entertaining their values.

One of my favorite movies starring Denzel Washington, called *The Book of Eli*, portrays a postapocalyptic time where crime and famine run rampant. In the motion picture, a story is told where all books have been destroyed, including the Bible, and people rely on their basic survival skills to stay alive. The people operate in utter chaos without hope of knowing how to regain order to establish society as it once was. Denzel's character possesses the only copy of a book that survived the war, and his sole mission is to get this information in the right hands so that order may be restored in the world. In his possession, Denzel holds and is able to detail the Bible verbally. It is a wonderful story. If you haven't seen it, I encourage you to check it out. It is my opinion that our society is making a gainful push towards a lifestyle without boundaries, as depicted in the movie. More and more, people are encouraged to live freely, let their emotions control their actions, and ultimately refute systemic structure (humanistic worldview). This type of mindset can truly be dangerous if too many people take heed and allow their emotions and natural instincts to flow without reins. The Bible speaks of such times in 2 Timothy 3:1–5:

> This know also, that in the last days perilous times shall come. For men shall be lovers of their own selves, covetous, boasters, proud, blasphemers, disobedient to parents, unthankful, unholy, without natural affection, trucebreakers, false accusers, incontinent, fierce, despisers of those that are good, traitors, heady, highminded, lovers of pleasure more than lovers of God, having a form of godliness but denying its power. And from such people turn away. (KJV)

The definition of perilous is full of danger or exposed to imminent risk of disaster. Disaster is characterized with widespread death and destruction. As I stated earlier, God gives warning that carnality is death, whereas spirituality breeds life and peace. More commonly we are seeing disagreements amongst husbands, wives, and even children against their parents. People are more unthankful and self-centered despite their abundance of blessings. They push for more possessions and money and boast about what they have instead of sharing. We see teens and young adults upholding the mantra "you only live once" (YOLO). YOLO is simply a mindset that endorses pleasure and thrill-seeking in the form of partying with sex, alcohol, and instant gratification. If you only live once, why limit yourself with boundaries and thoughts of future consequences.

Despite the push of the humanistic worldview, God continues to speak to His people and those who are lost as well to show them the absolute truth in Titus 2:11–12: "For the grace of God that bringeth salvation hath appeared to all men. Teaching us that, denying ungodliness and worldly lusts, we should live soberly, righteously, and godly, in this present world" (KJV).

We are definitely living in interesting times and, therefore, we have to be mindful of how culture and times are shaping our behaviors so that we are better able to avoid the pitfalls and disengage from the untruths.

Social/Temporal Context

Contexts are synergistic in nature and are often interwoven. In any given scenario, there may be several different contexts at play. Understanding this synergistic engagement is key to grasping the depth of how much we are influenced by our contexts daily.

To illustrate, one of the most popular stories in the Bible is the story of Moses. I'll add that it happens to be one of my personal favorites as well. In Exodus 2, Moses was born in a time (temporal context) where Pharaoh (social context) ordered all males born to Hebrew families to be killed at birth. Fearing for her child's life, Moses's mother constructed a basket and sent his young sister to float him along the riverbank to safety. Eventually, Pharaoh's sister found Moses's basket and she decided to raise him in the house with Pharaoh. Moses was like a son to Pharaoh (Egyptian) and a brother to his son. Upon learning that he was Hebrew, Moses became conflicted when seeing another Hebrew being beaten by an Egyptian. Moses murdered the Egyptian, a man whose origin he thought he shared at one point. Feeling lost, confused, and fearing for his life, Moses fled from Egypt and developed a reliance and close relationship with God.

Eventually, God commissioned Moses to return back to Egypt to free the Israelites from the bondage they were under. He would return home not as Pharaoh's friend but foe (God's side). Moses was able to converse and negotiate with Pharaoh since he essentially grew up with him. This story is miraculous but gives light to how powerful context can be in the development of who we are and our destiny in life. Moses was the best man for the job of freeing the slaves because of how and where he was reared. One of the most valuable things to note is that he was born under a decree to kill all Hebrew male children. Subsequently, Moses was raised by a stranger who nurtured him and facilitated the development of essential skills required to be a soldier and strong man for that particular time. Despite the enemy's attempt to eradicate him at the outset, he was still used for the Kingdom of God to facilitate physical freedom for the Israelites. Today, he remains, historically, one of the greatest religious figures of the Jewish and Christian faiths.

Personal Context

We all have unique circumstances based on personal contexts of gender, age, racial background, heritage, and ethnicity that shape our thoughts of who we are. No experience is identical, and that's what makes us all so special. One's personal lens is guided by individual situations, which may vary widely. As an African-American woman, I can identify with how being labeled a "black woman" has shaped my thoughts about myself and how I expect others of a different racial background to view me.

There have been moments in work settings where I felt like I had to be twice as good and work twice as hard than someone of a different race to prove my worth. As a black woman in corporate America, I have often found myself amongst a select few and felt isolated. Under these circumstances, the pressure is enormous, as my mere being is under an invisible microscope. Where did the pressure come from? No one has ever sat me down in an interview and stated the qualifications for this job requires black women to work twice as hard. Are you up for the challenge? This has never happened, so why do I think that way? I'll tell you where it came from. It came from within.

At a certain point in my life I developed the perspective that African Americans are viewed as less than their counterparts, and it is my personal responsibility to prove my value. Some of you have personal stories that are pretty average with typical childhoods full of play, education, and positive family experiences. Others may have less flattering tales of childhood and could provide stories that will cause anyone with a heart to shudder in disbelief. Perhaps you were a victim of rape at the hands of a close relative while growing up or of a stranger as an adult. Maybe you come from very impoverished circumstances where your basic needs, such as food and clothing, were not met, or you suffered neglect and abuse from a drug-addicted family member. Maybe you've grown into adults, and your past has directed you onto a pathway that constantly breeds continuous conflict and turmoil. Your personal context continues to hold you bound, mentally. Understand that we cannot control how and where we are born, but we can control our thoughts about it.

Unfortunately, if a negative viewpoint lingers unattended long enough, disease may fester, and the viewpoint takes on a life force of its own and is extremely difficult to break. Often, a person's incorrect thinking is accompanied with a mental/spiritual stronghold. A stronghold is defined as a place where a particular belief is fortified or strongly defended or upheld. Strongholds have to be broken and meditating on God's word can help us do that. Moreover, there are times when a person may fortify a particular thought from irrational logic to help them manage their personal affairs effectively. Often, diseases like depression, substance addiction, anxiety (fear disorder), and personality disorders have spiritual roots, which are rarely considered with our natural eye. In the United States, the prevalence of mental illness is growing, and the causes are not just genetic and physical in nature. They can just as easily be stemmed from cues in our environment. This is why it important to know and analyze what is shaping your perspectives and views. We have to be self-aware and reflect from time to time to ensure our values are Gods values.

I hope you see the point I'm trying to make about the strong interaction with your environment and the vital role it plays in shaping your views of others as well as views of your personal identity. Please visit AprilTeleeSykes.com to receive a nature versus nurture analysis under Uniquely Purposed in the resource section. Your awareness of contextual influences is critical so that you do not allow the enemy to tell you what you can or cannot be based on your circumstances. Like I've said before, you are always learning something whether you know it or not. The most intelligent and successful person you could think of may be unknowingly operating in a state of deceit by following worldviews that are contrary to the Word of God. It is important to understand that deception is clever and, often, your natural reasoning is the platform for believing a lie. You may not seek or solicit certain information, but it falls in your lap.

Your natural assertions deemed by your environment rarely align themselves with what God says in His word about handling a situation. Isaiah 55:8 says His thoughts are higher than our thoughts and His ways are higher than our ways. Hopefully, you are beginning to gather a deeper understanding of what is shaping your thoughts daily so you can more easily sift through the information that's bombarding your senses. The better you train yourself to sift through the garbage external factors may present, the more in control of your thoughts and behaviors you will become. As stated earlier, 50 percent of what we do is determined by environment (nurture). It is your job to understand the environment and contextual influences affecting your thinking. Understanding your mental processing better prepares you to properly react to what's thrown at you. Properly managing contextual influences propels you to build the lives you and God could be proud of—the life you were predestined to live from the foundation of the earth.

CHAPTER 3

FAMILY IDENTITY

"What can you do to promote world peace?
Go home and love your family."
—**Mother Teresa**

Our families are the most essential social context we will ever encounter on this side of heaven. They are the first people we met. They introduce us to our culture, standards, values, and the outside world. They are our mother, father, sister, brother, grandma, cousin, or uncle. The health of our family is often observed in our behaviors, actions, and perspectives. The good, the bad, and the indifferent. We all have experienced that awkward moment in the grocery store line when a highly agitated child embarrasses their parent with a temper tantrum or some other disrespectful behavior. If you are like me, you might have inwardly thought to yourself, "Wow, I wonder what they are doing with them at home?" While working for a staffing agency, I once encountered a three-year old tell me to, "shut up—bit$#". I was interviewing his mother for a potential job and he literally cursed me out. His mother said nothing. I was in shock. Truthfully, I was ready to spank the child myself but refrained and redirected my energies towards his quiet mother. I explained that his behavior would not be tolerated in this setting and the interview would have to end, if she didn't get better control of her baby. Most of us will agree that when observing bad behavior, we immediately look for the parent. Honestly, we cannot always blame the parent for children's bad behavior. However, kids are sponges and absorb everything they see and hear. Often, they will embarrass us at the most inopportune time, just like that three-year old. Adults have to be careful what they model at home. Consciously or un-consciously we are teaching and never should underestimate the impact of the family unit.

I am sure, at some point, you have heard the expression "it starts at home". The expression, simply implies that the hub of our first stages of learning occur within the four walls of our homes. Ultimately, this means parents and/or guardians are the chief educators for children in cultivating many of the life skills, personality traits, behaviors, and characteristics necessary to be productive citizens in society—not the public-school system. Yep, cat's out the bag! It is the parents' chief responsibility to facilitate positive behaviors, adequate language skills, healthy self-esteem, and a good moral compass for their children to interact with others and become successful adults in their surrounding environment. Proverbs 22:6 says,

"Train up a child in the way he/she should go: And when he is old, he will not depart from it". Have you ever noticed that certain families have generations of wealth, success, and prosperity that are passed along for decades? Often, generations are blessed by the actions of their ancestors and parents. The information and instruction that is passed along to them assists them in being victorious and successful in life. When you have the tools and experience at being prosperous, you are able to model the behaviors required to obtain and sustain it. Nothing is more meaningful then teaching your children about faith in God. What follows is wealth, peace, and good fortune. God instructs the generations to praise Him for His works and declare Gods mighty acts throughout the ages (Psalms 145:4). Generations praise Him when they are taught to do so, within their families and culture at home. The proverbs tell us that true wisdom begins with understanding the fear of the Lord (Proverbs 9:10). God's way and laws lead to a peaceful and prosperous life. Our lives often are an example of our honor of the Lord and an obedience to following His word. Our children are the primary benefactors of our obedience to Him. When we read Deutoronomy 28:1-14, we see a list of the blessings God promises His children for obeying his instruction. Take a moment to read over them and write them down one by one.

Deutoronomy 6:6-8 says this,

"And these words, which I command thee this day, shall be in thine heart. And thou shalt teach them diligently unto thy children, and shalt talk of them when thou sittest in thine house, and when thou walkest by the way, when thou liest down, and when thou risest up."

Just the same, if our lives reflect a lifestyle of sin and disobedience to God's instructions, we inadvertently teach our children through our disobedience and pass along curses. These curses can be found in Deutoronomy 28:15 and are observed with lack, poverty, and distress. When we follow God's instructions—we work to establish the right foundation and environment for our children to have the best chances of success. A two-family home is what God designed for our family structure. This is increasingly becoming more difficult as the standard and look of the family continues to shift. Single parent homes are becoming more common and the rate of divorce is steadily maintaining at fifty percent. Fifty percent of marriages are ending in divorce and some are choosing not to marry at all. It's ideal for children to be raised in a two-parent home. Statistics show that children raised in a traditional home setting with married parents are more likely to attend college, are physically and emotionally healthier, and are less likely to live in poverty in comparison to children living in single or cohabiting parent homes. Additionally, they are less likely to participate in adverse behaviors, such as drug use or sexual activity. If this is true, then why is it, even in the body of Christ, are we struggling to establish and build healthy family units? I'll tell you why: because the family is under a spiritual attack.

The Art of War

I am pretty sure by now you can see that the family is in a world of trouble. So, the question then becomes, "Why the family?" Because we are in a spiritual war, and our adversary, the devil, is doing everything in his finite power to win. The devil's strategy is pretty evident and has been used for centuries in battle. It is called divide and conquer. In 1994, Chinese scholar and businessmen Ralph D. Sawyer translated with a historical introduction Sun Tzu's Art of War. Sawyer outlined how many battles during the era of Sun Tzu were won by creating division within a military organization and then sequentially capturing the weakened soldiers. It's pretty clever, right? The devil knows that it is significantly easier to fight and capture a single entity or a weakened defense then an army of armed, united soldiers. Families are broken, divided, singular, and unarmed for this spiritual battle. More often, family members do not even realize they are fighting.

It says in Ephesians 6:12, "For we wrestle not against flesh and blood, but against principalities, against powers, against the rulers of the darkness of this world, against spiritual wickedness in high places" (KJV). We get so caught up in fighting each other in relationships that we don't see with our discerning eye who is the real enemy. When you know who/what you are fighting, then you are better equipped to come up with a strategic plan of attack. One of the first methods of the enemies' attack on the family has been to distract them.

In the United States particularly, parenting styles and priorities have shifted. Today, many parents spend a great deal of time outside of the home due to high financial pressures and other impeding responsibilities that help man the ship. Sadly, parents with all good intentions to provide for their families are too distracted and overwhelmed to place child rearing as the top priority.

At times, managing life circumstances may become so difficult that it leaves little to no time to adequately raise our children. Additionally, people are having children less often than they did three to five decades ago and/or are waiting much later in adulthood to start a family. Unfortunately, I fall into that category. Traditionally, men would spend more time outside of the home. Today, both men and women are equally tasked with the responsibility of providing for the family and are gone at least eight hours of day. For the first time in years, some parents were allowed to work from home, which was a change of pace for the working parent. The workload was not less and although they were home—their heads were buried in their laptops and computers. Being distracted by work is understandable and unfortunately a necessary evil but there are other distractions, which are extremely selfish in nature.

There are some parents who may have bad habits, such as drinking and/or abusing drugs (illicit or prescription). Substance abuse is a direct insult on the family unit. Prescription drug abuse, specifically opiates, is a growing epidemic in the United States with over 54 million people over the age of twelve who have used prescription drugs for nonmedicinal purposes. Adults are not the only ones that are self-medicating with prescription drugs—children are as well. Children with emotional and psychological issues seek ways to chemically escape. We often observe this in homes where neglect, physical and sexual abuse is present. Unfortunately, the addiction follows them into adulthood and the cycle repeats.

Children may have to be removed from the home, causing another set of psychological issues to deal with. This may place them at further risk for future abuse as a means of coping or escape from an undesired living situation. No one wins when children are displaced from their parents' homes and move in with elderly grandparents, aunts/uncles, or into foster care but it happening every day. It's a sad circumstance for all parties involved and the scars can be long lasting. This is spiritual warfare at its finest, often undetectable, unrecognizable, and swept under the rug.

I want to be clear that most people are doing their best to have healthy family structures and raise their children right despite the current social environment. They strive to have a suitable work–life balance that allows them to pour into their children as much as they can but the cost of living and inflation make it so hard.

Our monthly expenses continue to increase and require a second job to maintain the household. Unfortunately, our growing financial obligations have caused a huge strain on the entire family structure. The financial strain increases when you factor in single-parent households. This is why faith and prayer are so important. God is notorious for being a provider and stepping in just in the nick of time. I am grateful for his provision and guidance to ensure all of my needs are met for me and my family.

Parents versus Teachers

Approximately seven hours of your child's day is spent at school. That is a significant amount of time away from home and around people other than their parents. The question becomes, who are their classmates and who are their teachers? Consider that your child may have as little as one instructor or as many as seven depending on their grade level. Students in grade levels six through twelve typically switch between teachers and subjects; therefore, your child may have several adults who are involved in their learning. In addition to teachers, you also have your child's classmates, which may be just as varied. Any parent with a sound mind should be very interested in knowing who is at the school and responsible for teaching their child. Do I agree with this teacher's or school's values? If parents took the time to really assess this amount of influence outside of their homes, every PTA meeting would be filled to capacity. Due to the demands of work and monthly living expenses, families are faced with the tough decision of placing their children in the school system at very early ages. Often, parents unknowingly rely on schools as the primary means of education for their children for that reason alone. Parents have increasingly grown accustomed to learning occurring outside of the home and sometimes, because their schedules are filled with other conflicting responsibilities, adults rely on schools to do much of the teaching that should be happening simultaneously in their homes.

This way of thinking has to be reexamined. Although your teachers may be competent in their various subject matters, their responsibilities within the classroom have grown. The individual attention required to facilitate building character and life skills is spread thin teaching the core curriculum while managing thirty other students. Additionally, all teachers are not in the business of teaching because they are passionate about childhood learning and development. Some are in the education system by default, and it seems like a good way to obtain a living wage after completing college. However, their reason for teaching should not be your concern. Quite frankly, it is not the responsibility of your teachers to instill character into our children but to educate them on math, reading, science, etc. This does not diminish the positive and/or negative influences your teachers may have in the development of your child. I say positive or negative because you may not always agree with your child's teacher's perspective on life, and when they stand in the front of their classroom to present a lesson, whatever bias they hold will fly out of their mouth as freely as birds in the air and into your child's ears.

As a parent, you want to be the key influence on your child's perspectives, viewpoints, and subsequent outcomes because your child's learning is your chief responsibility. Like I mentioned earlier, we are to "Train up a child in the way he should go: and when he is old, he will not depart from it" (Proverbs 22:6 KJV). You should ask yourself, "Am I teaching my child things that I want them to retain in their adulthood?" If you are not thinking about these things during your interactions with your children, readjust your thinking and begin to do this. Standing idly by and allowing other influences outside of the home to teach your children life skills will ultimately lead to an array of outside influences and morality issues that you may not agree with manifesting in your child's life. Most parents can testify that adult children have a tendency to share their grown-up problems and issues with them. If they have a problem with the law, a financial woe, or a dispute with a spouse, the issue will typically find its way into your lap. You really don't stop parenting when they turn eighteen. Sounds romantic to think that you would, but it is not realistic and rarely occurs this way.

One of the largest influences outside of your home is other children. They may or may not have parents actively involved in teaching them what you think is morally sound judgment. Furthermore, they have teachers who inadvertently or sometimes boldly influence your child's education with their viewpoints. What if the teacher shares a viewpoint that is the complete opposite of yours? This occurs more frequently in the public-school systems. If you have children, I am sure you have had that moment when your child comes home asking questions about some adult topic and wondered to yourself, "Where the heck did they get that from?"

Aside from other children and teachers, these influences are found on television shows, in music, and on the internet. I remember distinctly being influenced through television when I was young. One of my favorite television programs was *The Cosby Show*. It starred an African-American comedian named Bill Cosby who played an OB-GYN physician named Cliff Huxtable who was married to a beautiful lawyer named Clair Huxtable. The couple had five children, whom they were successfully raising and steering into adulthood. At the time, I was the same age as the youngest character, Rudy, and identified with many of the age-related life changes she experienced on the show. Most importantly, I observed positive images of her elder siblings graduating from high school and then attending college. This was a complete contrast of imagery found in my home. Although there were five of us, we did not have the same fathers, so there was not one patriarch (male head) assigned to our family for guidance. Additionally, no one in my immediate family had attended college, so my first exposure to that thought stemmed from the images I experienced on that television show.

Every week, I tuned in and was privy to watching two successful African-American parents raising their children together in a comfortable home. My mother, eldest sister, and several other close relatives became pregnant in their teens and subsequently dropped out of high school, so college life was not a part of my teen pep talks. By the grace of God, I avoided this trend and graduated from high school and then college five years after that. I later went back to school to get my master's degree. Thankfully, *The Cosby Show* was a positive television program airing during my youth, and I was able to gain valuable insight about a way of family life that I may not have been otherwise exposed to. It saddens me to observe the controversy surrounding the creator of the sitcom, Bill Cosby, but sometimes we make poor choices that creep up to bite us in the bottom later. Whatever his personal flaws may have been, the impact he made on the African-American community during the 1980s and '90s was undeniable, phenomenal, and much needed.

Unfortunately, much of the television programming that currently exists is not as positive as it once was and it requires considerable adult discretion when watching. Many of the commercials and content is jam packed with propaganda that is steering the viewer to believe and feel a certain way which is often contrary to biblical principles. We all have to be vigilant and take careful consideration what is being taught to our children/youth through the airways.

Attack on the Family Structure

There is a growing epidemic of dysfunctional family units in the United States. Unfortunately, some of us realize this major issue, but still find ourselves in a broken family situation due to confusion regarding gender roles, failed relationship or marriage for a variety of reasons, such as finances, infidelity, child rearing differences, religion, cruel treatment, and/or outright, blatant selfishness. With the exception of those interested in casual dating (sex) without commitments, I am certain that many of us do not dive into relationships or a marriage with the intent of ending the union. However, many of us, with all of our intense efforts at maintaining a happy family situation, find ourselves amongst the statistics of another failed relationship or marriage with kids in tow.

As the prevalence of brokenness in our families continues to grow, society adapts to the dysfunction by redefining the family identity. New terms emerge, such as co-parenting, nontraditional, and blended families. These terms become the new normal for many families. By definition, the word "family" is a basic social unit which involves two parents and their children (offspring) living together in the same household. In the United States, this is considered the traditional family structure. However, times are changing, and now the structure of the American family has many alternative forms. As of 2014, statistics show an estimated 46 percent of children living in two-parent homes in comparison to 73 percent in 1960 and 61 percent 1980. Children living in single-parent households rose from 9 percent in 1960 to 26 percent in 2014. Parents choosing to remarry has trended differently, with a miniscule increase from 14 percent in 1960 to 15 percent today.

More interesting is a new trend of cohabiting parents accounting for 7 percent of family structure, which was nonexistent in 1960. This may be partly due to parents just choosing not to marry at all. The growing fear of separation and/or divorce is the contributing factor to the trend of just living together, sharing bills, and raising children without a contractual agreement within the institution of marriage. Today, the covenantal agreement between husband and wife is losing its authenticity, and what was once referred to as sacred vows are no more than empty promises. In fact, statistics show that 45 percent to 50 percent of first-time marriages in the United States end in divorce. For persons on their second and third marriages, the number increases significantly to 60 percent to 73 percent. These numbers may sound astonishing to some but, more and more, single-parent households are becoming the new normal and a common reality.

Most people do not go into relationships with the intentions of not trying to make it work but sometimes that is the reality they are faced with. People are connecting with each other before dealing with emotional baggage and mental hang-ups from past broken relationships (parental, familial, or sexual) before they've had the opportunity to mature emotionally. These unresolved issues prevent them from being successful independently, let alone as part of a healthy union. Sometimes, we get married to the wrong person for all the right reasons or get married to right person for all the wrong reasons. Whatever the case, the relationship ends in divorce. Consequently, we break the passionate promises vowed in the presence of family and friends at the wedding alter. By 1997, 80 percent of marriages ending in divorce were filed under "irreconcilable differences." The term means that two people are unable to come into agreement to reconcile a difference. Simply put, if I don't agree with the thinking of my spouse, then I have a reason to leave the marriage. I can break our truce or vow thus becoming a trucebreaker. Initially, abuse, adultery, or an abandoned spouse were the only bases for ending a marriage. Interestingly enough, those few reasons are more aligned with biblical principles. I believe there are only three states in America (Arizona, Arkansas, and Louisiana) that offer this type of marriage as an option at the onset. Although covenant marriage is a viable option in these states and resembles God's intent for marriage, only a few couples choose to approach their vows in this way.

Approximately, 73 percent of people end their marriages because of "lack of commitment." That is a high number with unfaithfulness. However, with forgiveness, repentance (a change of heart/direction), lots of prayer and God, even broken marriages because infidelity can be restored. Our marriages and families are in trouble because God is no longer in the driver seat and societies values are taking over. Many of the characteristics we as men and women have acquired through our sinful nature prevent us from having healthy and positive relationships with each other. This is not everyone but often either both people or someone in the union suffer from selfishness, pride, ungratefulness, lack of affection, aggression, and unholiness. It is no wonder we have a difficult time getting on one accord and ending the marriage. If we can fix our hearts and minds, we can cure our relationships. Sometimes, that may require extra support from a marriage counselor, individual therapy, an elder, or even a good book. There is plenty of content out there on the topic. If you are interested in strengthening your marriage or preparing yourself while you wait, then I suggest you search out notable authors like Willard Harley, Jr, Gary Chapman, Henry Cloud, or Myles Munroe. Additionally, I believe understanding the significance of our roles in a marriage and the household provides us with wisdom on why we are better together than apart. God created us different, with different needs on purpose. We are meant to complement each other in relationship, not compete.

Man Identity

Man, one of God's greatest and most revered creations. God was so kind and gracious that He designed man in His own image and likeness. Before woman was created, God was intentional about pouring into man, his identity and daily functions. God gave Adam a job, authority, instruction to protect, and the tools to provide for the rest of creation. In Genesis 1:26, God begins to detail the role of man with giving him the responsibility of having dominion over the fish in the sea, birds of the heavens, the cattle, all the earth, and all the creepy things that crawl upon it. When we read a little further in Genesis 2, we learn that He gave man the job of tending and keeping the garden of Eden. In these mandates, you see two of a few basic characteristics of mankind being shaped—which is man "the protector and the provider." The definition of "protect" is threefold and includes keeping safe, aiming to preserve, and restricting by law access to or development of land so as to preserve its natural state. I don't think God could have been any clearer with the job description. God created man to execute a portion of His affairs and bestowed him with the weight of tending to things situated on earth.

There is an innate weight of responsibility a man holds with living up to a predecessor of divinity. Having God El Shaddai (God Almighty) as your predecessor may be intimidating if you haven't the faintest idea who your father is, or if you feel you are too insignificant to ever fill his shoes. God, the Creator of all things, designed man to dream, create, and reign here in this life. If any of you add the suffix of junior or senior to your name, you may understand this better than anyone else. You are always looking to regard the legacy in the highest esteem by being as great or greater than your father. This applies to those who come from very humble beginnings just as much as those who are born into a family of privilege or royalty. God's desire for man had not changed as much as the perception of the creation (mankind) in their Creator's identity. Some men have lost sight of who they are because they don't know their spiritual father all that well, nor understand how they could ever compare or begin to live up to the stature of Him. Unfortunately, man has struggled with his identity in God since the beginning, when Adam and Eve disobeyed Him by eating from the tree of the knowledge of good and evil. Hence, the awareness of their humanity came crashing down like a flood. In their knowing, they hid from God, and from that point on, the spiritual relationship became strained. If we know anything from earthly relationships, it is that you cannot hide from someone and get to know them at the same time. Consequently, God punished man for his disobedience to His mandate to rule over EVERYTHING on earth. It says in Genesis 3:17:

> Because thou hast hearkened unto the voice of thy wife, and hast eaten of the tree, of which I commanded thee, saying, Thou shalt not

eat of it: cursed is the ground for thy sake; in toil shalt thou eat of it all the days of thy life; thorns also and thistles shall it bring forth to thee; and thou shalt eat the herb of the field; in the sweat of thy face shalt thou eat bread, till thou return unto the ground; for out of it wast thou taken: for dust thou art, and unto dust shalt thou return. (KJV)God's punishment to mankind was to labor and work for their survival. Until that point, food was not a matter of concern for Adam and Eve. I'm not certain of their means for obtaining nourishment prior to the fall, but I imagine they did not get hungry, or food was provided (manna and quail) from heaven, as described in Exodus 16:4–16. God provided manna to the Israelites for forty years until their exodus from Egypt was accomplished due to their griping and complaining to Moses and Aaron about God leaving them in the wilderness to die.

Since the fall of man, God has demonstrated a natural propensity towards provision for their households. It is in this verse where another one of man's primitive characteristics was established—being a provider. Men are divinely ordered to be providers and should have a natural propensity towards work and providing bread (subsistence) for the home. Have you noticed how most men you know can become obsessed with their jobs or careers, even to the point where they run themselves down? The word God spoke over men in the garden still stands today, and men must work. Many Scriptures thereafter give examples for men in their work and responsibility of providing for their families. Paul states in I Timothy 5:8, "But if any provide not for his own, and specially for those of his own house, he hath denied the faith, and is worse than an infidel" (KJV). In 2 Thessalonians 3:7–10, another Holy Spirit–inspired passage, it says:

We were not idle when we were with you, nor did we eat anyone's food without paying for it. On the contrary, we worked night and day, laboring and toiling so that we would not be a burden to any of you. We did this, not because we do not have the right for such help, but in order to make ourselves a model for you to follow. For even when we were with you, we gave you this rule: "If a man will not work, he shall not eat." (NIV)

This clarifying Scripture gives light to how men may inappropriately displace their roles and responsibilities by not working, providing for themselves or their immediate families (i.e. children, spouse, or elderly parents). Today, we are seeing this misalignment in society. Especially, in the African American community. Men have to be careful not to allow culture to pull you out of your role. The African American household was fractured at its onset with slavery and many men were stripped of their dignity, respect, and position as leader. Without the best version of a man in the home to model, a young man is lost and ill equipped to play his role when it is his turn. Generations later, we see some men display effeminate characteristics; holding onto an entitlement mentality; spreading their earnings thin amongst multiple residences with two or three mothers or, even worse, allowing a woman to be the sole provider of their household.

As seen in the garden of Eden, this way of thinking is out of order, out of alignment, and has dire consequences—such as being cursed with hard labor and being kicked out of the garden. Like it or not, men were created first and, by design, are purposed to be leaders in their homes. Men, be strong, courageous, and clear about your true identity. Yes, women are beautiful, confident, and strong but do not allow mainstream media to tell you that women do not need you. She indeed needs you but functioning in your God ordained assignment. God created woman from Adam's rib to be a helper and for her to be unified with man (Genesis 2:21–24). When considering the anatomy, understand that the ribs protect the lungs, a vital organ to our existence. Without the breath of life, the living soul will perish, and just as well; without each other, our existence will be no more. Man and woman need each other to survive and replenish the earth. Moreover, when men and women operate outside of the order that God created them, discord in the family unit typically occurs.

Woman Identity

Many women can attest to the high demands of the workforce today, how it leaves little time or energy to do much else but stare at a wall for an hour or two just to collect one's thoughts and feel human again. Now, this is not the case for everyone; there are some superhuman women who manage to assist with homework, clean the house, attend to the needs of their spouse, run errands, and fix dinner after a long, hard day at work, all without breaking a sweat. To those who are able to accomplish such a feat, I take my hat off! Understand, this type of woman is a unicorn, and most women struggle to thrive in such a multitasking household. It is hard to be responsible for two places at the same time, but the modern woman has no choice but to try. Although tough, it is certainly doable with great discipline and organization. There are some women who are single mothers by default and are responsible for the entire household without the help they need or desire. It becomes even more challenging as a woman and we decide to either take on the full responsibility of being the provider for our households or struggle through impoverished circumstances. For many, the burden of caring for the home and raising the children alone is extremely difficult. Some stop trying altogether and rely on governmental assistance to obtain the necessary resources for households.

As I mentioned earlier, the modern woman lives in a world where she works and tends to her family with the greatest intentions. She is the twenty-first-century woman who is accomplished and is able to afford many things, such as cars, clothes, large houses, shoes, and new technology to support her family and lifestyle with or without a man. She is resilient, qualified, and independent enough to take care of the entire household with limited support. Unfortunately, she is not afraid to let the man know it! More and more, women are realizing that, with high ambitions and perseverance, they are able to accomplish anything, even aspiring to become President and Vice President of the United States.

I need to emphasize that God's intentions were for both distinct male and female roles to be in place at home for our families to effectively and efficiently operate. Independence was not God's natural design, nor was reliance on government assistance. Scripture says it is not good for man to be alone (Genesis 2:18 KJV). The traditional female role of housewife or stay-at-home mom seems beneath some women and it is sometimes viewed as lazy or old school. Although the liberation of women is great and shows progress from previous generations, it does not mean a traditional role in the house should be regarded as backwards thinking. This could not be any further from the truth—it takes a strong woman to manage her household affairs. In fact, God has a lot to say about the role of the woman and the optimal management of her home, family, and husband. In Proverbs 31:10–31, Solomon describes the woman:

Who can find a virtuous woman? For her price is far above rubies.
The heart of her husband doth safely trust in her,
so that he shall have no need of spoil.
She will do him good and not evil
all the days of her life. She seeketh wool, and flax,
and worketh willingly with her hands.
She is like the merchants' ships;
she bringeth her food from afar.
She riseth also while it is yet night,
and giveth meat to her household,
and a portion to her maidens.
She considereth a field, and buyeth it:
with the fruit of her hands she planteth a vineyard.
She girdeth her loins with strength,
and strengtheneth her arms.
She perceiveth that her merchandise is good:
her candle goeth not out by night.
She layeth her hands to the spindle,
and her hands hold the distaff.
She stretcheth out her hand to the poor;
yea, she reacheth forth her hands to the needy.
She is not afraid of the snow for her household:

for all her household are clothed with scarlet.
She maketh herself coverings of tapestry;
her clothing is silk and purple.
Her husband is known in the gates,
when he sitteth among the elders of the land.
She maketh fine linen, and selleth it;
and delivereth girdles unto the merchant.
Strength and honour are her clothing;
and she shall rejoice in time to come.
She openeth her mouth with wisdom;
and in her tongue is the law of kindness.
She looketh well to the ways of her household,
and eateth not the bread of idleness.
Her children arise up, and call her blessed;
her husband also, and he praiseth her.
Many daughters have done virtuously,
but thou excellest them all.
Favour is deceitful, and beauty is vain:
but a woman that feareth the Lord, she shall be praised.
Give her of the fruit of her hands;
and let her own works praise her in the gates. (KJV)

The scripture is describing the strength of a woman and her role in her community and household. Women of virtue possess an ability to be business minded, busy working, and always concerned about the affairs of her home. Her children grow up and call her blessed, and her husband sings her praises as well.

As you can see, God's intention for the woman is a strong one, and she exudes many of the characteristics of the twenty-first-century woman. However, she is designed to be this for her husband and family. With so many financial demands on households, one of the greatest blessings God bestowed on mankind—children and family—has taken a backseat in pursuit of Western civilization's American Dream. Women are finding less time to be inside their homes when they are working as hard or harder than the men to provide for it outside of the home. The scenario of children rising up and calling their mothers blessed like the scripture suggest is less frequent, and some children rise up and call their mothers everything except a child of God. This is further perpetuated when men view and call women degrading, unflattering names. The woman is losing her reverence in her home, and in order to take it back, she has to begin understanding and being fully engaged in her role as the woman of her home. Whether you want to accept it or not, men are watching and need you. I cannot begin to tell you how many times I have heard men make general statements about how unkempt some women keep their places and how disappointed they had been by the offense.

Unfortunately, with all of a woman's explanations for not maintaining cleanliness in her home, men have a natural propensity to expect women to manage their home dwellings. God has placed such a unique role on women that He uses the Apostle Paul to advise the older women to pass along their wisdom to the younger women so that they know how to treat their husbands and raise their children (Titus 2:3–5). In fact, Paul calls this sound doctrine since the way we teach future generations is through physical example and consistency. Women, your children need you to nurture them into God-fearing adults. This is not just the responsibility of the clergy or Sunday school teachers, nor of friends or media devices. Children and men alike rely on their mothers and wives for a softness and acceptance they may not receive outside the home. Husbands need a woman's support so that he feels respected out in the world. Men need respect, and this is a fundamental truth for all men despite race or background; however, some men may be at more of a deficit of respect than others. These men may be highly sensitive in this area and may be unaware of how to communicate that need effectively. Men may seek respect in maladaptive ways, such as cheating or having difficulty committing to relationships, which further burdens the entire family. Men are created to be the head of the house, and God calls wives to be under their submission since the fall in the garden of Eden (3:16). In Ephesians 5:22–24, Paul says wives are to submit themselves unto their own husbands as unto the Lord, for the husband is head. Just the same, men have to be obedient to the word and love their wives as Christ loves the church. Christ was unrelenting with His love and willing to sacrifice His life for the church. Sacrifice can be painful and goes against the natural propensity for self-perseverance. It is the opposite of selfishness. How does this look? It means a man seeks to address the woman's needs before his own. He is attentive to her needs and desires that may differ completely from his own. He may go to a musical play when he'd rather watch football. Okay, I may be taking it too far with the musical play over football example, but the point is sacrifice.

In some cultures, women are better at being submissive than others due to values passed along generationally, especially in Hispanic, African, Indian, and European women. Just the same, there are other cultures that struggle more with submissiveness and pass along strong family values to their children and young ladies. Black women are on the top of that list, unfortunately. I'm a black woman and can attest to the many unfair cultural factors, which has led to this hard exterior and mental toughness. If I am transparent there are times, when I internally battle this persona. Overpowering and domineering women are not God's design for the partnership of a marriage. We have to counter culture and learn ways to respect our men, even when they lack the tools or finesse to rightfully obtain it. We have to face that African-American men have been placed at a disproportionately disadvantage due to slavery, segregation, and the residue left behind. Sometimes black men lack healthy male role models due to father absenteeism and the lack of financial resources to provide for the household at the same level as the black woman or men from other cultures. I empower and implore those black men, who have developed the right tools for successfully leading a household to share their knowledge with their brothers. Become mentors and encourage our men in the areas of finances, communication, education, and leadership that require development. Women, the best way to keep the drama down in our lives is to avoid the drama before it enters the gate. When a man shows you that he is not quite ready to be the head of the house, believe him. Please leave him alone and allow him time to figure out how to handle this responsibility before you cohabitate and engage in sexual relations with him. If he needs you to be his mother and guide him into manhood, then he's just not ready to be in a serious relationship like marriage. Let him go, to let him grow. I am preaching to myself as I minister to you. It may require much patience but God is able to bring us the spouse that suits us best.

CHAPTER 4

WORD IDENTITY

"Words, in my humble opinion,
are the most inexhaustible source of magic we have."
—**Author Unknown**

I will begin this chapter by posing this simple question: What are you saying? I mean, really, what are the words that are coming out of your mouth? Words are powerful—period. I have to begin by saying that this particular chapter was not a part of the original outline for this book. However, the way God works, He will maneuver (through the Holy Spirit) and have His way to make sure His full message is conveyed. The more I learn about the word and power embedded within, the more it makes absolute sense why the Holy Spirit would prod me in this direction. Truth comes in knowing the influence of words in shaping our identity and how we ultimately build and shape our daily lives. So, in obedience, I am adding this chapter to give honor and glory to my heavenly Father by writing about the significance and power of His word and its influence on our identity.

Language and, essentially, the words we speak are powerful. Throughout Scripture, God is intently conveying this message about the power in our words. Unfortunately, this truth flies under the radar for many believers and unbelievers alike. I should know since I was one of those believers who just did not get it. I would cringe when I heard ministers, church folk, or my own precious mother saying things like, "You got to name it and claim it, April." My thoughts were, "Yeah, right"; "Ugh, God is not a genie"; or "How ridiculous! When are these people going to get it?" In reality, the question should've been, "April, when are you going to get it?" Reflecting back, I can laugh at my ignorance and realize that I had a lot to learn or unlearn.

I am sure, at some point in your life, you have heard the phrase, "Sticks and stones may break my bones, but words will never hurt me." This phrase is often used to negate negative feelings shaped by hurtful words spoken to or about you. It's catchy but couldn't be any further from the truth. In fact, words do hurt and leave a lasting impression within us that may or may not fade with time. If this mantra resonates with you and has found its way into your memory bank, please take a moment to reflect if people's words have never hurt you.

While researching the word topic, I came across this same example in Bill Winston's book *The Law of Confession*. Winston is a prominent pastor in the Chicagoland area who has built an amazing ministry on the principles of the law of confession and the power of God's word. His message about the benefits of operating with kingdom thinking resonates. "What is kingdom thinking?" you ask. I believe Jesus gives us the best way to grasp this way of thinking in Matthew 16:19, when He tells Peter: "I will give you the keys of the kingdom of heaven; whatever you bind on earth will be bound in heaven, and whatever you loose on earth will be loosed in heaven" (NIV). Jesus provides Peter this additional insight about how spiritual matters work, following an agreement about Jesus's identity as the Son of Man (Matthew 16:13–17). I was excited to know that God was speaking to me on this matter and desired for me to fully understand this fundamental truth. Essentially, our words have the ability to create, build, bruise, or tear down. Building and constructing is always wonderful, but words also have the ability to cause demolition.

In layman's terms, we can either use our words to edify or to tear down situations and people in our lives. Unfortunately, with so many false truths surrounding the gravity of what comes out of our mouths, most people say whatever they feel without any second thought to the repercussions of their words. In the heat of an argument, we may allow our emotions to get the better part of us and say offensive or hurtful words to our family members, friends, coworkers, and/or spouses. Unfortunately, after our emotions have calmed and the situation has resolved, we or the other party are often left perplexed and impacted by what was said during those heated moments. When our words hastily fly from our mouths in anger, disgust, fear, anxiety, and pride we are rarely truly ever able to retract the effect we have made, even with a sincere apology.

There are many things that have flown from my mouth that, after much contemplation, I wish were never spoken. I remember many arguments, either with an ex-boyfriend or family members, where I came back and apologized for what I said in the heat of the moment. Although my apology was hypothetically accepted, the significance of the words lingered as time passed. This becomes evident when a new situation arises and some of those things I said (and I thought I was forgiven for) very easily resurface. I'm sure you have experienced the same thing. If you are like me, you probably thought to yourself, "Goodness, why do they keep bringing up old stuff?" Moreover, there are words that have been spoken against me by people I loved that have caused quite significant damage as well, and at other times some very positive things have been said that have encouraged my soul tremendously.

In some cases, these words have reshaped the course of my life with the ending or initiation of relationships both personal and professional. For example, I remember the day I considered being an occupational therapist based on a verbal exchange with a near and dear family member. I had been working as a staffing agent for approximately four years and, for the most part, enjoyed my job. However, in the mid 2000s, my stepfather suffered a massive stroke and tasks like talking, writing, eating, and walking were difficult for him and, therefore, he required rehabilitation. Literature was provided to my family to educate us on what to expect from the rehabilitation team during his recovery. Occupational therapy was one of the therapies he would receive, and the leaflet shed light on some of the activities he would participate in during his therapy. I wanted to keep my stepfather motivated and progressing along, so, during my visits to the nursing home, I would have him do various tasks that the therapists would traditionally do with him, like writing and washing his face. During one visit in particular, my nephew saw me assist his grandfather in writing his name on a piece of paper. My nephew said, "You would be good at this job, Aunt April." "How cool would that be?" I thought. "Me, a therapist?" After researching the idea further, I ended up enrolling in prerequisite courses in 2009 and graduating with my master's in Occupational Therapy in 2013. Crazy, huh? Not really.

I'm here to let you in on a little secret and one of the most powerful truths you could ever grab hold of. Come close so you can really get this. Our words possess a spiritual root that far exceeds our natural abilities. In John 6:63, Jesus says, "The words that I speak to you are spirit, and they are life" (NKJV). How can words be life? And why did Jesus want us to know that? Could it be because we are made in the very image of God? The spirit of God is described as *ruach* in the Hebrew language, which means "wind" or "spirit." *Ruach* was present in the beginning of creation and hovered over the face of the waters, the sun, animals, and man when created. God is wind, God is life, God is the air we breathe, and God is the words we speak. It actually makes more sense when we begin to understand the power of words in this way. If I speak things into existence, then I'm ultimately operating in the likeness of God, our Creator. Through words I honor Him in my acknowledgement of His infinite power and the creation of the world. He receives glory when I choose to believe when He says I possess the same power and then begin to speak to my circumstances and expect them to change. This is the true essence of faith. According to Hebrews 11:1–3:

> Now faith is being sure of what we hope for and certain of what we do not see. This is what the ancients were commanded for. By faith we understand that the universe was formed at God's command, so that what is seen was not made out of what is visible. (NKJV)

I can neither see nor feel God, but by faith, I believe that He exists and is always there. Just like air, which I cannot see nor taste, but you better believe I know that it is there. Without it, this fleshly body I am encased in would collapse and become nothing but dust in the ground. Without it, I would suffocate and seek a resolve and way to breathe. Like air, my spiritual man seeks to be in relationship with God whom I cannot see and without whom my spiritual man will collapse and perish. It is my faith in God through Jesus Christ, which allows me to see Him working on my behalf in a very tangible way over, over, and over. God, in His awesome glory—invisible but reachable—is prodding and waiting to connect to us whenever we give Him the green light.

Something in us longs to connect to Him as well. All mankind possesses this force and yearning for connection to the ultimate life source. They may choose to ignore and suffocate it, but the seed exists and is always seeking resolve. Some people may reason away the gravitational pull toward this spiritual nature, but I believe one day we will all know the truth about this universe and our existence. This will be a glorious occasion for those who believed in the Word of God while on earth, but hellacious for others who did not. If you are trying to figure out what words or faith have to do with your identity, my reply is simple: everything. Everything we are and *are not* derived from the deep of invisibility or darkness, where the spirit of God hovered over the waters (Genesis 1:2). It was over the deep where God called out and named the first contrasting element: light.

Here is an interesting fact for all my scientist and analytical readers: In the story of creation, the first element God named in the abyss of darkness found in our universe was light. The very first element on the periodic table is hydrogen. Yes, hydrogen and helium (number two), are the major properties found in both the stars and sun that illuminate our sky (light). Pretty cool, right? Could be a coincidence, but maybe not. On this planet, everything and everyone has a specific name, an identifier to disassociate them from other things or people. We ascribe adjectives, which serve as descriptors to provide further distinction between people and things, to help us identify what someone or something is. In fact, the task of naming all animals and birds was one of the very first assignments God placed in the hands of mankind, as described in Genesis 2:19: "Now the Lord God had formed out of the ground all the wild animals and all the birds of the sky. He brought them to the man to see what he would name them; and whatever the man called each living creature that was its name" (NIV).

Whatever Adam decided to call the beast or bird became its name. There was no debating or negotiating between God and Adam; it was now the name. It is my belief that it was here in Scripture where God was teaching Adam of the power that he possessed through His words. God essentially said to him, "Just name it, and it will be as you say." It is the secret and mystery of the universe. What a beautiful gift. Unfortunately, it is also my belief that, upon disobeying God's instruction of not eating from the tree of the knowledge of good and evil, Adam forfeited the true value of this beautiful gift. In Adam's newly acquired knowledge, he (mankind) became hypersensitive to natural properties found in this world and desensitized to the spiritual. Adam and Eve saw and realized, "Oh snap, we are naked!" They became enlightened by their human nature. In a quest to discover more, they knew less. Unfortunately, mankind's perceptions only amount to a measly understanding of 4 percent of the universe, which is primarily the physical properties of the planets, sun, moon, etc. Yep, you got it. Scientists have researched for decades and are only able to rationalize about 4 percent of this world. They are limited by what can be measured with vision, hearing, taste, tactile, and proprioceptive sensory input. It's the metaphysical elements that have scientists perplexed and the atheists shaking their heads at all of us "crazies" who dare to believe there is something beyond what our eyes show us.

The question becomes, what are we missing? What are we not getting? An awful lot, it appears. Our universe is comprised of several elements consisting of gases, liquids, and metals. Oxygen (a gas) is one of those elements on the periodic table alongside hydrogen, helium, and nitrogen. Oxygen is one of the very last elements God utilized to create mankind. Genesis 2:7–8 states, "And Jehovah God formed man out of the dust of the ground, and breathed into his nostrils the breath of life; and man became a living soul" (ASV).

Our breath (oxygen), produced in our lungs is vital to our very existence, but guess what? We cannot see it either. You and I could not and would not be if the breath of life were not circulating throughout our bloodstream to other essential organ systems, such as our muscles, brain, and heart. Additionally, our speech is a direct derivative of the oxygen (air) in our body created within our lungs. The words we speak are produced through the mechanism of pumping air (diaphragm) across our vocal cords to create vibrations, which create sound escaping through our mouths. Our breath has a dual responsibility with providing life within our bodies and simultaneously responsible for allowing the voice and tone for our speech. I wonder if this is mere coincidence as well, or something deeper. I hypothesize that God, in His infinite wisdom, strategically made oxygen responsible for both roles, because oxygen is more powerful than we could ever comprehend.

Jesus did describe words as a spirit in the book of John. John the Baptist explains this truth best in John 1:1 when he says, "In the beginning was the Word, and the Word was with God, and the Word was God" (KJV). I find this Scripture fascinating because it details the value of something that we as humans sometimes take so lightly: our words. In John 6:63, Jesus states, "It is the Spirit who gives life; the flesh profits nothing. The words that I speak to you are spirit, and they are life" (NKJV).

In this Scripture, Jesus tries to provide the disciples with an understanding of His life and ministry. Jesus wanted the disciples to know that the miracles He performed were influenced by spirituality and not His natural abilities. Jesus knew that there were some disciples amongst Him who did not believe in the things He was saying. It is my belief that our words are transformative and life altering. It is with our words that we are able to confess Jesus as our lord and receive salvation; it is with our mouths that we can curse a fig tree from its root to prevent its growth from ever occurring again; it is our words which cause healing to occur, and it is with our mouths that we can cast a mountain into the ocean. If we ever grip this revelation of the truth and begin putting it into practice, our natural lives would forever be changed. As I'm sitting here writing these words, I can tell you that I'm only beginning to scratch the surface of this truth and adequately apply it to my daily life.

In 2006, author Rhonda Byrne wrote a book called *The Secret*. The author describes the law of attraction and the effect of thoughts on life outcomes as it relates to money, relationships, health, and happiness. I'm not sure if you remember this, but everyone started talking about this "secret" phenomenon of speaking to the universe. The idea is, if you meditate on a subject or thought long enough, it will manifest physically. People all over the world began to write and speak aloud their affirmations to help shape their lives. This concept flew, because celebrities who live rather lavish lifestyles heavily endorsed the idea. What person wouldn't want to live like a superstar or millionaire? Surely, if they followed a model that was utilized by Will Smith or Oprah Winfrey, it would propel them into similar success by simply speaking to the universe. Interestingly enough, Rhonda did nothing but reintroduce a spiritual truth found in the Bible and then wrap it up in a secular package. If the world can take hold of something that God has clearly outlined in His word, surely as believers we should take a clue. God, since the beginning of time, has empowered mankind to create and control our world through our words.

Language is powerful; it shapes the thoughts of people that hear it. God said that faith comes by hearing and hearing by the Word of God (Romans 10:17). Our faith begins in our thoughts, which in the Bible is described as our heart. Proverbs 23:7 says it like this: "For as he thinks in his heart, so is he" (NKJV).

Our thoughts are essentially manifested through our actions, which are based on what we heard. When you hear good things about yourself, like you're beautiful, smart, and/or so talented, you may form a belief that may propel you to try or do something outrageously big like trying out for American Idol or applying to medical school. On the other hand, what you hear could work negatively against you, since sometimes the people responsible for cultivating us don't realize the truth about their words and the gravity they hold. Out of ignorance, they may have called you a harsh name like stupid, ugly, or even worse, good for nothing. You cannot begin to comprehend the damage such words have on a person's self-esteem and self-worth. Maybe you experienced a parent, teacher, friend, coworker, or family member who has said such negative things to you and have left an unattended wound in your soul. I'm telling you today that you have to find out what God says about you and begin to say those things to yourself instead. You will find out what He says about you in the Bible. "For the word of God is living and active. Sharper than any double-edged sword, it penetrates even to the dividing soul and spirit, joints and marrow; it judges the thoughts and attitudes of the heart" (Hebrews 4:12, NIV).

Search the Scriptures and begin to say them aloud so you can hear it loudly and clearly. You may have heard someone referring to this process as speaking affirmations. Whatever you label it, it is good practice to speak out loud positive words to yourself. What I believe and say about myself will be manifested outwardly, and you are no different. If you could come to a true revelation and understanding of what that means, your life's outcomes will be boundless. The Scripture in Genesis 11:1–6 does a great job of illustrating this point with the story of Babel:

And the whole earth was of one language and of one speech. And it came to pass, as they journeyed east, that they found a plain in the land of Shinar; and they dwelt there. And they said one to another, Come, let us make brick, and burn them thoroughly. And they had brick for stone, and slime had they for mortar. And they said, Come let us build a city, and a tower, whose top may reach unto heaven, and let us make us a name; lest we be scattered abroad upon the face of the whole earth. And Jehovah came down to see the city and the tower, which the children of men built. And Jehovah said, Behold, they are one people, and they have all one language; and this is what they begin to do: and now nothing will be withholding from them, which they purpose to do. (ASV)

As you see in this story, God makes emphasis on the power of language and the effects of being on one accord with our speaking. Their speaking was directly linked to their thinking, purpose, and intended goals. He says there is nothing that will be withheld from them, which they intended to do. By getting familiar with the Word of God and then repeating what He says, we are on one accord with Him. His word says that there is nothing we cannot do if we do this. One accord is to have a harmonious union of sound or consent of will amongst two individuals or groups. This truth is important for us to grasp since it serves as a standard for our families to operate in as well. It is the division and discord that has so many marriages and families in disarray. If you can begin thinking alike, you will start saying and then begin doing the same things. This behavior will ultimately transform your families and other relationships into what God intended for you from the beginning of time.

Like a child, I'm learning to utilize this information to transform my physical reality. I have developed so many haphazard habits with my speech over the years that I found myself reteaching myself the definitions of words so that I truly understand what I'm about to allow to fly out of my mouth before it reaches the air. For instance, if you are like me, you may have used the term "I love him/her to death" when describing someone you really love. Why say love them to death when the meaning of death is so finite? Shouldn't you want to love them to life? Let's do a quick exercise and break down the definition of two contrasting words, "life" and "death."

According to Merriam-Webster, life is the quality that distinguishes a vital and functional being from a dead body and the principle or force that is considered to underlie the distinctive quality of animate beings. Death is defined as the action or fact of dying or being killed, the end of life of a person or organism, the state of being dead, and no longer being alive.

How many have used the expression "I'm dead" when someone expresses something humorous or comical? Seems cute and harmless, but death's meaning is still dead or without life. We have to be careful how we use these words, especially commonly used colloquialisms we hear in everyday language. I know it seems harmless, and you may be saying to yourself, "It's not that deep. It's only a joke." I would have to ask you, "Who told you that?" It really is that deep. I believe the longer you ignore the truth about the power of your words, the longer you will leisurely float around saying whatever comes to mind and allow your thoughts to drift far from shore and off course. Unfortunately, floating causes you to create circumstances in your life and in those around you that are not as flattering as the life God desires.

I have many examples and I am sure you do, as well, of people speaking negatively about their children misbehaving by calling them "bad"; calling themselves or other people "stupid" or "dumb" when a simple mistake is made; stating predictions based on evidence of probable causes such as poor weather conditions. You may conversationally say, "It's about to get really nasty out there," or, when feeling symptoms of a cold or flu, say aloud, "I think I'm getting sick." Many of these things seem innocent when they easily fly out of your mouth, but the outcomes don't typically manifest in that way after you say them. I actually have been reexamining these words and instead of saying what I see or feel, I attempt to state what I would like to have happen. Additionally, I found it is better to simply not say anything at all.

God actually wants us to become so saturated in His word to learn what He says about an issue, so we state it instead of the obvious. For example, now when I'm feeling cold symptoms, I've learned to say I am well and whole or, simply, I repeat Scripture like the one found in Isaiah 53:5: "But he was wounded for our transgressions, he was bruised for our iniquities; the chastisement of our peace was upon him; and with his stripes we are healed" (KJV). There are several other Scriptures that believers may reference to declare healing over their body. If you do not have them committed to memory, do not fret—you can enter healing verses into an online search engine or look in the glossary of your Bible to find what you need.

Aside from dealing with minor sicknesses, there have been other moments in my life where I've been afraid about an outcome and/or situation causing harm and I have learned to say Psalms 91: "He, that dwelleth in the secret place of the Most High shall abide under the shadow of the Almighty. I will say of Jehovah, He is my refuge and my fortress; For he will deliver thee from the snare of the fowler, and from the deadly pestilence" (ASV).

I am growing into an understanding of believing what God says about it more than what I feel or think. I mean, He is the Ancient of Days and the Alpha and Omega, so His wisdom is infinite. Relying on my measly thirty-something years of knowledge is nothing compared to an all-knowing God. I thank God for teaching me to be a better steward of my words and what I say out of my mouth. As I reflect on some of the things I have said in the past, I realize how reckless I was unknowingly being. I am finally learning to guard my tongue, or in layman's terms, "watch my mouth." Yes indeed, "watch your mouth!" I remember my mom telling me that a lot when I was growing up, but that's a different context from the point I'm making here. In Proverbs 13:3 it says, "The one who guards his mouth preserves his life; the one who opens wide his lips comes to ruin" (NKJV). In another Scripture it says, "He who guards his mouth and his tongue guards himself from trouble" (Proverbs 21:23, AMP).

In practicing to do this, I have seen some amazing things happen. A recent example is when strong hurricanes were frequenting the peninsula of Florida. One in particular, named Matthew, was headed to the coast of Florida in the fall of 2016 and had the entire state in an uproar. According to news reports, this storm was wickedly powerful and had already caused major havoc in Haiti with a death toll reaching approximately 1,000. How devastating and horrible for the people of that country. Matthew's projected path was set for the United States and was to touch down first in the state of Florida. The trajectory was not looking good for the state and, within a few days, the city of Jacksonville was projected to experience a devastation similar devastation to Haiti.

My natural reaction was to attentively watch the news broadcasts and to tell my friends and family that lived out of state what was going on and inform all of my local people I cared about to run. I actually felt the Holy Spirit telling me that this storm was terrible, and it could potentially cause severe damage. I began to pray in tongues and declared that the city of Jacksonville was covered, and Hurricane Matthew would force me to flee. Interestingly enough, I was scheduled to attend a wedding in my home state of Illinois, so I would be out of harm's way if I caught an earlier flight, but I didn't want the storm to overtake the city where I lived or harm the people that I consider family and friends. My prayers were fervent and made with much supplication.

On the eve of the storm, with the projection to hit the Jacksonville coast, I used a new developing story that the storm "could" lose some power and not directly hit. I spoke life to that story and declaration and took my faith a step further and posted on Facebook that the storm was downgrading to a category two or three, would turn east into the Atlantic Ocean, and would not hit our city directly. It was so great to see my prediction manifest into a reality. That storm literally hovered several miles off the coast of Jacksonville as if an unseen force was keeping it at bay. I came home and learned that my neighborhood's power was out for no more than 30 minutes, and that much of the city was not affected with the exception of flooding at the beach and damage to their homes. It was definitely NOT the catastrophic storm that had been predicted.

I cannot speak to why Haiti was devastated in such a horrible way or to the damage that occurred directly below or above our city. Did they speak to the power of the storm as it was forecasted on the news? Did they say, "Run for cover, it's going to hit us hard"? I do not know, but maybe they did. It's our natural reaction to say what we see. "Look, here comes a storm!" It was our Lord Jesus Christ who provided the perfect example of how we are to respond to the storm when it appears, and that is to be undisturbed in rest and tell it to be quiet and calm (Mark 4:38–39). However, I will say that I know a few other believers in the city of Jacksonville, Florida who shared similar faith declarations and actually believed they can speak to natural circumstances and cause them to supernaturally change. It takes discipline to guard your mouth and unshakable faith to say the opposite of what your senses perceive, but it can be done. In fact, the Word of God says it is extremely wise for us to do so.

Solomon's Wisdom

If you are familiar with the biblical story of King Solomon, then you know he was the son of David. King Solomon, like his father, found favor in the sight of God and was blessed to have a close fellowship with Him. Solomon was asked by God, "If you could have anything in the world that your heart desires, what would it be?" His reply to God was, "I want wisdom so I can be a better king." Wow, that's admirable. Now of course, God, being the provisionary that He has always been since the beginning of time, granted him his heart's desire of bountiful wisdom. Solomon's wisdom was abounding, and from it was birthed the Book of Proverbs, which is affectionately known as the Book of Wisdom by biblical scholars. It is in the Book of Proverbs that Solomon repeatedly provides us with Scripture regarding the power of our tongue. Ultimately, being aware of the power of our words and carefully speaking our thoughts is regarded as wise to God. He gives Solomon insight on being an effective leader by teaching him that one must understand the power of one's words. I can think of one or two world leaders who could take a lesson from Proverbs.

Our words are powerful but, more importantly, God's words ARE. In fact, Scripture makes it clear that we need God's word to sustain our lives just as much as food. In Matthew 4:4, He replies to the tempter following forty days of fasting with this word: "It is written: Man shall not live on bread alone, but on every word that comes from the mouth of God" (NIV).

Jesus was in the wilderness, near the brink of starvation, but He understood that while food for our natural body is good to have, the Word of God, which feeds our spiritual being, is far more of a necessity. In fact, it was after Jesus was tempted in the wilderness that He was able to work tremendous miracles through healing the sick, casting out demons, and walking on water. I need you to get this. First, Jesus brought His body (flesh) under submission to His spirit and He was able to make the supernatural occur. That is so powerful. Jesus understood His words were a spirit and there was power in quoting what God says before proceeding with a motive. This was Jesus's ministry, and this is what the body of Christ is to imitate. In the name of Jesus, we are able to achieve the same results and allow the supernatural to occur.

Negative Words

Another popular Scripture you may have come across reads, "Death and life are in the power of the tongue" (Proverbs 18:21, KJV). It is not necessarily a literal death or life, but a metaphor for negative or positive things happening from the words we speak. Negative words are considered curses and destruction in biblical Scripture and, in the context of words being a spirit, it makes sense why they are such. On the other end of the spectrum, positive words are "blessings." I mean, we all have been there before, on the receiving end of someone's negative words, and leave the conversation with feelings of inadequacy, anxiety, or even anger. Just the same, you may have encountered a person who speaks uplifting words that edify you and make you feel like you can conquer the world.

Negative words can cut your soul like a knife and leave a person with internal scars and bruising. Complaining and bickering is another negative way we speak that causes death and turmoil in our lives. The Israelites give us the best example of how murmuring and complaining could cause devastating consequences in Numbers 14. I want to you to read the story of the Israelites in the wilderness in greater detail. However, for now, I want to illustrate how bickering caused them to forfeit their opportunity to enter into the promised land sooner. Numbers 14:26–30 reads:

The Lord said to Moses and Aaron: How long will this wicked community grumble against me? I have heard the complaints of these grumbling Israelites. So tell them, "as surely as I live, declares the Lord, I will do to you the very things I heard you say: In this wilderness your bodies will fall—every one of you twenty years old or more who was counted in the census and grumbled against me. Not one of you will enter the land I swore with uplifted hand to make your home, except Caleb, son of Jephunneh and Joshua son of Nun." (NIV)

You can see how God allowed the very thing they were complaining about to occur. They never made it to the promise land. They wandered aimlessly in the wilderness for forty years and eventually died. Their outcome was a direct reflection of their inner fears and lack of faith in God's deliverance. It was unfortunate because, instead of being grateful and thanking God for their deliverance from slavery in Egypt, they used their words to speak out their fears and complain about the circumstances of being in the wilderness. The Israelites serve as an example of what not to do while going through obstacles or challenging life circumstances. The consequences of their negative words proved to be unfruitful. Usually, seeds of fear, doubt, and disbelief are at the root cause of ungratefulness, negativity, and complaining.

Those who call themselves Christians are just as guilty of this as anyone else. Christians could easily be found complaining, gossiping, and griping about things and people they don't like in the church such as, "Why is she/he wearing that?"; "Why didn't the usher sit me here?"; and "Why are they singing that song?" Let's do a quick self-check to determine if you need to clean up your words. Are you one of those people who rarely have anything positive to say or often complains about things that do not go well? Okay, maybe you don't call it complaining, but maybe you are known for "keeping it real." Is that you? Maybe you consider yourself highly perceptive, "woke," and speak out against things that are just not right. If you are, please, take a hint from the story of the Israelites and learn to bite your tongue. I love the old saying, "If you don't have anything good to say, don't say anything at all."

Outside of watching what we say aloud, we must equally be on alert about the words we manage internally. We are constantly playing words in our mind regarding our self-worth, ideals, plans, and emotions about our surroundings. Truly, we have internal conversations about everything. This is particularly important to know since the soundtracks you and I play internally are fueling our outward realities through our belief systems. If you only believe what you personally see, feel, and experience then you shrink your thinking. We have to dare to dream and visualize past our current situations. Dreaming is so important since our actions and behaviors follow what we believe. We essentially walk out what we talk (outwardly and inwardly). Examine what you are saying to yourself inwardly because it has a way of manifesting itself in life.

I cannot tell you how many times the pep talks within myself, positive and negative, have shaped a decision I've made. Essentially, all of my decisions have stemmed from those self-given pep talks. I have talked myself into doing some foolish things based on a fear or skewed reality I created internally. I assure you that if you change your thoughts, you'll change your talk and, ultimately, you will change your life. Solomon wrote in Proverbs 23:7, "As he thinketh in his heart, so is he" (KJV).

It is important to assign appropriate values on your thoughts since your thinking propels you in a direction. Your thinking is the prime facilitator towards an action and motive. If you allow your mind to drift away freely without control, you could be steering yourself in the wrong direction, away from the path that God designed for you to be on.

Paul gives us the antidote for keeping our thoughts in check in 2 Corinthians 10:5: "Casting down imaginations, and every high thing that exalteth itself against the knowledge of God and bringing into captivity every thought to the obedience of Christ" (KJV). Paul is telling us that we need to examine our thinking and check it against what God says about the matter. I think I may have said that earlier, but I cannot emphasize that point enough. You cannot check your thoughts against God's thoughts if you don't know what He says about you, the universe, your neighbors, fear, love, or life in general. If what we think does not align itself with the Word of God, then we are most likely thinking incorrectly.

2 Timothy 3:16 says, "The scripture is given by inspiration of God, and is profitable for doctrine, for reproof, for correction, for instruction in righteousness" (KJV). In 2 Timothy 2:15, Scripture says, "Study to show thyself approved unto God, a workman that needeth not to be ashamed, rightly dividing the word of truth" (KJV). Understand that one of the best ways for God to communicate to us about the universe and how we should conduct ourselves in it is through Holy Ghost–inspired Scripture. I understand that reading may not be everyone's forte, but we live in the age of technology where physically reading a book is substituted with watching videos, eBooks, and audio commentary. This makes reading the Word of God easily accessible to everyone. Whatever your preference, it is time to get familiar with the information in some form or fashion.

In concluding this chapter, I would like to reiterate the value in evaluating your behavior as it relates to the utilization of your words. It behooves us to gain a deeper understanding of God's word and being mindful about our thinking so that we say the right things. Paul tells us how to do this in in Philippians 4:8, which says:

> Finally, brethren, whatsoever things are true, whatsoever things are honest, whatsoever things are just, whatsoever things are pure, whatsoever things are lovely, whatsoever things are of good report; if there be any virtue, and if there be any praise, think on these things. (KJV)

God provides us with a way of streamlining our thoughts, so we speak correctly and positively about people and life events. It is of extreme importance to do so, since our perceptions are primary motivators toward our actions. Moreover, we instinctively move by what we know (understand and think) or what we don't know. We should strive to seek diligently after wisdom so that we are better equipped to think on things that are true, honest, pure, and just.

The sole purpose of Proverbs is to provide a book of concise and expressive teachings to help guide us into life's truths with words of wisdom and insight. In today's information age where computers, media, and other digital devices give access to an infinite amount of ideas, perceptions, resources, data, and propaganda, it is all the more vital to guard yourself and your children's minds from negative words, filth, and deception. Knowing the truth and being wise in your understanding of acceptable and unacceptable ideas can be a matter of life and death. Discovering, speaking, and operating in God's truth is the key to the effective management of your identity, purpose, and, ultimately, what God designed your world to be before the foundation of the earth.

CHAPTER 5

MEDIA AND TECHNOLOGY IDENTITY

"In the age of technology, there is constant access to vast amounts of information. The basket overflows; people get overwhelmed; the eye of the storm is not so much what goes on in the world, it is the confusion of how to think, feel, digest, and react to what goes on."
—Author Unknown

In this chapter, I chose to combine the identities of media and technology because the two are inextricably intertwined, meaning disentangling them would be extremely difficult. Without the use of technology, media would be difficult to disseminate to the masses, and without the masses, there would not be a demand for media. The global entertainment and media markets have grown substantially over the past century, and expansion is inevitable. Trillions of dollars are spent worldwide on media products, ranging from music, television, internet, and public broadcasting. Have you ever just sat back and wondered what you would possibly do with your time if you didn't have the television, a computer, radio, cellular phone, or tablet device sitting in front of you? Would your days be severely boring and utterly unproductive without these devices? Does your daily routine revolve around checking emails, social media statuses, watching TiVo prerecorded programs like *Power*, *The Real Housewives*, *The Walking Dead*, *Wheel of Fortune*, or *Days of Our Lives*? If the answer to any of these questions is "yes," then this chapter is especially written for you.

Unfortunately, many Americans spend much of their day outside of working hours engaged in these sedentary activities. They truly would feel utterly lost if they were not able to log onto Facebook, Instagram, or Twitter to check their friends' or family members' statuses from their cell phones or watch a good "read" on reality television. The growing necessity for technology and our devices in society is almost comical if you sit back and think about it. I mean, how did we ever get along before cell phones and the internet?

You know what, I think I remember—we waited. We waited around a radio, sometimes in large groups, to listen to our favorite weekly scheduled programs. We waited for a loved one to return home from a long trip to hear about it. We waited for company to stop by; we waited until our parents prepared a hot meal off the stove; we waited for our food to be harvested. We waited to receive a love letter in the mail. We waited until we returned home or drove to a pay phone before we made a phone call. We waited to research information at the library when we needed to learn something new. We waited to have sex with someone until we were married. We waited until we returned to work the next day to pick up a task that we were handling the previous day. We even waited until someone got off the phone before we spoke to them.

The younger generations may be scratching their heads at the notion that people could live their lives in such a slow (boring) pace. With so many ways to reach and connect with a person, why on earth would a person need to wait? I actually remember the time when you might call someone and if their phone line was busy, you would wait ten minutes or so to call back. I grew up in the '80s, and my explanation of waiting is probably less significant than someone's who grew up in the '40s when communications by mail was common. Patience is definitely relative. However, the truth is, we are increasingly becoming more and more impatient as a society, and our need for instant gratification has increased.

Commercials, marketing strategies, and global companies seeking to earn more capital (money) tell us we need more products, and we believe them. Having the newest and latest cellular or smart device in our home is a must, then before you can blink, an updated model is awaiting to replace the one you just purchased. (Darn, just when you thought you were the coolest person on the block ...) Companies have become wise with leasing options for devices since they know that people's desire to have the newest model will drive their decision to forgo ownership of the older one. A marketing strategist's primary role is to research the spending habits of certain demographics and sell them products in order to influence companies' profits. Our need for the latest and greatest gadgets, homes, cars, and personal gains keeps us chasing our tails in a never-ending rat race. We will never catch it and there will always be something new and better.

Subsequently, the need for more and our utilization of the latest technology has caused us to lose sight of one of the most valuable and exhaustible resources we possess in this life—our time. I challenge you all to take a moment to consider all of the minutes, hours, or even days you have dedicated to screen time alone. Then I would like you to imagine what other productive things you could have accomplished with the time you spent in the virtual reality of your televisions, laptops, or cell phones. If you haven't heard this in a while or ever before, your time is valuable, and so is the time of your loved ones. Tomorrow is not promised and, therefore, we are to cherish each moment since it could be the last.

God reminds us of how temporal our lives are. James writes in James 4:13–15:

Go to now, ye that say, To day or to morrow we will go into such a city, and continue there a year, and buy and sell and get gain. Whereas, ye know not what shall be on the morrow. For what is your life? It is even a vapor, that appeareth for a little time, and then vanisheth away. (KJV)

The Scripture serves as indication of just how finite (having limits or boundaries) our lives are in the scope of eternity. If our lives were nothing but a vapor in the grand scheme of things, you would think we would treat each moment we live and share with others as precious and something we cannot get back. I mean, if life is only a moment, try to make the best of it.

Have you ever found yourself having dinner with a spouse, friends, or family and stayed so glued to your personal device (phone or tablet) that your dinner conversation was deduced to a couple of comments you made about a celebrity's Twitter page or a developing news story reported on CNN or WorldStarHipHop? I have to admit that I am guilty of doing this. I just think it is the most ridiculous and pathetic thing ever. What about this scenario: Have you been at a concert, but instead of sitting to enjoy the concert—you view it from your cell phone screen so that you can Snapchat or live post on Facebook? I've deduced that social media should be renamed antisocial media. Seriously! We are no longer spending time with each other because we are too busy spending time with our devices and technology.

Essentially, we are developing horrible social habits all the while conditioning antisocial behavior. We are creating a culture, which minimizes human interaction and a physical need to maintain constant stimulation. Our brains rarely get a chance to break. It is no wonder that more and more American adults are suffering from depression, anxiety disorders, or some other form of psychological distress (roughly 8.3 million or ~3.4 percent of the population). Americans are becoming socially introverted and bombarded with nonstop stressors from our cellular application alerts, family or coworkers' phone calls and texts, and no down time to process it all. Moreover, we are growing into a culture that inherently makes it difficult to obey the second greatest commandment of all, which is to love your neighbor as yourself (Mark 12:31).

I was having a conversation with someone regarding our emergence of antisocial behaviors in the United States, and his observation of this phenomenon was intriguing. He described his experience getting on a MARTA train in Atlanta, Georgia, as one where people wearing business suits/dresses glared down at their phones while they waited to enter a train car. In their ears were Bluetooth-operated ear buds and, like robots, everyone entered and exited the train car without speaking to or giving eye contact to each other. He found it interesting that they were able to do this without bumping into each other. Just like that, a form of transportation, which, in times past served to provide a means for exchanging interesting stories or, at best, good people watching, was now diminished to nothing but a means of getting from point A to point B.

Unfortunately, these moments of diminished human interaction are not exclusive to strangers on subways. Lately, we are too busy to go grocery shopping so we may place an order online to have it delivered. I am not a huge fan of shopping, so I am guilty of this preference as well. We might arrange for our children to have play dates on Skype and FaceTime, or we conveniently obtain medical advice from a telehealth professional to avoid a traditional doctor's office visit. If you think spending time with each other is too hard, then you can only imagine how much time we are spending with God. We are crowding our lives with so many things that don't matter. Things that are constantly perishing, all the while pushing away the everlasting Father of the universe and our loved ones. If you are one of those people who are struggling with both physical and spiritual time management or have found yourself in emotional distress, I have the perfect Scripture to help you out if you take heed.

The Apostle Paul gives us one of the best descriptions of how we are to spend our time in 1 Thessalonians 5:12–18:

> And we urge you, brethren, recognize those who labor among you, and are over you in the Lord and admonish you, and to esteem them very highly in love for their work's sake. Be at peace among yourselves. Now we exhort you, brethren, warn those who are unruly, comfort the fainthearted, uphold the weak, be patient with all. See that no one renders evil for evil to anyone, but always pursue what is good both for yourselves and for all. Rejoice always, pray without ceasing, in everything give thanks; for this is the will of God in Christ Jesus for you. (NKJV)

If you are spending time engaging in the aforementioned activities, you will be hard-pressed to be angry, complaining, dissatisfied, sad, overworked, and stressed. Additionally, you would simultaneously be spending more time in relationship with the Creator, God. This here, ladies and gentlemen, is Time Management 101. The good news is that it also is the antidote for depression, self-worth deficits, anxiety, egos, hate, bickering, and depleted time resources. If we are truly, positively concerned about the welfare of others and simultaneously praying without ceasing (talking to God), then we would have less time to browse the web, compare lifestyles, seek likes, or respond to all of our text messages, email, and social media alerts, which are ultimately stressors.

The enemy is truly a craftsman of deceit and distraction. It is pretty clever, if you think about it. You would think that by having new technology to make our lives easier we would have extra time for the things that matter, like our Creator and the people we love. However, with the additional time we gain through the use of microwaves, vehicles, planes, and computers we become increasingly too busy to enjoy the moments spent with our loved ones and, sometimes, even the possessions we crowd our lives with. It's really sad, when you think about it. Maybe you are one of those people who has been able to afford a more lavish lifestyle, but you are never home or have time to enjoy it. If so, it may be time for you to reflect on what takes the highest priority in your life and ask yourself some tough questions about readjustment. Like I mentioned earlier in the book, we are to be vigilant and alert since we have an adversary out there who is looking for someone to devour (I Peter 5:8). It is extremely difficult to be vigilant when you are distracted with a phone in your hand every free moment or binge-watching series on Netflix or working around the clock.

Sometimes, we are not the only ones to blame for demands on our time through technology. I find it interesting how those outside of our families acquire demands on our extra time more than those within the four walls of our homes (spouse and children) or God. CEOs and large corporations offer great benefit packages where they may provide a vehicle or cover your gas mileage, cell phone, pager, and laptop to ease the financial burden that comes with getting these companies' objectives accomplished. All of these company perks are granted in exchange for full access to your time. Your paid cell phone is directly connected to your company email where your boss may have a great idea at 9 p.m. that just has to be shared with you or, worse, he/she establishes an impossible workload that keeps you busy on your laptop until the wee hours of the morning.

It is not the intent of most people to work their lives away; however, people easily get duped into it when the money and perks are presented to them at the onset. They take the bait of acquiring more and sacrificing their peace of mind for the dream job. If you have unknowingly isolated yourself from the outside world by burying yourself into your work, then you are a perfect target for the enemy. It's all a distraction from what is most important. It is easy to seek after what looks or feels good when your values or identity in God the Creator is not deeply rooted. I'm sure you have heard this expression before: "If you don't stand for something, you will fall for anything." This mantra is so true and, unfortunately, the enemy knows this better than anyone. As I said before, his sole intent is to kill, steal, and destroy. Unfortunately, whether you are too busy with work or busy playing with your devices, you are vulnerable for a spiritual attack. The spiritual attack is to get you from accomplishing God's perfect will for your life and enjoying the benefits He has laid aside for His children. The spiritual attack begins in our thoughts and causes internal confusion and chaos.

I want you to think back to the garden of Eden. The devil posed a question and alternative reasoning to Eve, which got her to thinking and pondering differently from God's instruction (Genesis 3:1–6). God's word is a trusted source, and He is trying to keep your thinking free from distractions, unrighteousness, and untruths. If you find yourself having trouble thinking straight or are overwhelmed with emotions, it's time to refocus your priorities since you are more than likely unknowingly under a spiritual attack. God promises to keep us in perfect peace when we keep our minds focused on Him (Isaiah 26:3).

The word "peace," by definition, is tranquility, quiet, and freedom from disturbance and war. This disturbance is an internal war occurring inside of us and is typically categorized by uncontrolled thoughts, feeling unsettled, and anxiety. God frees us from the enemy attack of worldly distractions and negative thinking when we keep our thoughts aligned with His, which happens when we spend time with Him in His word, not forsaking the assembly of the saints, and praying without ceasing. Additionally, it is important to note that, unlike most things in the world, time is something we cannot get back. Until Jesus Christ returns, we all have an expiration date and, therefore, our time is limited here on this earth. I advise you to treat it as such and become wise about how you spend it. Ask yourself how you want to respond to God about the stewardship of your time while on earth. Fortunately, man's creative genius continues to evolve, so the platform for the enemy's deceit becomes easier for him to insert, providing us with shiny options through our technology.

Pop Culture Identity

Pop culture is everywhere you turn these days. It's on our televisions, radios, computers, and even when we are at the checkout counter at the local grocery store. It seems that everyone wants to be connected to the rich and famous and people who live extravagant lifestyles. Pop culture is defined as culture that is popular (pop) to the masses. It is dictated by what the general population values, believes, and/or finds interesting.

If you are familiar with music of the '70s, '80s, and '90s, then you may recognize a musical icon by the name of Michael Jackson. He was known for singing popular songs like "Billy Jean," "Thriller," and "Man in the Mirror." His songs appealed to people from all nationalities and attracted millions of fans across the globe. Jackson was before his time in that this type of popularity on a global scale was rare in the decades when he was most active. This popularity eventually inspired him to acquire the title "King of Pop." He was an icon and contributed greatly to pop culture during his time, influencing millions of fans with his dance moves, sequin-emblazoned glitter gloves, leather jackets, and the infamous Jheri curl.

I did not consider myself a big Michael Jackson fan, although, I loved his music and would often attempt to "moon walk." Just for the record, I was truly unsuccessful at it, but that will not stop my future attempts when the opportunity arises. Nevertheless, I did rock a Jheri curl for the early part of the '90s (Lawd!). Maybe you did, too. I sometimes look at those old pictures and laugh at my juicy hair and think about the many pillowcases and collars I ruined. It was a popular hairstyle at the time and widely accepted as attractive by both men and women in the United States. Michael Jackson had one; my best friend had one; and, therefore, I had to have one, too. Unknowingly, we are being sold ideas.

Whether it's a perspective on how to digest current events or images of what our lifestyles should be through mass media outlets. In the 1930s and '40s, celebrities, including Ronald Regan, sold us cigarettes and household products. Movie stars made cigarettes attractive. We later found out that cigarettes cause lung cancer, and now marketing media campaigns like "truth" ads are put in place to counter the positive imagery cigarettes once held. This example of following pop culture should be a lesson to all in being careful of following pop culture trends, because what is popular today may be deemed hazardous and harmful later in life.

Today, we continue to be sold products through imagery and famous entertainers, which has proven, over time, to be the greatest marketing asset to businesses of various kinds of products. Magazines, Instagram pictures, and television provide images of athletes, singers, and actors/actresses smiling while driving the newest automobiles, wearing the trendiest clothing or shoes, and/or utilizing the latest electronic devices. With the spread of technology, our pathways for obtaining information broadens, and we are constantly bombarded with celebrity images and ways successful people live as we follow them on their social media feeds. Reality television, Tik Tok, and Instagram have turned the *National Inquirer* into a modern day dinosaur. We are allowed glimpses of celebrities wearing their fancy designer clothing, eating at fancy restaurants, smoking or drinking their favorite poison, raising their privileged children, and arguing with each other over petty issues online and/or on their reality shows. With every new fashion design, disagreement, car purchase, or home, a culture is being established for what a person should be doing, wearing, driving, and living to be deemed successful.

For many years, entertainers obtained supplemental income by being hired to represent *Fortune* 500 companies to endorse a brand. Times have shifted a great deal, and many entertainers have a greater understanding of their influence on pop culture and forged pathways from celebrity into business ownership, stock holding, and self-branding. It has been quite interesting to watch these entertainers' careers evolve over the years, with talk show host Oprah Winfrey, model Gisele Bündchen, singer Jessica Simpson, reality show personalities the Kardashians, comedian Kevin Hart, and rappers Dr. Dre, Kanye West, Jay-Z, and Sean "Diddy" Combs. These are just a few of the names that come to mind who have used their influence to sell us products like vodka, shoes, basketball tickets, apparel, headphones, perfume, swimsuits/lingerie, and shoes. Some people watch their YouTube channels and interviews in amazement and for inspiration, which is not bad in itself if the entertainer's ideas and morals align with the Word of God. It is when we begin to take the words of the celebrity to heart and place it in higher regard than we do the Word of God that we run into trouble. This is easily done, especially when more of your time is spent ingesting the opinions and words of entertainers, observing and modeling their behaviors more than you pick up the Bible or gather for Godly worship and learning in small groups, Bible study, or church services (online or in person). Oftentimes, we look at the celebrity and covertly covet their lifestyles; therefore, modeling their glamour is sometimes more appealing than seeking God's wisdom.

News Media

As much as I love music, movies, and the daily news, I understand that the enemy uses these tools as ways to discourage and distract. Media is defined as a collective means to distribute communication to a large mass of people and includes mediums such as radio, television, newspaper, and the internet. Over time, segmentation, programming, and advertisements are aimed to target specific groups and fill our airways on a regular basis. We could essentially watch television and access the internet from sunup to sundown if we choose. American families sit in front of the "tube" and are entertained with programming, which includes an array of sports and their affiliated teams; cooking shows/competitions; fictional story lines about zombies and medieval times; celebrity reality shows; and news coverage. Follow me, if you will, and we will dig a little deeper into mass media and technology's influence on shaping our thoughts and identity.

First, let's talk about "The Media," specifically news reporting. The very first news broadcast was reported in Detroit in the 1920s. It was a short segment of approximately ten to fifteen minutes and was America's introduction to providing a larger audience with information through the air by radio. With any medium, it is the ability to reach the masses that makes it powerful, and radio was proving to be powerful with listeners tuning in across the city. Until this time, most communications were in written form via popular newspapers, such as the *Boston Herald*, *New York Times*, *Chicago Tribune*, the *Florida Times Union*, and the *Kankakee Daily Journal*. Okay, the last two were shameless plugs for my hometown and current city newspapers, but the point is that newspapers were it.

Initially, the news spread through newspaper outlets reached a smaller audience. Over time, newspapers have extended their reach. When radio was first introduced, topics were more community-centered and political. Additionally, broadcasts were not inundated with advertisements to incite buyers to purchase goods. This was the purest form of media communications. Eventually, news media transitioned from radio into television, and its reach extended much further than either paper or radio news could imagine. Television networks and their programming were limited at this time, but the imagery offered by television was much more impactful than its predecessors. The utilization of pictures and imagery on television proved to be powerful and could provide more commentary than three pages of literature. I'm sure you've heard the popular saying, "a picture is worth a thousand words." This statement is extremely accurate. Every picture produced on the silver screen provides us with tons of information to obtain and digest. Whether we were interested or not, we were being sold something with the images portrayed on television—an idea. The larger picture reveals the most critical point regarding news media, which is our understanding of the information we obtain from it.

As I discussed in the previous chapter, there is power in *words*. The media is full of words and even more words. Oftentimes, the more a story is saturated with gloom, despair, fear, and pain, the more sensationalized the story becomes. It is rare that news broadcasters report news stories that are upbeat and jolly. Maybe around the holidays, a story about a Good Samaritan doing a kind deed may get coverage, or a segment on ways to share cheer or holiday bliss will get airtime. It is also during these times that you are probably being sold something you don't really need, like bakeware, clothing, or trendy trinkets. Don't get me wrong; the news is beneficial, since it is a good idea to be aware of what is happening in the world and the community around you. However, it is of extreme importance to think objectively about the information and words you and your family are so frequently digesting. More importantly, you must be careful not to allow all the negative stories and/or imagery from secular programming to become what you think about.

Many times, news stories covered on one network will have a differing bias from another network's coverage. Most people following politics will agree that Fox News is politically conservative in its views. Therefore, mostly Republicans watch and listen to its stories. Similarly, CNN is tailored to more liberal audiences, so more Democrats will enjoy their programming. Then there are the subtle biases and negative images that may fly more covertly under the radar, which affect the way one thinks about a particular group or idea. If most of the images of African-American males on the news or other media programming include some involvement in negative behavior, such as crime or violence, then one begins to perceive that particular group as predisposed to that behavior. You may have never had a negative encounter with an African-American male but find yourself intimidated or nervous when he walks close behind you or onto the elevator with you. Where did that fear come from? A biased image is where, and now your perception has been flawed. It is of extreme value to understand how media shapes your thinking about not only yourself but also your view of others. So often news stories are written to bait the viewer into being fearful or to sell something.

The Bible gives us a way of processing the information we take in, whether good or bad. Proverbs 3:21–26 says this:

> My son, preserve sound judgment and discernment, do not let them out of your sight: they will be life for you, an ornament to grace your neck. Then you will go on your way in safety, and your foot will not stumble; when you lie down you will not be afraid; when you lie down, your sleep will be sweet. Have no fear of sudden disaster or of the ruin that overtakes the wicked, for the Lord will be your confidence and will keep your foot from being snared. (NIV)

It is our job to discern and have sound judgment to avoid getting entangled in fear or by deceptive stories presented to us. This way, we avoid becoming entrapped in negative circumstances and are able to have peace to sleep at night. Our thinking is reflected in the daily decisions we make. Therefore, we must be vigilant in guarding our eyes and ears.

Social Media

If you think television is a monster, then you must know that the internet and, subsequently, social media is a four-headed beast. I remember when the World Wide Web was new, and most people did not own a computer in their homes. There were only a few people in my immediate circle of friends or family who owned one. As for the rest of us, we were privy to the utilization of computers with the internet in more public arenas, such as the library, computer lab at an educational institution, or at our professional workplaces. Although I consider myself a fairly young person, the reality that the internet, as we now know it, has been around for approximately twenty-five years is crazy to think about. What's even crazier is the understanding that there is a group of millennial adults who only know this way of obtaining information and connecting with others.

I remember going to my college's computer lab and getting my first taste of online chatting through chat room sites. There were many chat rooms of varying interests, such as teen chat, politics, gender specific, or African-American. As a new college student, I found it exciting to talk with people from all over the country who shared some particular commonality and interest with me. Reflecting back, I would spend several hours on those sites chatting about life experiences and nontrivial subjects. Those chatting websites expanded my web of influence tremendously and provided access to people from all walks of life. There were also AOL accounts where we would dial up and receive instant email messages from people who shared the site. It was exciting to log in and hear the catchy phrase, "you've got mail." I would think to myself, "YES, I got mail! I wonder who it's from?" It was so refreshing to speak to people near and far whom you may or may not know. Hollywood even made a cute movie (*You've Got Mail*) starring Tom Hanks to fashion the idea.

Fast forward to today, the phenomenon of online chatting has grown at a rapid pace, and we are able to connect with anyone in the world instantly, and it is widely accepted in most developed countries as a way of communicating. Moreover, we no longer have to wait to get home to dial up to the internet or even log into a Wi-Fi network on our computers. Most of us have mobile devices, and people of all ages and backgrounds have replaced landlines with portable computers in the form of cellular phones—mobile phones with operating systems, which allow us to receive and send messages, emails, make phone calls, and access the World Wide Web at any moment. In many ways, it is quite resourceful to have my cell phone or a tablet with the internet to find information, get directions, or stay connected to loved ones. We can speak and even see anyone across the globe through technology whenever the need persists. High school or college classmates and distant family members are now just a simple click away. It makes a family or class reunion less exciting, but it is definitely nice to be easily connected to people you know and care about.

Do you remember when you or your parents would freak out over the house phone bill due to long distant calls? If you can relate to this question, then you also remember the emergence of the calling card. To get your hands on a calling card and a cozy pay phone was like hitting the lotto. Oh, how far we have come. Making long distant calls is a thing of the past, just as well as showing up to someone's house unannounced. Funny enough, my dad did not get that memo on unannounced house visits until the day he left the earth. My dad would casually mosey to and from family members' homes without warning well into the new millennium. I digressed for a second, but he was funny in the way that he disregarded some of the latest social norms.

Dating and socializing has changed significantly as well. Most of us browse several social networking and dating sites, such as Twitter, Facebook, Instagram, Snapchat, Tinder, Blogger, YouTube, eharmony, and Skype to stay connected to loved ones, friends, or future mates without a second thought. Technology has become so sophisticated that corporate meetings may be conducted virtually from different countries, and healthcare can be done remotely in rural areas with limited medical accessibility through Telehealth. If you grew up in the 1980s, you may have had glimpses of these times in the movie *Back to the Future*. I eagerly anticipated being able to video chat with friends, colleagues, customers, and loved ones without physically being able to touch them. Well, the time is here, and we have officially arrived, so to speak. We are essentially living and thriving in the Information Age with minimal warning and very little instruction, to say the least. I mean, there was no big roll out. Back to the future just suddenly happened. There should've been a roll out. Having a little bit of forethought or insight on the effects of technology would have been nice.

Often in the business sector, when a new company initiative is introduced, the company makes sure everyone on the team is on the same page and has a glimpse of the direction the initiative will take the company. Not us; technology just arrived, and we moved along with our lives and welcomed the next new app (application) or technological advancement with limited education. The ramifications of how this would affect us and our children were rarely talked or thought about. Whether you have taken time to think about these things or not, it is impacting you more than you can imagine. As technology continues to grow, it is important that you consider more than the convenience of it all. Online predators—cyberbullies trolling the internet with intentions to bully and incite followers with hateful and persuasive language—are preeminent threats. We should take serious notice since it is affecting your children and loved ones more than you know.

Cyberbullying among adolescent youth is a real problem in public schools. Approximately one out of three children have experienced some form of cyber threats, and over 50 percent of youth have been involved in some type of bullying online through means of posting on social networking sites or sending mean or sexually suggestive text messages. People have less of a filter behind a computer or cell phone and more easily share sensitive and private information, pictures, and videos of themselves. Some children use social networking sites to obtain validation and increase their self-esteem by receiving likes for wearing tight or little clothing while posing with duck lips, posting hateful comments/videos, or divulging personal information. The more people following them the better since they can receive more likes and, sometimes with YouTube videos and blogs, they may even earn a little extra income. The positive reinforcement of a "like" fuels more negative behavior.

There are other times when information meant to be for one person is shared with others without the permission of the victim, and the deception is even more devastating. Children send sexually suggestive text messages and pictures to their new girlfriends and boyfriends and have to worry about what the scorned individual will or will not do with the information once the relationship ends. In the wrong individual's hands, explicit pictures and language can then be reposted/retweeted and used to get laughs from other students for weeks or longer, which leaves the victim with feelings of depression, rejection, worthlessness, and even thoughts of suicide. Children are not the only ones impacted by this. Young women, especially, and men of all sexual orientations and ages post overtly provocative pictures of themselves to receive "likes." These young ladies may even pose nude, or close to it, to gain popularity on social networks like Twitter and Instagram. We live in a time when people are obsessed with vanity, and celebrities' social media pages have provided an outlet for anyone to become famous or popular. In either scenario, your child or young adult is placed in a vulnerable position to be bullied or harassed for an unknown length of time since the information could remain online indefinitely.

The larger issue at hand is the number of children at risk for committing suicide due to cyberbullying. Approximately 20 percent of children bullied consider suicide as a way out, and one in ten will attempt suicide. This is alarming since over 80 percent of youth are walking around with technological devices, and roughly 50 percent of those with devices will be bullied at some point. Additionally, children are at risk of becoming victims of child pornography, sextortion, or, worse, human trafficking. Sexual predators and offenders lurk the internet seeking to lure teens with threats of exposing pornographic pictures or videos found in chat rooms or on social media sites. In an effort to prevent family and friends from learning about their explicit sexual activity, the children are coerced to perform sex or engage in prostitution without pay. Human traffickers are on the internet to recruit and exploit young men and women for financial gain, so beware. Oftentimes, an underlying need to seek gratification and self-worth for others being interested in them in this way.

I am sure we all want to believe that our children are smart enough not to post pictures of themselves in sexually compromising positions but often children do not possess the maturity to think of the ramifications of their actions and they click and send images with simple motivations of cute emoji responses. Aside from these obvious threats to youth and young adults alike, there is also the silent threat of premature or overexposure to adult situations and information, which leads to desensitization to violence, drugs, sex, and crime, which pollutes the mind and leaves people with a warped sense of what is and is not morally acceptable. There are higher instances of children displaying aggressive and sexual behavior at younger ages. The larger picture is this: adults have a responsibility to understand what type of social networking and internet activity their children are engaged in and how they are processing all they are exposed to, so that behaviors can be better redirected before things spin out of control. Young adults must be informed of tactics geared at causing them emotional, psychological, and even physical harm. Parents have an obligation to protect their children from all possible threats, including those found in the cyber world or virtual context within our media and technology.

CHAPTER 6

SEXUAL IDENTITY

"Just because something isn't a lie does not mean that it isn't deceptive. A liar knows that he is a liar, but one who speaks mere portions of truth in order to deceive is a craftsman of destruction."
—Criss Jami

America is increasingly becoming more and more oversexed! Every day, I pick up a magazine, turn on the television, listen to the radio, or view a post on someone's social media page and I am reminded of this very fact. The question then becomes: Why is everyone obsessed with sex? Sex, in all its various forms, deeply penetrates the various media outlets. The more sexual content that is produced, the more society wants to see and have at it. Secular artists rap and sing about it, then create music videos featuring half-naked women dancing to further express their feelings toward the subject matter. The movies we watch would not be complete without a good sex scene. Websites and social media sites provide enough pornography to make *Playboy* magazine seem like a Disney brochure. You may start to wonder why everyone is so sex crazed. If you are like me, you begin to question which came first, the desire for more sex or the oversaturation of sexual content? I am not really sure, but I speculate it is the latter.

For centuries, there has been a natural propensity toward sexual pleasure seeking in cultures around the world. God has a lot to tell us about sex, and we have many examples of mankind's destructive behavior with the subject matter throughout the Bible, such as Sodom and Gomorrah, King David and Bathsheba, King Solomon, and Paul teaching to the church of Corinth, just to name a few. All in all, God knows we are having sex and sees how easily deceived with it we are.

Sexual freedoms are not foreign in places like India, where the *Kama Sutra* is woven into the fabric of the culture, offering over 200 sexual positions, or in Brazil, where legal prostitution, sexuality, and sensuality are society's norm. In fact, many countries, like Finland, France, Belgium, Costa Rica, Amsterdam, and Germany, have regulated legal prostitution. Regulated, meaning most sex workers have to register themselves and have documented medical checkups.

However, with the United States being founded on Christian principles and values, prostitution has been, and remains, illegal. Most sexual deviations in the United States have been considered taboo, immoral, and are often frowned upon in society.

Oh, how things have changed! With all the sex we are seeing, hearing, seeking, and feeling, it becomes difficult to process and filter the overwhelming amount of sexual information without becoming desensitized to it. What is more disturbing is that the oversaturation is not exclusive to adults; children of all ages are subject to just as much sex as grown-ups and are less equipped to manage the ramifications of poor choices related to sex. As we continue to press forward into the twenty-first century, everyone's moral compass becomes increasingly more skewed. Lawmakers make it difficult to decipher what is or is not morally acceptable with the passing of laws, while media gatekeepers inundate our senses with overtly sexual content and images of acceptable behaviors, relationships, and so forth.

Increasingly, society's discretion toward sexual matters has greatly diminished, and most people struggle to have a point of reference for morality anymore regarding the topic. What once may have been considered taboo in our society is now considered status quo and normal behavior. As I mentioned before, sexual immorality is one of the main contributing factors to broken family units, and the result is a society of wayward belief systems across the nation, which are passed along to our children. Confusion regarding our sexuality and orientation is becoming more prevalent, with statistics showing a trend of increased homosexuality and bisexuality in the United States. With so much information and mistruths being disseminated in mass production through television, radio, music, and other media forms, it is vital that Christians demonstrate their light in society by holding true to the values spoken to us in the Word of God. There is a high level of variation of ideologies that are surfacing and gaining popularity globally and within our American communities. Unfortunately, these ideologies have crept their way into Christian church pulpits, and believers are struggling as much as nonbelievers to know the truth about sexual identity.

I have to be transparent by stating that tackling sexual identity has required the most courage, considering my own personal struggle with the subject. I truly understand sexuality is a touchy topic, and there are some who will look to scrutinize and condemn the message. I get it. It is one of the most intimate acts we engage in as humans. It's easy to shy away from discussing it. There are so many people, including children, who are negatively affected by the sin of sexual perversion. We cannot turn on the news without a story of a priest and other adults in power molesting youth. Children and women are being taken from their homes and countries, their bodies sold on the black market to satisfy willing and buying customers' sexual lusts. Let's be clear, there would not be a market if there was not a demand.

Moreover, kids who are the product of premarital sex are being raised in broken homes and suffering the negative effects of financial hardships and neglect from absent parent figures. Men and women walk around with hidden guilt and shame, afraid to be honest with themselves about their attraction to the same sex. Some of them opt to cover and hide their true feelings while engaging in risky sexual behaviors to satisfy the urge. The body of Christ has to stand firm on the Word of God and be bold in teaching truth to everyone, saved or unsaved. Many Christians are scared to speak out about sex in the church or anywhere else in fear of offending someone. Sitting quietly idle will not help people get set free. I cannot tell you the amount of conflicting information, absorbed daily, regarding Christians' participation in sexual relations that parallel or are very similar to the world's perspective. Most people seem to have turned a blind eye to the social woes stemming from sex. We see more and more people assimilating to the world's systems, or just flat out living in denial about the negative ramifications of their sexual choices. Unfortunately, the world system is failing everyone, and people are in need of the truth whether they are ready to admit it or not.

Scripture tells us these two invaluable things: "Without knowledge the people will perish," and "How could people hear if they do not have a preacher or teacher?" Therefore, I pray I serve in those two purposes by providing knowledge to believers and unbelievers by teaching those who have an ear to hear. Paul instructs believers to spread truth in love (Ephesians 4:15) so that we can help mature followers of Christ grow into spiritual adults. Therefore, know that, although at times I may sound mildly assertive, my heart is full of love and without condemnation. Many of us unknowingly have skewed perceptions of sex that we were taught or haphazardly stumbled into by chance as children or young adults. Many would argue who and how a person chooses to share physical intimacy with is a personal matter and a choice belonging to the individuals involved. Who is it harming anyway? I believe that is a good question and I hope this chapter provides the reader greater insight of the implications of our sexual choices and how harm occurs. The truth is no one has the right to judge anyone, and not one person on earth is exempt of sin—whether it be heterosexual, bisexual, homosexual, or other sexual perversions (bestiality and incest). The sin is choosing not to love as God instructs and exalting our approach to love our way above His.

I must reiterate, I am not a judge, and it is not my intent to condemn anyone, but provide truth in love. I do not possess a heaven or hell to place anyone in, so this information seeks to enlighten. First and foremost, sex falls under a multitude of sins that man and woman commit. Sin is sin but I can attest that sex sin is truly weighted. Sexual desires and lusts carry some of the heaviest consequences while living on earth. Prayerfully, some of you will develop a paradigm shift that catapults you into making wiser decisions related to the sexual relationships you choose to enter into moving forward. For others, it may give a benchmark of how you should behave in the relationships you are blessed to be in before and after marriage. Despite personal belief, there is a personal and spiritual impact to the decisions we make related to our sexual identity. However, we all have assurance through the words of Paul with this redemptive truth found in Romans 3:23–24: "For all have sinned, and come short of the glory of God; Being justified freely by his grace through the redemption that is in Christ Jesus" (KJV).

That being said, I am a sinner, as we all are, saved by grace. I thank God for His grace that I do not deserve. Let's just be clear, I am in the perfect position to write this chapter since I have had my own struggles with sexual immorality, so, truly, I have no stones to throw here. It is through the grace of God, activated by the Holy Spirit within, that I continue to mature in this area so that I can see clearly and make wiser decisions relationally and sexually. If I had been obedient, I would have saved my virginity for my husband. We can toss that one to the wind. If I'm honest, I wish I would have waited and saved myself for my future king. I've carried some very heavy burdens emotionally, socially, and spiritually because I did not. I would have waited to learn more about the spiritual, mental, and physical ramifications of sharing myself sexually with partners I dated. In the end, maybe it surmounted to a good time. My self-esteem was through the roof until I started messing around and having premarital sex in hopes of catching a husband.

Let me help you out; having sex does not help you get married but delays the process. For some who were married, maybe you can be honest with yourself and testify as to how having sex prematurely placed pressure on you to stay in an abusive relationship or marry the wrong person! It is invaluable to have a deeper understanding of the issue of sexual immorality and how its effects on society include increased crime rates, growing division among families, economic woes, depression, and prevailing health crises. These woes have propelled me to dig a little deeper into God's word to understand what He says about the subject matter in order to establish truth in such an obscure era. As my wisdom has grown in what God deems best, I have learned why it is important to abstain from sex before being in a committed marriage. There is so much information floating around, some new and some old. That is why understanding the terminology is invaluable.

First and foremost, I would like to establish what "sexual identity" means. Sexual identity is the unique combination of a person's sexual gender, orientation, preferences, and roles and their effects on a person's identity. It is important to note that one's sexual identity is not exclusive to one's romantic or erotic (sexual) attractions. A major component of one's sexual identity is shaped by our perception of a person's gender roles and their associated social behaviors. Having a clear picture of one's gender identity is important to establish and understand one's role in society. What does it mean to be a man or a woman? It affects the way people talk, dress, behave, and engage in daily tasks.

People across racial and cultural backgrounds perceive a vast portion of their identities through the lens of gender. Social and political factors play a big role in this perception, as people may determine what they can and cannot do based on laws and culture established within their community. The United States happens to be one of the most liberated countries in the world. Therefore, opportunity limitations related to gender, social standing, and/or race are seen far less than in other countries. It doesn't matter if one grew up as a young woman in the slums of New York or young black man from the projects of Chicago, with hard work and perseverance, one can become the CEO of a *Fortune* 500 corporation. This is one of the primary reasons America is affectionately known as "the melting pot" with immigrants from all over the world seeking to live in "the land of the free" with countless opportunities.

Although society plays a significant role in the development of one's gender identity, the family in which one is raised plays the largest role in the perception of gender roles and associated behaviors. Children watch adults play out these gender roles daily in families, whether functional or dysfunctional. Children are sponges and soak up all the good, bad, and/or indifferent. They perceive adult behaviors while performing these roles without exception. This is why, no matter how many times you say it, they will not be able to comprehend the concept of "Do as I say, not as I do!"

When a male child observes his father getting up early in the morning, putting on his work outfit, and heading out the door, he is inadvertently learning how a man provides. When he sees him take out the trash, mow the lawn, or fix things around the house, he is gathering information related to tending to a home. On the flip side, when he grows up with a father absent from the house, he may easily perceive that a family can survive without a man in the home. Subsequently, he could later choose not to be in his own children's lives when he creates offspring. Everyone is different, and some children are able to look at their parents and do differently. I have met outstanding fathers like Bishop George Davis and other young men who grew up without their biological fathers in the homes. Kudos to you who find a way to fight through those tough circumstances and stand up and become the man God intended you to be.

A young man also learns when an adult male figure comes by occasionally to take the young person to the park or drop some money off to his mom, followed by remarks about how she is "lazy and good for nothing." They are also learning when they never see that father figure come by at all. When a young girl watches intently as her mom effortlessly prepares breakfast for everyone, she is establishing a point of reference for how to nurture a family. If a young girl observes her mother work two jobs to make ends meet and sometimes leave leftovers in the refrigerator for the children to reheat or order pizza when she finally returns home at eight or nine o'clock at night, her mother is teaching. Just the same, if a mother drinks and parties all night and then sleeps in the next morning, leaving her young ones to fend for themselves for something to eat before school, they are inadvertently learning a way of being a woman. In turn, children begin to understand what are viewed as acceptable behaviors in their gender roles, as well as expectations for behaviors from the opposite sex.

As I stated in chapter three, men and women have distinct roles within a family and society. Traditionally, men are characterized and are more often seen as masculine, protective providers, and leaders. Women, by contrast, are viewed as feminine, nurturing, yielding, and possess a natural propensity toward matters inside the home. As time and generational shifts occur, so do the lines that hold onto a gender-specific standard. Gender roles are increasingly becoming murky, if we want to be honest. Children are encouraged to explore tasks and ideas that deviate from what has been traditionally assigned to their gender. Society is shifting to an era in which people want to believe that identifying with a specific gender role may be self-limiting and outdated.

For example, traditionally, most people distinguished the sex of their babies by using the colors pink, for girls, and blue, for boys. Several years back, men started wearing the colors pink and purple as a trend, which, in the past were considered feminine colors. More recently, men's fashion has evolved to include skinny jeans, rompers, heels, long tees (resembling dresses), and colorful beaded jewelry traditionally worn by women to accessorize their outfits.

I must be clear that some of the feminine-looking clothing has been seen in other cultures, such as ancient Rome, with male soldiers wearing leather lappets in war, and Scotland, where men wear kilts for special occasions. And I would be remiss if I did not mention how in the United States men flirted with feminine fashion in the late 1970s and in the 1980s. Men in pop culture adorned themselves in blouses and other garments typically viewed as fashionable for women, but it was not popular among the masses. The flashy feminine fashion trend eventually faded before jeans and flannel shirts, typically worn by lumberjacks, became the norm among most men in the United States. Modern-day Western culture is more accepting of men wearing more feminine clothing. It appeals to a broader population, including athletes, businessmen, clergy, and the average man across the globe.

Additionally, the woman and her role in the 1950s looked much different from the role of the woman in the new millennium. The woman in the 1950s typically tended to the house and children while her husband worked. This role has been replaced with the working mom, who adds to the family budget by working outside the home. This has become the new normal. Many women, including myself, decided to defer establishing families to become educated so that we could contribute to the household income. Most women in our society today have to work in order to stay financially afloat, but the reality remains that working outside of the home makes it difficult to tend to family matters at the levels we desire. Some employers might even shame women for their need to leave early to check on their sick child. Additionally, the trend for men and women marrying in this generation is at a far lower rate—approximately 46 percent at older ages between twenty-seven and twenty-nine years in comparison to our predecessors with approximately 62 percent of their population married by twenty to twenty-one years of age.

Although our desire to obtain education, success, and postpone marriage may have changed, our desire for a sexually intimate relationship has not. Statistics show that roughly 93 percent of men and women have engaged in premarital sex by the age of thirty. In the United States, a measly 3 percent of couples choose to abstain from sex until marriage. I wish I could say I was part of the latter statistic. Unfortunately, I fall into the former 93 percent that engaged in premarital sex. I was seventeen when I lost my virginity to a high-school flame. This statistic denotes that most people engage in sexual relations before exchanging marital vows with someone. Having sex outside of marriage is definitely not seen as taboo as in previous decades in the United States. Once upon a time, it was frowned upon and even considered a disgrace to engage in sexual activity before marriage. Even more upsetting was getting pregnant without a father present. This scenario would send a young lady into hiding. The shame was severe.

Some of you might say, "So what? People are having sex! Whoop dee doo! What's the big deal?" Okay, so you don't think it is such a big deal. Well, let us explore some statistics and social factors that will give you some food for thought. Right now, 40 percent of children are born to unwed mothers in the United States. This translates to 40 percent of American households without a father figure living inside of the home. This does not include those who eventually marry but divorce with children in tow. More than ever, single-parent homes are common, and the negative implications become a dull ache at the heart of America's social woes. Data show that single mothers are the highest disadvantaged group in the United States. Approximately 30 percent of single-parent homes live below the poverty line, and about 37 percent live in poverty. Poverty is a real and tangible issue when viewed through the lens of ramifications it presents.

Okay, so let's define poverty for those who are far removed from such a lifestyle. Poverty is the inability to have the material resources for meeting basic needs, such as food and shelter. Poverty often leads people to meet these needs in unconventional ways, such as prostitution, government dependency, illegal drug distribution, stealing, and so forth. Ninety percent of women on welfare are single mothers. Seventy percent of gang members are children born into poverty, with more than 50 percent of those incarcerated. Additionally, roughly 64 percent of youth suicides are children raised in a single-parent home. Moreover, children from single-parent homes experience higher levels of substance abuse, and roughly 85 percent of children diagnosed with behavioral disorders come from single-parent homes. Is it still not a big deal? I don't think so. Many people living in poverty are distressed and complain, but very few people talk about the elephant in the room with true substance or resolve.

So, what is the elephant? The elephant is the broken family unit. Mother Teresa's quote in chapter three is spot on in this respect. If we are truly going to solve some of the issues we see in America, we need to start in our homes. People complain about the symptoms of social issues but never address what is causing them. Political parties argue that welfare and government assistance is an expensive crutch and places a Band-Aid on a gaping wound. Fathers outside of the home complain about having to pay child support and their subsequent difficulty establishing themselves independently. Some men may have a strained relationship with their child's mother, which makes it difficult to see their children or have meaningful conversations about child rearing. Consequently, women suffer the responsibility of being the primary caregiver, providing all of the children's bare necessities, such as a home, food, and clothing, with little to no spousal/child support. Moreover, they carry the stigma of being a single mother, which impacts future relationships with potential viable helpmates.

Sometimes, women will establish a relationship with a new mate to make ends meet but inadvertently run the risk of exposing their children to sexual and verbal abuse and other dilemmas, like running away, teenage pregnancy, and dropping out of school. Maybe the children grow up with negative feelings regarding the absent parent and the neglect from having that missing piece of their family. Dealing with daily dysfunction or discord in a home might leave a child with unanswered questions about their own sexual identity, decreased knowledge of how to model gender roles or become a productive citizen in society, and negative images of family life—and the vicious poverty cycle continues. In some cases, mental disease may settle in with major depression, gender dysphoria (incongruence with their biological sexual organs), sexual disorientation, experimentation with drugs, and the development of addictions, and other mood disorders. These issues may leave children and young adults in a vulnerable position without the tools to process it all, hence, the reasons for some of the statistics I stated earlier.

I do not believe that anyone at the outset of a relationship seeks to engage in sexual activities that ultimately negatively impact the emotional, physical, or mental well-being of themselves or their children. However, the consequences of engaging in dysfunctional relationships may render this effect. Similarly, no one wishes to have and raise a child alone or as a co-parent—it just happens, and people deal with it. Some enter into sexual relationships with the intention of keeping things strictly physical but end up in a world of emotional hurt and mental garbage to sort through. Unfortunately, sex was never intended to be so casual, and there are strings attached whether you choose to see them or not.

The enemy is clever at leading us into sexual discord with one another. Cultural influences found in music, television, and laws relax our moral standards, and we begin to believe distorted versions of truth are acceptable and harmless. Many people, including myself at one time, were grateful for the advances in medicine that made our sexual escapades outside of the marital union more inviting with the utilization of contraceptives like birth control pills, condoms, and, more recently, the morning-after pill. On the extreme side, people may choose to terminate a pregnancy when sex leads to such unexpected consequences. Over the past few decades, the sexual revolution in the United States has grown, and people casually engage in sexual interests with whomever they feel and whenever they feel with minimal thought for the negative consequences of their actions. Paul warns us of such behaviors in Romans 1:28, "And even as they did not like to retain God in their knowledge, God gave them over to a reprobate mind, to do those things which are not convenient" (KJV).

God, being omniscient, understood the hardships we place on ourselves with wayward thinking and behavior toward sexuality. With every attempt to reduce the act of sex as nothing more than a natural animalistic urge that we cannot control, there is a spiritual component that we fail to recognize. Sex is a spiritual covenant that was created by design for a man and women. This spiritual covenant occurs when the hymen of a woman breaks upon the penetration from a male penis to consummate their marital bond. A covenant is an oath, a contract, which binds two parties together. Anything outside of the bond of marriage is considered immoral or sexual immorality.

Sexual Immorality

I will not assume that everyone reading this book has spent their days of youth and/or adulthood attending Bible school to understand terms like "sexual immorality," so I will give a brief description of the term to ensure that we are all on the same page. The Greek word for sexual immorality is *porneia*. This is where the English word pornography is derived from. *Porneia* or *pornos* means the selling off of sexual purity and includes promiscuity of every type. Sexual immorality is an all-inclusive term. I believe sexual immorality is a gateway to the broken family unit. Unfortunately, our relaxed moral values regarding premarital sex and divorce in this country easily promote single-parent homes. It is primarily the rise of non-covenantal relationships that leads to men or women raising children alone. Additionally, it is one of the contributing factors of children living in poverty or as orphans.

Aside from the social ramifications of poverty, there is the growing global issue of human trafficking, which stems from poverty. Human trafficking is the exploitation of people for services or sexual acts in exchange for money. Unfortunately, there is a high demand for this form of commerce, and business is booming. Human trafficking differs from prostitution in that victims are subjected to abduction and sexual coercion. Young women and children are sold into modern-day slavery for labor and satisfying sexual deviations of the buyers. The demand for those persons trafficked is high and reaches past the borders of the United States. Human trafficking for sex can be found in almost every country around the globe. Its reach extends to developed and underdeveloped countries. According to an article published by the United Nations Office on Drugs and Crime, 79 percent of human trafficking cases account for sexual exploitation. People are paying top dollar for virgins and, unfortunately, many virgins are underage.

Why is sexual immorality so prevalent? I believe society's relaxed social standards diminish the novelty of traditional sexual practices. I need to be transparent about my involvement in noncommitted sexual relationships in the past and their negative impact on my life through early adulthood. When I was nineteen years old, I met a young man and convinced myself that he was my soulmate. We were both in college and shared so many things in common that I thought he was everything I needed in a husband. I chose him, not the other way around, which is outside of God's will.

Although I knew he was not ready for marriage, I thought I could convince him into being ready for marriage by showing him how good a wife I could be. I owned the wife role by cooking, cleaning, and sexing him in every way imaginable. I needed him to know that I was wife material so he would ask me. Although I knew it was wrong to have sex before marriage, I continued to do so with him because I convinced myself that, eventually, he was going to figure out what I knew: that we were meant for each other and good together, and he should marry me. It wasn't too long before I became pregnant. He and I were both still in college with only a year or so left. Having a baby was not a part of the immediate plan, so we decided to terminate the pregnancy. I figured we would get pregnant again when we eventually got married, so having the abortion was best. He gave me the money, I went to the clinic by myself, and the abortion was performed. I thought to myself, "That was easy," and "It wasn't a real baby yet anyway." I can recall someone reassuring me, "It's just tissue!" I found out from my ultrasound that I was approximately six weeks pregnant.

The night following the abortion, I had a nightmare in which someone was chasing me down to steal the baby from me. I was running as fast as I could. Dreams have an interesting way of subconsciously telling us things. Unknowingly, I had already allowed the enemy to steal the baby from me.

Fast forward to today, and I've asked God for forgiveness. I am forgiven, but I cannot help but wonder what my child was meant to be and do. I was tricked into believing that, if you get pregnant and are not ready to have the baby, you can "easily" get an abortion. I found solace in the belief that the baby conceived in my womb was simply undeveloped tissue and not real. I believed a lie!! I saw an ultrasound performed on a woman on television and saw that the baby had a heartbeat at six weeks. A heartbeat!! There is no condemnation from me toward anyone who has had an abortion; I'm just telling my story of my pain and my hurt. The law of the land permits it, and women like myself are able to abort a child as a part of planned parenting. It seemed so simple at the time but, twenty years later, I still think about my baby. I think about what he/she could have been, and what my child would be doing at this stage of life had I not gotten that abortion. Would he or she be entering college or the military or deciding on some other life pursuit? Unfortunately, I will never know.

In addition to forfeiting my motherhood at that time, I struggled both spiritually and emotionally in the relationship with my ex for years without ever getting married. I spent many years of my life mentally, emotionally, and physically connected to a man to whom I was not married. There was so much invested in that relationship despite the marital status. I felt we were meant to be together. We were already acting married; it would be just a matter of time before he eventually asked. I had the most difficult time moving away from that relationship, even when it had proven to be unhealthy. I am certain that, in God's plan for my life, He did not intend for me to spend several years of my life in a non-covenantal relationship, but I did. Surely, that was not God's best for me.

At times, I wondered who I overlooked, or who had overlooked me while living in Godly disobedience. The truth is many of us today enter and exit casual sexual relationships with soul bonds to people more often then we want to acknowledge. Understand, when we enter in and out of sexual (heterosexual, bisexual, or homosexual) relationships, we are creating soul ties with multiple partners. We are behaving adulterously with little regard for fidelity or commitment to the spiritual components God created within us. God speaks wearily about the adulterous individual and makes many correlations of marriage to God's relationship with man. God desires that we stay committed, to be faithful to the man/woman of our youth. We have to withstand the fiery darts of our lustful thoughts while in relationships with each other.

God created our model (example) of covenantal marriage when He created Eve for Adam and as much as our flesh may want to debate multiple Eves or relate to each same sex partnership, it is not the model, so it will more than often result in some discomfort or negative consequences. God is all knowing and, in His infinite wisdom, understands that we lose in the natural realm by straying from our commitments to our spousal marriages, but, additionally, we perhaps lose something more in the spiritual realm when we break our promises to each other. We possibly more easily fray our connection and commitment to God with our disobedience to His instructions. With our infidelity, we nurture disloyalty and a love-with-conditions belief system even with God the Creator.

Thankfully, God is committed to us no matter what. His love is unconditional in spite of our flaws and sinful nature. In our sin, He found a way to redeem us and place us back in relationship with Him. He redeemed us through His son, Jesus Christ. By design, we were created to love each other unconditionally as well (Mark 12:31). Everyone longs to be loved because we were made from love. We are meant to be unified and to coexist with each other and allow for grace to make up the difference when our loved ones fall short of our expectations. Man is not good alone, and we are better together. God presented other helpmates to Adam, but the other creatures were not good fits or suitable (Genesis 2:18–22).

In fact, I want you to look at the Scripture, because God made Eve different from the other creatures He presented to Adam. God formed from the ground the beasts of the field and fowl of the air, which He presented to Adam. However, He made Eve from Adam's flesh by removing one of his ribs. God could have taken any other part of the anatomy, but He took a rib. Why the rib? From what I understand of anatomy, ribs have a pretty unique role in the body. They support the vital organs of the human anatomy, housing both the lungs and the heart. Eve is to protect his heart and support man's primary life source, which is the oxygen from his lungs. Adam is incomplete without her, since she carries a piece of him. It is in this way that the man should be seeking after his wife and not the other way around. God presents, and the man can accept or reject His presentation as he did with the animals. Ultimately, he is searching for that person who is able to support his life source and protect his heart. Our God is truly amazing when you consider the details. God made Eve from Adam, and they are intrinsically designed for the other. In this way, men and women are both spiritually and physically wired for each other. God presented to Adam and Eve in the garden when He said, "Now be fruitful and multiply." Sex is an amazing concept, created by the Lord Almighty. When done God's way, in the union of a loving God, ordained marriage can be beautiful and satisfying on many levels.

Solomon wrote this verse in Proverbs 5:18–19: "Let thy fountain be blessed: and rejoice with the wife of thy youth. Let her be as the loving hind and pleasant roe: let her breasts satisfy thee at all times and be thou ravished always with her love" (KJV). This Scripture alone gives women a hint at the thoughts of a man and his desires for his sexual pursuit. Therefore, married women, it is not abnormal if your man is interested in sex often since Solomon is advising your man to be satisfied with you. A man should and does seek pleasure and refuge in being sexually satisfied; it is a part of his physical nature. God ordained this desire to be for his wife, not for anyone else outside of the covenant. This is what Pastor Michael Todd from the Transformation Church calls the "Sex Container." If you have not had a chance to check out his six-part series on "Relationship Goals" on YouTube, then you are truly missing out on a treat.

Sex is wonderful when done with someone you are equally yoked to and within the boundaries of what God ordained for a marriage. For single men and women, an equally yoked person shares your faith in Christ, and they are working toward the common goal of glorifying God in all ways, including life purpose and with their bodies. If you are dating someone who is pulling you away from the things of God or requesting things of you that go against the moral standard God provides, then this would be considered an unequally yoked relationship. If the person you are entertaining is suggesting otherwise, you should run. Assume that this is probably not who God designed and presented to you. If God is not presenting the person, then he/she may be hand delivered by His adversary, Satan. Hebrews 13:4 says, "Marriage is honorable in all, and the bed undefiled; but whoremongers and adulterers God will judge" (KJV). Marriage is God's standard for relationships, point-blank, period. Do not let anyone talk you into believing you are old-fashioned or unrealistic for desiring to live your life in obedience to your wonderful and beautiful God. God's way does not serve as a punishment, but as a way to get His blessings to you.

We desire sex because God uniquely designed it for all creatures: humans, animals, and vegetation with the capability to procreate. Yes, sex is definitely enjoyable but, ultimately, it is how we reproduce offspring. It is how we maintain life's existence and accomplish God's charge of being fruitful and multiplying. Procreation with humans requires seed and an environment to be fertilized. We require two different sexual organs to make a child. Male and female are uniquely created to provide each other with sperm (seed) and a place for fertilization within the walls of the uterus to facilitate populating the world. In this way, procreation is purposely heterosexual.

More and more, we are tricked into believing the notion that we are better off by ourselves, we can make life work with the same sex, or almost together as co-parents. Mankind, in all its ingenuity, has designed ways to reproduce offspring alternatively through donors, surrogates, artificial insemination, and oocyte cryopreservation. Unfortunately, this has allowed some people to be deceived into thinking there is no real need for God's original design for reproduction anymore. Do not get me wrong; the advancement of science and fertility has been a blessing in offering alternative methods for couples to conceive. I am amazed at how far science and technology has grown in even the short time span of my life. However, it becomes problematic when people develop a mindset that God's intent for procreation of the family is dated or no longer required. Scientists are working overtime to reinvent creation. Currently, research illustrates progress toward transgender womb surgeries, which would allow uterine transplantation to facilitate pregnancy in transgender females.

As science presses forward, we see genetically modified fruits and vegetables, seedless vegetation, hormone-injected animals, and cloned species. Ultimately, mankind has invented ways to reproduce vegetation and animals that are look more desirable and produce greater profits. Unfortunately, we are now observing this growing awareness of genetically modified organisms (GMOs) and hormone-injected animals in our food industry, which may be causing harm to our bodies. Those who are aware are upset. Companies are now expected to be more forthcoming and accountable regarding the impact these organisms have on people's health. What do GMOs have to do with sexual orientation, you might ask? It's about tampering with the genetic reproduction of our food source. It's about man's prideful propensity to be like God. More importantly, it's about mankind's ability to generate alternatives outside of God's will, which oftentimes lead to destruction.

Sexual perversion, promiscuity, and adultery present mankind with alternatives to God's will of relational fidelity in a marriage. These alternatives remind me of when Moses demonstrated God's wonders to Pharaoh, and the magicians (illusionists) duplicated similar acts of lesser power to the people (Exodus 7:10–12). Yes, it may work, but it will never be able to sustain life at the level God created. Following God's mandate to be fruitful and multiply has always been meant to happen between a man and woman. If all of humanity chooses differently, then mankind could eventually become extinct. It is important for me to state this, because there is a growing population of people, especially among youth, who believe identifying with a specific gender is not necessary and even self-limiting. This person no longer wants to be identified with a particular gender or its associated roles. The name for this is gender nonconformity or gender fluidity. This is truly deceit and eventually will lead to some form of internal conflict.

Emotionally, most men and women are wired differently. The unit is meant to facilitate each other and help to establish balance within a family unit. Gender roles and labeling are important to a person's psychological health. As I stated earlier, children are the primary beneficiaries when parents are committed to sustaining a healthy structure in the home and actively participating in rearing their children together on one accord. When considering the vast amount of psychosocial issues associated with the traditional family unit, one must wonder how gender identification and dysphoria shape a young person's ideas of their identity and ultimately affect what they can or cannot achieve.

Sexual Orientation

Sexual orientation is related to the genders to which people are attracted. Unlike sexual identity, orientation of sexual nature is the physical act or desire for sexual intercourse with another being. The very first account of sexual intercourse occurred between Adam and Eve following the fall in the garden of Eden (Genesis 4:1), "And Adam knew Eve his wife; and she conceived, and bare Cain, and said, I have gotten a man from the Lord" (KJV). The word "know" translates to the Hebrew word *yada*, which means to perceive, acquaint, become known, and/or understand something or someone in an intimate way. In times past, you would date, engage, marry, and finally "know" your partner through consummation of sexual intercourse. Consummation on the wedding night (sexual relations) was how couples established the greatest intimacy and came to know one another.

I want you to note the order of how the Scripture states that Adam took his wife and knew her and then Eve conceived and had a child. As I mentioned earlier, God spoke the word in the beginning, which was for man to be fruitful and multiply. Now, the way in which we bear children may not be the original concept, but the mandate was already in place. I actually found it interesting that Adam and Eve did not come to know each other in a sexual way before they were disobedient. They were roaming around in the garden of Eden, naked and not afraid, until their eyes (minds) were open to their human nature (physical naked bodies). It is my belief that these two were living in a place of such spiritual richness that sex was not a necessity or given any thought since their pleasure came from intermingling with God. When Adam and Eve saw their nakedness, they saw each other differently, maybe now in a sexual way. As time progressed, Adam and Eve began to populate the earth with their offspring who were called the sons of man, giving life to God's decree for human multiplication.

Scripture tells us that the daughters of the sons of man were so beautiful that the sons of God came to know them in a sexual way. It is not exactly clear who the sons of God were, with the exception of Satan in Job 1:6, but one could reason that these could possibly be fallen angels or demons (Genesis 6:4). The offspring of these two beings intermingling resulted in giants or Nephilim. Spiritual beings attracted to and having sex with humans was the beginning of skewed sexual orientation. The Nephilim and their offspring were so corrupt that God did three things: He regretted making mankind (ouch), shortened the lifespan of man, and eventually destroyed the world through a flood, sparing only clean animals, Noah, and his family. As you can see, mankind has been struggling with its sexual attractions since the fall in Genesis 3.

Essentially, sexuality and attraction could arguably be one of the sins that begets perverse or wicked behavior from our species (Genesis 6:4–5). Therefore, it is safe to say the issue of sexual orientation and perversion is not new and neither is homosexuality. In fact, it can be dated as far back as Noah with his son Hem. Following the great flood, Noah began growing a vineyard and produced wine from it. One day, while in a drunken stupor, his youngest son noticed him drunk and naked. Amused by the sight of his father's nakedness, he went to get his brothers so they could see him as well. The eldest brothers were not amused and covered their father, as they should, and diverted their eyes to look elsewhere. Now, it never says that Hem engaged in sexual intercourse with his father, but it suggests that seeing his father in this way served as a pornographic image, and he then lusted after him. The mind is a powerful thing and, if unchecked, it can direct you into mischief and activity that is sinful in nature. That is why it is important to understand the impact and dangers of pornography. Be careful what you look at, because the lust it produces is dangerous. It is dangerous enough to steer you into perversions of sexual relationships with children, family, and so forth. Noah's son Hem was punished with the inheritance of land in Canaan that was accursed. Noah cursed the land of Canaan by saying that they will be slaves to the other brothers' inherited territory.

The land of Canaan has experienced much conflict over the years and is today called the Middle East. Additionally, Sodom, which is known for being destroyed with Gomorrah, was situated on the southeast border of the land of Canaan. Sodom and Gomorrah are the places Abraham's nephew Lot was living. Sexual perversions, including homosexuality, were heavily practiced in these two places, and God sought to destroy them by fire. The men were extremely perverse in this region. In fact, they threatened to kill Lot in order to get to the angels who were sent to warn him and his family to leave before the city was destroyed (Genesis).

Again, this is another instance where humans and angels have been suggested for possible intermingling sexually. Due to the close proximity of these two regions, it could be surmised that some homosexual customs and practices may have been passed along between the people who were settled in this area. Unfortunately, these customs and practices of sexual perversions were not destroyed by the flood (seed of Hem) and did not end in the fire of

Sodom and Gomorrah. Since that time, many prominent societies have engaged in sexual acts with multiple partners, including same gender and underage youth. Places like Rome, Spain, Greece, and Brazil are notorious for their freedom to explore their sexuality. Polygamous relationships, multiple sexual partners, and same sex activities are not as taboo in these countries. Men of status or with power would often have young male or female concubines outside their marital union to satisfy their sexual desires or deviant behaviors. However, the young United States has historically not been as liberated sexually. Due to our country's Christian roots, we have for many years been considered a more sexually conservative country than our predecessors. As time presses forward, many of our original beliefs and customs have become relaxed, and some citizens refute the country's premise of placing Christian values upon the general population as it relates to sex.

In 2015, the United States Supreme Court's ruling to accept same-sex marriage in every state has propelled several societal changes in our once conservative country. Since then, there is a heightened sensitivity to how the country views the LGBT (lesbian, gay, bisexual, and transgender) community, and new laws are affecting the public and private sector in a variety of ways. The LGBT community is considered a protected class and a minority. Therefore, anything perceived as unjust or discriminatory holds consequences. It has affected how grocery stores, schools, dressing rooms, churches, and other public places conduct business with many changes to teaching materials, bathroom labels, marketing strategies, movie productions, etc. Many people, especially Christians, are having a difficult time assimilating to these new laws since they are influencing so many levels of daily living. It impacts what is being taught in schools, television programming, commercials, consumer rights, and business commerce. Just in case you are one of those people who feels like you have walked into the twilight zone when you turn on the television or pick up a magazine, I'd like to define some of the terms used to identify sexual orientation and associated behaviors.

Heterosexual: A person who is sexually attracted to someone of the opposite gender/or sex

Homosexual: A person who is sexually attracted to someone of the same gender/or sex

Gay: A homosexual of male sex

Lesbian: A homosexual of female sex

Bisexual: A person who is sexually attracted to both men and women

Transgender: A person who identifies and expresses a gender identity different from the sex they were born with

Pansexual: A person who has no boundaries or sexual preference with regard to biological, gender, and/or gender identity

According to a survey conducted by the Centers for Disease Control and Prevention, the incidents of bisexuality rose from 2 percent to 5.5 percent in men and from 14.2 percent to 17.4 percent in women from 2006 to 2010 and 2011 to 2013, respectively, with both genders showing an increase of roughly 3 percent for bisexuality. Moreover, 12.8 percent of the women and 2.8 percent of the men surveyed who identified themselves as heterosexual reported having some type of sexual contact with the same sex. The survey included approximately 9,000 men and women between the ages of 18 and 44. According to the census of 2015, only 1.1 percent of the United States population reported being homosexual women and 2.2 percent reported being homosexual men. Now, what does this all mean? What I found to be interesting is the amount of people who are engaging in homosexual activity but are not necessarily identifying as gay. Some may argue that people would prefer to identify as bisexual or heterosexual because there is less of a stigma attached to them, and I'm sure there are some who fit into that category.

However, I think it's a little deeper than that. I believe the numbers for bisexual orientation and homosexual encounters are higher because more and more people have fewer boundaries regarding their sexual behavior. Today, people are more willing to experiment with sexual perversion. In turn, some are growing increasingly more disoriented with their sexuality and practice sexual fluidity. Children are growing more desensitized to same-sex interactions and, during critical times of development (youth and adolescence), inherit a nonchalant attitude towards their sexuality. Children operate within the boundaries of these blurred lines because they disagree that there should be lines in the first place.

A 2014 article published in the *International Business Times* says millennials (persons between eighteen and thirty-five years old) are the gayest generation ever, with a survey conducted among youth where 7 percent reported they are either lesbian, gay, bisexual, or transgender whereas only 3.5 percent of people over the age of thirty-five identify with being a part of the LGBT community. It is anticipated that approximately half of generation Z will identify as being straight or heterosexual. So, the question becomes, "Are more people being born gay, or is it a social shift?" The question stands as to whether sexual identity is genetic in origin or if the sexual orientation of this generation is influenced more by social standards of what is sexually appropriate or inappropriate.

This question is of extreme importance, because if you are not careful, you can develop a belief system that is shaped by worldly influences and not the Word of God. In a world where truth has become so obscure, it is of extreme value to have wisdom. In all you're getting, obtain understanding (Proverbs 4:7). If you do not have a good understanding of what truth is, you can easily be tricked into believing a lie. Deception is subtle and often mingled with abstract understandings of information to incite your reasoning into believing an ill-guided perception. It was the very first trick of the enemy in Genesis 3 where suggestions or questions were provided to present confusion. If one is not careful, anyone can easily be deceived into accepting gray-area reasoning and developing a perspective that places them at risk to make destructive, life-altering decisions.

The enemy's tactics of deceit are sometimes illuminated like a glowing neon sign, but other times the deceit is found in subtle inferences. For instance, in researching the topic of sexuality, I was given misleading definitions of the terms "heterosexual" and "homosexual." I was conveniently provided an opinion of a definition when I placed heterosexual in an extremely popular search engine. A few sources provided the definition of heterosexuality as, "considered normal sexual behavior, but it is not normal." I was thinking to myself, "What now?" Why would heterosexuality not be normal?

Moreover, when researching the definition of homosexuality, I read the definition but not one preference for consideration of abnormal or normal sexual behavior was given. What a pretty clever trick to deceive and distort people's perceptions. A young person researching the topic, maybe out of curiosity or a need to complete a school assignment, would be provided with information full of bias and someone's opinion. How will young people decipher what is honest and true? The answer lies with parents, guardians, and, most importantly, Christians. If you are a parent who believes, then you need to make sure you are reading the Word of God so that you are certain of what is absolute truth. Additionally, you should take heed of what materials are being taught at your child's school.

In this present time, it is not enough to just fill the seat on the pew and be fed what you need to know from a pastor. Unfortunately, there are many doctrines being preached today that minister the opposite of what the Word of God teaches about sex. When you are sound in your position of truth, then you are better able to guide your child's thinking before these types of questions arise in a school setting without your knowing. Today, you hear more and more of your child's teachers addressing sexuality and their opinions of sexual orientation in front of the entire class. Furthermore, most assignments and school projects require children to have internet access to complete them. Parents need to be in the know about what their children are learning, whether it's from a handout, textbook, the internet, a friend, or a lesson given by the teacher. There is so much information accessible to your child through these media, and parameters should be placed on which websites they are allowed to visit.

Both children and adults are equally subjected to untruths from television, radio, celebrities, news reporters, and even ministers (false prophets). The difficult talk with your kids about the "birds and the bees" has evolved into a talk about the "jungle," which requires a more in-depth conversation. There is no longer room to beat around the bush! Unfortunately, parents do not have the luxury of casually avoiding this difficult conversation as they once did if they want their children to develop healthy perceptions regarding sexuality. As humanists, activists, and media gatekeepers push secular worldly views onto mainstream society and, subsequently, your children. Adults need to be intentional in the conversations they have with children. Families must be equipped to know what is deemed acceptable sexual behavior according to the Word of God. This comes by reading and hearing the Word of God. You may not know this, but God has a lot to say about sex. I mean, He did invent it. Additionally, He realizes it has been the Achilles' heel of mankind for centuries. Many mighty men of God have struggled because of sexual lust, including King David, King Solomon, and Samson, just to name a few. Of course, we are not exempt from the lustful sin of sex. God teaches us in 1 Thessalonians 4:3–5, "Keep yourselves from sexual promiscuity. Learn to appreciate and give dignity to your body, not abusing it, as is so common among those who know nothing of God" (MSG).

God wanted us to understand that it is not common practice for mankind to sexually abuse their bodies, and we should set ourselves apart from those who do not know God as we do. The enemy is using sexuality to hurt and kill many people, including our youth, with feelings of hopelessness, anxiety, fear, shame, and emotional chaos. This is not what God wants His children to feel. In fact, the words tell us that Jesus came so that we would have life and have it to be full (John 10:10)—a full life that does not include shame, self-defeat, sickness, and low life expectancy. Disobedience to God's way leads to destruction and death. Did you know that those in the LGBT community have a higher prevalence of depression and, subsequently, increased rates of suicide? Gay men are three times as likely to suffer from depression than heterosexual men. According to the Centers for Disease Control and Prevention, approximately 29 percent of LGBT youth are diagnosed with depression, placing them at a higher risk for having suicidal thoughts.

Even more staggering is this number: eight out of ten new cases of HIV were among young gay and bisexual men. Those statistics are horrific and sadden me. Some may argue that the depression stems from society's stigma of homosexuality and perceived discrimination within the minority group. I cannot argue with that logic since there is a heap load of shame, guilt, or fear that may be associated with coming out as gay or lesbian. Some live with a fear of losing the respect and love of those closest to them and have a difficult time accepting the alternative lifestyle. Unfortunately, just like with the vice of alcoholism and drug addiction, the enemy will use everything in his power to pull you outside of your purpose, whisper lies about your self-worth/value with the end goal of ultimately destroying you. If he can convince you to harm yourself through depression or lack of self-control by acting on your sexual impulses, he will! Unfortunately, when you turn yourself toward sin and away from God's will, His voice becomes increasingly faint. Eventually, you may find yourself so far inside of a lifestyle that you don't recognize or hear His voice at all. In fact, Paul says this in Romans 1:26–28:

> For this cause God gave them up unto vile affections; for even their women did change the natural use into that which is against nature. And likewise also the men, leaving the natural use of the woman burned in their lust one toward another; men with men working that which is unseemly, and receiving in themselves that recompence of their error which was met. And even as they did not like to retain God in their knowledge, God gave them over to a reprobate mind, to do those things, which are not convenient. (KJV)

God loves us unequivocally, but when we chase sin, God allows us to explore our free will and sometimes lose our mind (reprobate) in it. As much as the enemy may lead you to believe differently at the onset, SIN is not as fun as we think, and it is extremely inconvenient. It is inconvenient to pay child support every paycheck to two different women; it is inconvenient to have an abortion; it is inconvenient to see your kids every other week; it is inconvenient to hide your love interest from family and friends; it is inconvenient to desire to be a parent but not have the physiological capacity to do it; it is inconvenient to have your child live in a foster home or with grandparents; it is inconvenient to be addicted to drugs and alcohol to dull emotional pain; it is inconvenient to desire to have children but have to seek alternative methods; it is inconvenient to raise a child as a single parent; it is inconvenient to need medications for the rest of your life for chronic illnesses contracted from sex; and it is inconvenient to not have a loving spouse to share the responsibilities of life with until you die. The moral of the story is this:

SEXUAL IMMORALITY IS EXTREMELY INCONVENIENT! It is not God's best, and He desires for you to have life in abundance.

We often get tricked into believing that God's statutes are too strict and He's holding out on us. This is and has always been the root of the SIN issue from the beginning in the garden of Eden (Genesis 3:1–4). We want to know what God is keeping from us and see if what He told us is true. We desire to trust ourselves to handle our world independently from Him. God loves us as a parent does a child. When parents give their children parameters, it is with good intent and with the purpose of protecting them from something harmful. If God says to run from sexual immorality, it is because He understands the natural ramifications of engaging in it and, most importantly, the spiritual benefits you forfeit to the enemy. God's kingdom is worth fighting for and provides a rest from worry, fear, and shame. When faced with the challenge of battling lustful desires related to sex, consider the ramifications that your heavenly Father is protecting you from. He's protecting me from a broken heart. He's protecting me from sexually transmitted diseases. He's protecting me from alienation. And He's protecting me from raising a child alone. Unfortunately, sin does have appeal, and it is not until we are lured into a deadly trap that we realize the harm it can cause.

Now for those who may say, "I'm not ready to relinquish or give up my sexual desires yet. Sex feels too good and I am enjoying my life right now. I will settle down when I get older. You only live once!" Remember, God does not promise always, and you could shorten your life expectancy with your actions. Paul provides this word of wisdom in 1 Corinthians 6:9–12:

> Don't you realize that is not the way to live? Unjust people who don't care about God will not be joining in his kingdom. Those who use and abuse each other, use and abuse sex, use and abuse the earth and everything in it, don't qualify as citizens in God's kingdom. A number of you know from experience what I'm talking about, for not so long ago you were on that list. Since then you've been cleaned up and given a fresh start by Jesus, our Messiah, and by our God present in us, the Spirit. Just because something is technically legal doesn't mean it's spiritually appropriate. If I went around doing whatever I thought I could get by with, I'd be a slave to my whims. (MSG)

In essence, Paul is saying living without boundaries or self-control means you do not care about God and are unwise. We do this when we take on the mindset that we can do whatever we please because we are saved by grace. We are basically allowing our body/flesh to control our behaviors and we miss out on experiencing the kingdom of God. God desires for His kingdom to be here on earth and rejoined to the spiritual connection that was lost in Eden. It is not beneficial and profitable for us to allow ourselves to do whatever our flesh desires because our body is perishing (dying) and is only concerned with the now. If our flesh is leading us, it will push us to the grave early, whether it is with indulging in unhealthy food, habits, alcohol, or sexual pursuits. Please do not let your flesh rule you. If you are like me and have fallen short in the area of sexual lust more than a few times, then there is good news. God's grace is sufficient, and when we are weak in the area of sexual temptation, He is able to strengthen us (2 Corinthians 12:9–10).

Thank God for grace! Especially for those who are believers in Jesus Christ and the sacrifice He paid for our sins on the cross. We are covered by grace when we are disobedient to God and ask for His forgiveness. The goal in your Christian walk should be to take your lustful thoughts and passions and submit them unto God. He will give you the power and strength to withstand those physical desires when you struggle with sexual lusts outside the will of God (a covenant marriage). He will help you renew your mind to establish new routines and habits to prevent you from repeating immoral sexual acts in the future.

Ask Him to forgive you; ask Him to come in and strengthen you in those areas where you have been weak and tempted in the area of sex. It does not matter how big the sexual immorality—whether it's pornography addiction, prostitution, promiscuity, fornication, homosexuality, or adultery. He is faithful to forgive us, and He will never leave you or forsake you. May the peace and blessings of God rest and rule in your life with your sexual identity from this point on and moving forward. Amen!

CHAPTER 7

PERSONAL IDENTITY

"When purpose is not known, abuse is inevitable."
—Myles Munroe

Perhaps many of you reading thus far have been waiting for a grand revelation related to your very own personal identity. What I am here to tell you is that understanding the previous chapters is the base ingredient for deeply understanding your own identity and, most importantly, transforming your identity into what God intended for you from the foundation of the earth. God's intention has always been for man to function free of fear and shame and with supreme authority over everything on the earth. Like I said before, sin caused us to forfeit those rights in Eden. Praise Jesus for winning it back for us. So often, we find ourselves carrying burdens and attitudes of defeat as if we are victims of circumstantial situations beyond our control. We place blame on things happening to us or on people who may have neglected, hurt, or damaged us emotionally, spiritually, and physically. Sometimes, the pain is so significant that we even blame God for allowing such circumstances to happen. No doubt, some of you reading may have experienced some unimaginable hurts and difficult life scenarios that, at times, make living challenging.

I would like to encourage you with this: for every challenge, there is someone else that faced the same situation and overcame it. We all have a choice of whether to fold, cower, or press forward when life serves us undesirable situations. Unfortunately, you immediately forfeit your chance at winning when you quit and give up at the sight of opposition. With every challenge in life, we have an opportunity for promotion to a new level or to remain stagnant in the same place. We gain personal growth by learning forgiveness and finding strength from one of the greatest treasures we can experience here on earth, unconditional (agape) love. Without true guidance, understanding, and a transformation of the mind, a person allows his senses to drive his perceptions, emotions, and decisions related to this world.

So often, people live in perpetual fear, anxiety, shame, hopelessness, and powerlessness and eventually die never realizing or displaying his/her total potential. You were not created to reflect an image of fear and powerlessness. You were always seen through the lens of your heavenly Father, which is greatness. "So God created man in his own image, in the image of God created he him; male and female created he them" (Genesis 1:27, KJV). Therefore, our natural earth suits (our bodies) are loaded with an ability to sense and perceive life with our five senses, which are secondary to our spirit man. Our flesh shall surely perish when God's breath of life leaves us. The truth is, your individuality and personality may be unique to you and every experience (good or bad) but we do not reach our fullest potential on earth until we put on the image of God our father, which is a spirit. In Matthew 6:9–13, Jesus instructs us to pray this way:

> Our Father, which art in heaven, Hallowed be thy name, Thy kingdom come, Thy will be done, on earth as it is in heaven. Give us this day our daily bread. And forgive us our debts, as we forgive our debtors. And lead us not into temptation, but deliver us from evil: For thine is the kingdom, and the power, and the glory, for ever. Amen. (KJV)

God desires for us to pray this prayer and seek to have His kingdom of heaven here on earth. As God's children, we are blessed to walk in spiritual authority, power, forgiveness, love, and His perfect will for our lives when we trust in Him above everything else. The identity crisis stems from natural losses resulting from not understanding our spiritual identity well enough to look and walk in the image Christ modeled for us while He lived on earth. The attack on our identity occurs when we take on the labels and names given to us by God's archenemy. Often, these labels greatly differ from what God originally created, which was a "masterpiece," "wonderful," "forgiven," "beautiful," "chosen," and "loved." We are more than the labels placed on us by our families, society, and even ourselves. Even with good intentions, these people may have a tendency to mislabel you and undermine your worth as seen through the eyes of your Creator. Your identity far exceeds the negative labels of "broken," "unworthy," "mistake," "convict," "afraid," "hopeless," "homosexual," "fat," "ugly," "unwanted," "stupid," "white," "black," "crazy," or "sick." This twisted identity is not new and has been happening for centuries.

Today, we are definitely in a heightened state with everyone across the globe comparing and sharing information about what is acceptable, flattering, or valuable. The television shows, social media pages, magazines, and "daddy issues" have many young people and even older individuals comparing themselves to unrealistic beauty and social status standards. We are seeing more and more people unsatisfied and depressed about their looks and lifestyles. It's crazy because we compare ourselves to pop stars, celebrities, and social media models who struggle with their own insecurities just as much or even more than their fans and followers. They too are suffering in silence from feelings of inadequacy and pain. Some disfigure their bodies they were born with on an unrelenting search for perfection. The search for perfection is perpetual and leads to a continued disfiguration of our bodies or, worse, pretending things are one way when they are not. I believe self-perfection, grandeur, and idealism play a major role in feelings of inadequacy, sadness, anxiety, and poor self-worth. As mentioned previously, social media has given everyone the platform to fuel the feelings. We see more youth today with anxiety and mood disorders than ever before. Let's be clear, there is not a perfect person with the perfect life on this earth, so give yourself a break! It just does not exist. Paul advises us against comparing ourselves to others in Galatians 6:4: "Don't compare yourself with others. Just look at your own work to see if you have done anything to be proud of" (ERV).

In another Scripture, Paul warns that lust drives us toward emulation or the desire to copy, match, or surpass a person or achievement, typically through imitation. When I first read this, I was amazed because I remember desiring to have the vocal abilities Mariah Carey, Whitney Houston, and even my younger sister had, and being disappointed of not touching their gifts. I would grab my broom (pretend microphone) and dance across the room crooning to maybe half of the lyrics they created on their songs. It was interesting to see that God had no interest in me sounding like those songbirds, since their gifts were uniquely crafted for them. He created them with their own uniqueness of sound and beauty as He saw fit. Whitney and Mariah have sold millions of records worldwide, and their body of work will remain a gift to all who live after them. That does not mean that I am not without worth or value.

He created you and me with our own set of gifts and abilities that are unique to us. God gifted me with a desire to write and a love of music that will be used on the platform that He designed specifically for me. I have a weighted voice that I am discovering more and more about every day. I love to worship God, so I volunteer in the choir, praise team, on mission trips, and any other capacity God allows. I am cool with that and happy to celebrate the gift of music with my praise and worship. It is all for His glory anyway. There is only one you, and you are *uniquely purposed* to be a gift to humanity. You are not a mistake and not sent here sit idly on the sidelines watching everyone else live out their dreams. I urge you to discover what your unique purpose is and pursue it with all the zeal and passion your heart can muster. God does not want us to waste time trying to be something He did not create us to be or give up and not live at all.

Being inspired by a celebrity to develop your uniqueness is fine but coveting and comparing their lifestyles to yours is truly useless! So often what we envy and desire to have is not as glamorous as we think. Our job is to desire and strive to learn what God created us to do and deliver it to our generation. In this way, you really do not have time to compare yourself to anyone except who you are today and who God desires you to become. Christians must endeavor to learn as much about the kingdom of God (heavenly places) so that we can assume our roles as ambassadors for our heavenly Father. The kingdom of God is magnificent and lives within those who believe. We are able to live in authority and accomplish the miraculous and extraordinary when we live with the mind-set that the Holy Spirit matters over everything, since it is eternal. From this perspective, we are quick to seek the guidance of the Creator to sense and perceive life with a deeper lens than our natural eye.

There is a spiritual culture (kingdom living) that Jesus mastered while here on earth that He earnestly desires for His brothers and sisters to grasp ahold of. He has provided us the blueprint for governing ourselves in this, both in the spiritual and natural realm simultaneously. We must strive to adapt to the Jesus culture above all competing contexts (virtual, physical, cultural, and social). This includes the context of family. The things Jesus did, such as heal the sick, give sight to the blind, and reach the lost, were gifted to His followers after His death. It is not until you have the deepest understanding of who you are in God through Christ Jesus that you are able to fully understand your destiny and purpose in life; experience an undeniable love; and stifle the effects of fear. Fear is crippling, and God needs us to conquer this emotion so that we can dare to believe in our creativity and try. When we have an understanding of God's love, it better equips us to effectively walk in our purpose, resist the enemy's tactics, find rest, and operate under a grace (supernatural anointing). This allows us to experience our best life while here on earth. This is the true essence of freedom! Being mentally and spiritually equipped is of extreme importance because every day you wake up and walk out your door you are warring against spiritual forces of darkness that want to prevent you from accomplishing what God intended for you. Those forces whisper lies about your identity, telling you there's nothing to live for; you don't have to fight; live life without boundaries; and no one would notice if you weren't here.

LIES! Satan is the father of lies, and there is no truth in him (John 8:44). There are many people who want us to believe truth is ambiguous and fluid. Fluid shifts and moves with the feeling or mood for the day. Fluid leaves us unsteady with our footing and off balance. Unattended fluid eventually will lead to slips and falls. One of the definitions for fluidity is defined as changeability, unsettled, and unstable. It is what God considers to be double mindedness. God warns us about being a double-minded person and says that he/she is unstable in all their ways (James 1:8). Fluid is dangerous and is unstable. Fluid is not firm and does not offer any support or footing. Unfortunately, foundations of fluidity make it difficult to stand and eventually will cause you to sink and drown, flail in desperation, grasp hold of anything (ideas or people) you think could save you, or, best case scenario, find refuge by swimming back to land. Too many of our youth are being tricked into believing the lie that making their own truth is better than following sound wisdom from mature adults or God's instruction. Proverbs 1:7 says, "The fear of the Lord is the beginning of knowledge: but fools despise wisdom and instruction" (NIV).

Ignoring wisdom from God, your Creator, your elders, and those who know more than you through experience is outright foolish. Please, take heed to this advice, for it may save your life. The "truth" is like math—it either is or isn't. There is no room for interpretation or gray area. One plus one will always equal two, and two times two will always equal four. Always! Remember that God's way is truth, so do your best to listen and learn so you are not deceived. Jesus says that I am the solid rock for which you stand. God's intentions for you are a life of good health, peace, joy, and prosperity.

When we experience anything different from the aforementioned circumstances, we can accurately assign the blame to God's archrival, Satan. How does he primarily attack you? He attacks you with and through negative thinking.

Thinking is so vital since it drives motives and actions. We are always deciding something. We can either make a decision to stay misinformed or become informed as it relates to truth. One of my favorite Scriptures to recite to myself is Hosea 4:6, which says, "My people are destroyed for lack of knowledge" (KJV). So many grand dreams have been buried in the grave, desires go unmet, and potentials fall to the wayside simply because of the lack of knowledge and poor thinking. I discovered that knowing is half the battle, and we have a responsibility to get in the know. It is important to know that whether you are seeking information or sitting by as an innocent bystander on the sidelines you are learning something. It's unfortunate when you sit back and allow people to dump information on you without seeking understanding or truth from what they are dishing out.

One of our best resources as Christians to gain knowledge to win in this life is the Bible. Imagine yourself working in a hospital for several years as a custodian. You know and understand the layout of the hospital like it's the back of your hand. You are also pretty familiar with most of the staff and even have a general understanding of the roles of the nurses, doctors, therapists, and social workers. You come to work on time, and your managers often praise you for the good work you do. However, upon arriving at work, you clock in as usual, but instead of advising you of your normal floor duties, your supervisor tells you that one of the physicians called in sick and management requests you fill in for the day. Would you try to wing it and risk hurting patients in the meantime? I'm pretty confident that you would not. I'm sure you would look at the supervisor as if he grew a horn in the middle of his head and became a unicorn. Why? Because you did not train to be a doctor and you don't have the knowledge or licensure to effectively treat patients.

Life is no different than this scenario. How do you expect to be effective in life if you never train or read the manual? Unfortunately, some of us approach life with an "I'll just wing it" mentality. Just winging it won't work in the hospital for a doctor, and it surely does not work well in life either. So, case in point, if you are a Christian, you should be reading your Bible so that you may adequately train yourself to do God's work and correct your thinking. If you are not a Christian, I will tell you that you are missing out on a jewel. The Bible has proven, over time, to be the best resource for education on life. It is the key to facilitating the transformation of the mind, obtaining peace, and protecting our souls.

Our soul is comprised of the mind, will, and emotions—it is often synonymous in the Word of God with the word "heart." The Hebrew word for heart is *leb*, which is described as the inner man, or mind, knowledge, thinking, reflection, memory, determination (of will), and moral character. Your mind, will, and emotions are generally the personal characteristics or qualities, which make you unique. Our soul is heavily impacted by the external factors in our environments, such as people, physical resources, family, culture, and temporal things. External factors can be considered things of the world, such as clothes, cars, food, husband, wife, children, and money. How we feel and how we process our world is managed through our soul. Our soul will feel defeated or victorious depending on what we tell it to perceive. Our desires and will are linked to these emotions, and we decide to act or not act within our soul. That's why we cannot leave our souls unchecked. We have to watch what we allow our souls to perceive from our environment and then filter it through the Word of God for the best outcomes. This is vital since it drives much of our actions. Christians expecting to get everything they need on Sunday morning is foolish and makes them a target for getting their behinds whipped by the enemy throughout the week.

I will admit, I have not always read the word (Bible) like that, either. It took a prophet, who I never saw a single day in my life, to call me out on this fact. I hate to say it, but, for many years, the only time I read the Bible was at church. As a young woman, I would go to church every week and wait for the preacher to give me a good word from a one or two-Scripture text. I had been going to church since I was in the second grade so I could quote Scripture that I remembered ministers singing or yelling through intermittently long breathed gasps. I guess at that point, I had enough word in me to get me through a one or two-hour span of a day, but not much after that.

As I said before, I did not pray because I thought I had committed too many sins that God would not listen to me. I was a fully-grown woman but, spiritually, an infant. I was sort of like Benjamin Button, a woman-baby. Paul uses infancy a lot for the early followers to understand their need to develop their relationships and faith for growth in the kingdom of God. Believe me, there are many older saints still wearing spiritual diapers. When we are unequipped for kingdom work, we are fair game for the enemy. The Bible says that we wrestle not against flesh and blood, but against principalities, against powers, against the rulers of darkness of this world, against spiritual wickedness in high places (Ephesians 6:12).

What's spiritual wickedness? I never really understood this verse in its entirety, so I was essentially clueless about what my adversary looked or sounded like. Additionally, I didn't have enough of God's word in me to combat any attack from this world of darkness or for the life trials that popped up on a given day. If all was going well, I was smiling and grinning from ear to ear. However, as soon as a serious life situation arose (a parent being sick, an unruly cashier at a restaurant, an unexpected bill being due, or an added caseload at work, I easily became frustrated or dismayed about that particular issue. I would wear that hardship on my demeanor like a pair of shoes or a nice dress. I was very unpredictable in my behavior and was easily swayed by my context, good or bad. The highs and lows of my emotions were easily traced back to the events that occurred within that day. Unfortunately, this is a tell-tale sign of an emotionally unstable person and a very sad place to be in. I carried a lot of anxiety during those times and tried my best to control EVERYTHING to prevent the rollercoaster of emotions from occurring.

Truth was, I was having the fight of my life and intermittent times of resting on the sidelines before getting back in the ring. I was fighting alone, I thought, and not allowing God's helper to assist with providing insight on how to beat my spiritual enemy. Life will kick your butt if you allow circumstances to drive your behaviors and emotions and not allow God to come in and give you a helping hand. Life, and the people who dwell with us in it, are very unpredictable and should have limited influence on how we choose to react to them. How we react to the events that happen to us determines the outcomes in our life. Responding appropriately and in a healthy manner will lead to success. Responding negatively to these events could lead to poor outcomes and damage. This was a lesson I had to learn the hard way and resulted in a few fractured relationships and hidden emotional scars. My mentor gave me the acronym E.R.O.S. (Event + Response = Outcome and Success) and I found it to be helpful in my daily and situational responses. I am nowhere near perfect, but I am growing in mindfulness of responding to daily stimuli.

I cannot stress enough the importance of controlling your thoughts and emotions. When these two things go unchecked or uncontrolled, they are typically the drivers behind poor decisions. The Apostle Paul gives us our best defense in controlling our thoughts in 2 Corinthians 10:5 through "Casting down imaginations, and every high thing that exalteth itself against the knowledge of God, and bringing into captivity every thought to the obedience of Christ" (KJV). Your mind is a battleground, and in order to win in this life, you have to be on defense about what you allow to shape and encourage your thoughts. Joyce Meyer wrote a book called Battlefield of the Mind and it really provides insight on how our thinking is under attack. I encourage you to read it at some point if you haven't already.

The enemy is aware of your identity and the power source accessible to you when you are spiritually connected to the Creator through His divine Holy Spirit. Therefore, he has demonic spirits on assignment to deceive your thinking with the ultimate goal of keeping you discouraged, doubtful, distracted, and, eventually, derailed from your purpose. I call it the devil's quadruple D's. Satan is the father of lies, and there is no truth in him (John 8:44). Let's take a quick look at these four spiritual attack strategies:

Discouragement

Discouragement is one the enemy's tried and true weapons of mass destruction. Have you ever found yourself hoping for something, such as a job, healing for yourself or family member, or acceptance into college, only to get smacked in the face with a big "no" or a delay? That "no" can be disappointing. Unchecked disappointment has a way of festering, but when we experience a series of disappointments, we may become discouraged.

Discouragement and disappointment are close relatives and can easily creep into our lives. Bishop George Davis says there are four sources of disappointment that usually are the driving factors in men and women feeling discouraged, which include:

- other people, such as family and friends;
- circumstances like sickness, divorce, or not getting a job;
- failing ourselves by not living up to standards or expectations we internally set; and

- God, when a prayer goes unanswered or we wrongly shift blame onto Him for a misfortunate experience.

When we are discouraged, we may have lost hope and confidence that our circumstances are able to change or ever get better. In this scenario, a person is at risk for depression. Being sad is one thing, but depression can be devastating to one's life. Discouragement in the form of depression may fool a person to stop trying with something that is clearly God-ordained or, worse, trick people into ending their lives through suicide. This is why we cannot walk around allowing our emotions to make decisions for us. Our emotions will lead us down a spiraling pathway into defeat and some form of death.

There are approximately 40 million adults living with depression in the United States, affecting approximately 18.1 percent of the population. The numbers continue to increase, and there is an increasing amount of evidence of children being diagnosed with mental illness as well. There are several risk factors, including poverty, low performance in school, single-parent families, and poor parent-child communication, which place children at risk for developing mood disorders.

Interestingly, many of the risk factors mentioned are contextual and preventable if parents begin to recognize and address these environmental challenges as the spiritual attacks that they are. Trust and believe the enemy is working heavily in the area of discouragement for people of all ages, so be on alert. Proverbs 13:12 says, "Unrelenting disappointment leaves your heart sick, but a sudden good break can turn life around" (MSG).

Just the other day, I watched a chilling video of a mother with her three kids inside drive their family minivan for several feet in the shallow end of the ocean. The mother's bizarre driving and behavior caught the attention of a bystander. While observing the van, the bystander could hear the children yell, "Help! My mom is trying to kill us!" When the man approached the van, he found three little ones in the backseat waving at the man and their mother in the driver's seat telling him, "Go away, we are okay." Clearly, they were not okay with their van mid-tire deep in ocean water. The mother then looked with a blank stare and turned her wheel left toward the large body of water. Her van lost its grounding and began floating with the waves.

Eventually, more people came along to assist in this rescue effort since the floating vehicle made capturing the kids more difficult. Thankfully, in this case, all three children were rescued. The mother escaped the car as well, only for rescuers to discover she was pregnant with a fourth child. The woman was eventually charged with attempted murder, and her husband was granted full custody of the children. It's such a sad story that one has to wonder what drove that mother to commit this heinous act?

Today, more and more family suicides occur and, oftentimes, the attempts are successful. It's sad to think that people are so unhappy with their lives that they are willing to escape by taking their lives and, sometimes, their innocent children with them. The statistics speak of the plea for help in a spiritual crisis. The church and body of Christ need to answer.

Distraction

Distraction is another area in which the enemy is having a field day hurting God's creation. People are so distracted today that there was a study published that described goldfish as having surpassed the attention spans of humans with the ability to attend for nine seconds. This study of approximately 2,000 participants revealed that humans are attending up to about eight seconds. This number is down from a span of twelve seconds of attention, which was reported in 2010.

This recent inattention stems from one of the newest distractions that most Americans are guilty of—the coveted smart phone. I have already talked your ear off about our growing obsession with the virtual context (world) that our cell phones allow us to live in, but I have to reiterate how much we are missing out on family time and God's plan when we can't attend for one minute without looking at our phones. We have to be better stewards of our time. On some phones, the amount of screen time used is currently being measured on an app. I encourage you to use this resource and, week by week, try to reduce your screen time if you can. You'll be surprised what you can accomplish when you are not so distracted by your cell phones.

Cell phones are not the only things that are distracting us, either. We can blame our busy lifestyles, work, social activities, and so forth. Friends, lovers, and family can also present distractions. This has happened to me on more than one occasion. I have noticed that, when I am extremely close to a breakthrough, whether it is personal, financial, or spiritual, a distraction pops up out of nowhere. If I decided that I was going to be productive and clean my house or finish a chapter by a certain timeframe, a distraction would mosey along and cause me to forgo my original plans.

Initially, distractions may seem harmless, but they are the easiest ways for you have your defenses down and allow the enemy to sneak into your territory and cause you to be ineffective in a certain area of your life. You are better able to catch a thief when your eyes are open looking for him.

Doubt

Doubt prevents us from experiencing the fullness of a relationship with God here on earth. For how can you build a strong or solid relationship with someone you do not trust? When we harbor feelings of fear, anxiety, and doubt in our hearts, we forge a wedge between God and ourselves. Our disbelief is a reflection of our lack of faith in God's ability and position over our circumstances. Without faith, it is impossible to please the Lord, because anyone who comes to Him must believe that He exists and that He rewards those who earnestly seek Him (Hebrews 11:6).

Faith is obscure to an unbeliever and unto the doubting heart. Doubt was the very thing the enemy used in the garden with Eve and Adam, and sin was the end result. Doubt is the opposite of faith and will prevent you from declaring healing over your body, speaking life over tough circumstances, cause you to say the wrong things in a spiritual battle, and will ultimately convince you to stop pressing forward when a breakthrough was right around the corner. I love this particular passage regarding faith and doubt in Mark

11:23, "Truly I tell you that if anyone says to this mountain, go throw yourself in the sea, and does not doubt in their heart but believes that what he says will happen, it will be done for them" (NIV). This Scripture is so powerful because it is the essence of us operating in our spiritual divinity passed onto us by our heavenly (spiritual) father.

The enemy has tricked many people into doubt and, therefore, they forfeit endless supernatural blessings available to them. Your belief system is so vital to your success or failures in life. If you can dare to dream and believe greater and bigger about yourself and purpose, you will not settle for less. Just the same, if you believe small or little about your self-worth and value, then you will not expect more. God says your faith is able to move mountains, so you can expect through His help and grace that you can accomplish anything you set your mind to, big or small, when you believe. When you imagine it, write it down, speak it aloud over and over, until you actually believe it, and watch your wildest dreams occur.

Derailment

Derailment is the ultimate end goal of the enemy. Yes, he presents circumstances and situations to discourage us, distract us, and leave us in doubt, but what he really wants is to get us so far outside of God's will that self-destruction is inevitable. Derailment includes depression, totally separating ourselves from the things of God, settling for a second-rate lifestyle, battling drug or alcohol addiction, losing custody of our children, going to jail, or ultimately committing suicide. Derailment is designed to get us so far away from the will of God that we stop striving and allow ourselves to be victims to whatever happens to us. The enemy is a professional at presenting distractions and evoking negative feelings to derail us.

Our physical bodies and our souls are under constant attack by the enemy, and with the right amount of negative external influences, such as the things we see, hear, and feel, he can lead us down a path of death and/or destruction that deters us from accomplishing our life's mission. In the heat of a moment, our emotions may get the best of us and we may engage in an argument or altercation with someone and become offended, finding ourselves behind prison bars. We could succumb to sexual lust for someone we find attractive. This lustful relationship may spin toward a downward spiral of uncontrolled circumstances that most have a difficult time recovering from, like unexpected pregnancy, poverty, settling for a Godless relationship, and/or even contracting a deadly disease like AIDS. In either scenario, these emotions have long-lasting consequences, which our God prefers us not to endure. Our feelings often evoke thoughts that we replay in our heads a thousand times and catapult us into action.

When we push away thoughts of doing and/or saying something different than what is stated in the Word of God, we are being obedient to Christ. Our obedience to God's word requires us to move quickly and be stern. Our obedience to the Holy Spirit's prompting is strongly connected to His promises of blessings and favor. Choosing to fix our minds and attention on anything outside of God and His word places a bull's-eye on our backs for the enemy and forfeits our abundance of blessings. Satan is envious of God's unfailing love for mankind and His desire for you to win in this life or in heavenly eternity. He knows his final destination will not be in paradise with God, so he pulls all the tricks out of the bag to deceive you so that he has company on his hell-bound journey. The devil continues to deceive you into believing lies about your identity, self-worth, and potential so you either do not try or so that you make poor choices that get you so twisted up that you cannot determine if you are coming or going.

Satan's quadruple D's begin with poor thinking or what my bishop calls "stinky thinking." As I mentioned before, our minds are the battlefield, and we win the fight when we figure out the enemy's playbook and begin playing offense instead of defense. Playing offense allows us to have an eagle's vantage point and use discernment when the enemy presents his lies and deceit to us. We close the door to distractions and shut off the negative thoughts of doubt and discouragement to prevent ourselves from being derailed as soon as the idea shows up.

One of the eagle's primary characteristics is its vision. An eagle's vision is keen, and its perspective is higher than any other bird. They observe situations around, below, and above to capture the bigger picture. They are able to see fifty miles away to spot another eagle headed their way. Their heightened vision gives them clarity and insight of what's to come. Eagles are also fearless in the face of adversity. During storms, they fly head-on towards the challenge, using the wind to propel them forward onto greater heights. Eagles are powerful since their ability to predict always places them at an advantage with their adversaries. This type of bravery, insight, and tenacity makes for great leaders in the faith and in life. It's time to step up our vision and altitude and soar above like eagles do.

We more easily recognize ideas that may be fostered by the enemy when we operate as eagles. We can quickly bring the thought under control, rebuke him, and replace the thought with the truth according to God's word. Jesus shows us how to do this in our own lives in Matthew 4:1–11. Every time Satan introduced a thought, Jesus would reply with, "For it was written," then preceded with the Scripture that negated what the enemy said. In this same way, we are to fight back our "stinky thinking" and win the battle that starts in our minds. This is not a typical way of handling our thinking, so it will take some practice and may be difficult at first. However, like all habits, we can develop it over time.

Typically, it takes approximately thirty days to form a new habit when we are consistent. The enemy's insertions of untruths do not just begin when you become a teenager or an adult; they sometimes start as early as conception. Believe me, he will do anything in his power to try and kill you on purpose to prevent you from reaching your highest potential. Unfortunately, our thoughts are not the only way he creeps in to attack us; he often manipulates weakened vessels in the form of closed-minded family members, spouses, and friends to unknowingly do his dirty work through sexual/physical abuse, drug addiction, alcoholism, selfishness, bitterness, and so forth. All of these things set the stage for an unstable personal and social environment in our homes where our initial learning occurs.

There are several examples of how this occurs in the present day, and we are seeing more children with behavioral and psychological issues than ever before. During my professional training for occupational therapy, we explored several psychological theorists who presented ideas to hypothesize human behavior. Martin Seligman, Abraham Maslow, and Erik Erikson are three psychological theorists who offered the most intriguing theories for personality development. I'd like us to explore two of them, since they shed light on some internal processes that relate to a person's perceived identity and thinking.

Maslow developed a hierarchy of human needs to better describe human beings' motivation in life. He described five levels of needs, which begin with physiological, safety, love, esteem, and then self-actualization. He created a chart to help us better understand the hierarchy of a person's most intrinsic and basic needs to feel successful in life. Further, he believed there were certain basic-level needs, such as air, food, water, shelter, and love, which had to be met before the person could move towards higher levels, which include self-esteem and self-actualization. As you will see in the chart shown, self-actualization is associated with a person's desire to strive toward accomplishing his life's purpose.

Here you will find Maslow's chart with its associated levels and what each level means:

Maslow suggests that a person will never reach a level of self-actualization and discovering their purpose if those foundational and base levels are not met. It is crazy to think, with the abundance of resources available in the United States, that there are people walking around lacking some of those base-level needs, but there are. Many of our basic psychological needs are met in a stable home environment, and that is why it is so important that we strive to foster homes where these are met and in abundance. Again, I believe this is the number-one reason the enemy is ravishing homes and family structures.

As I mentioned in a previous chapter, broken families and single-parent homes are often faced with poverty due to lack of resources. Poverty prevents us from having our basic needs met. Unlike in the 1960s, American lifestyles require more than one income to maintain the household. When a single parent is able to pull the resources together to make a household work (without the financial support from a partner or government), they often have limited time inside the home. Another base-level need that all humans share is the need for love and belonging. We all desire to love and be loved! Just like food and air, humanity is designed to desire love and relationship. Unfortunately, the need for love and belonging may diminish or be lacking in broken home units. A parent, in this case, desires to show love, but because of limited quality time or sparse resources, their actions may result in a child, spouse, or family member not feeling loved.

According to *The 5 Love Languages* author Gary Chapman, everyone has a love language and a way they interpret love. In his book, he describes quality time as a language of love, along with gifts, acts of service, affection, and words of affirmation. My love language is quality time, so it is important for my mom, family, and friends to support me by going to my plays, choir concerts, attending science projects—showing us how to bake, and spending time with us on family trips.

There are several reasons people are lacking love in their homes. We have to understand that, more and more, people are walking around with feelings of worthlessness and self-defeat. Being loved and knowing you have a sense of belonging are directly linked to your self-worth and esteem. Every person who exists on this earth is wired to feel love and acceptance. When you know and understand that you are loved, your strengths stand out more to you, and your flaws become little quirks that your loved ones deal with. You feel safe in that space and you gain confidence in your ideas and dreams. You will look for ways to make them come true. Our goals and dreams will always be eclipsed by our physiological and security needs for food, water, and shelter. God reminds and gives us assurance of this ability to provide this basic need for us:

> Therefore, I say unto you, take no thought for your life, what ye shall eat, or what ye shall drink, nor yet for your body, what ye shall put on. Is not the life more than meat, and the body than raiment? Behold fowls of the air: for they sow not, neither do they reap, nor gather into barns, yet your heavenly Father feedeth them. Are ye not much better than they? (Matthew 6:25–26, KJV)

God gives us assurance that He cares for us and will provide these basic needs when we place our trust in Him and seek first after His kingdom in the heavenly realm (Matthew 6:26–34). God needs us to know that He is more than capable of handling our basic needs and that stressing ourselves out about these things causes a burden that we need not bare. There are some of you reading who come from family situations where those responsible for your well-being failed to provide these basic necessities. God is very concerned with our basic needs and encourages His people to look after some of our most vulnerable populations, such as the orphaned, fatherless, and widowed. The lack of resources and growing up in a poverty-stricken environment can be devastating to someone's faith with leading them to search for options outside of God. Additionally, it may lead to a condition called learned helplessness.

Learned helplessness prevents a person from striving for a future with a better lifestyle when it is within reach. Learned helplessness is a conditioning of the mind that occurs from unrelenting hardship, pain, and stresses that may result in the person failing to attempt available options that may arise in the future. Basically, a person's belief system is that uncontrollable external circumstances are beyond their control and there is nothing they can do to prevent bad things from happening to them or having good things happen for them. The individual has experienced so much resistance and conflict in their past that, when a new environment and people with better options become available, they choose not to try them. They may hold a belief that everything occurring in this life is out of their control and they have to endure whatever is thrown at them. This mindset and way of thinking has Satan written all over it. The enemy loves the idea of you believing that you have no dominion or control over the things of this world. This belief system has many human advocates and activists scratching their heads at times.

Understanding learned helplessness is the key. Advocates and those who experience such thoughts have to intentionally seek ways to reverse the negative conditioning of the mind. Advocates may often see this with youth or people who have been in the foster care system, those sexually victimized, domestic violence victims, children in poverty, and those in the sex trade. Seligman suggests three deficits that arise from the pain of uncontrollable events: motivation, cognitive, and emotional.

The cognitive deficit is the idea and belief that negative circumstances are uncontrollable. The motivational deficit is the inability to realize or respond to available methods of escape from the negative situation. The emotional deficit results in depression and perceived hopelessness. Major depression is often the end result of learned helplessness. Those who suffer from personal helplessness are more likely to have self-esteem deficits. Youth and teens with low self-esteem perform more poorly academically. Academic self-esteem has a high correlation with later success. Students who feel they don't perform well in school will be less motivated to try to perform and, thus, perpetuate a cycle of poor school performance.

Self-esteem is established very early in development and is directly related to how successful we are later in life. It is important to have positive reinforcement in the areas we perform well and minimize criticism as much as possible. Teachers, parents, and community leaders should strive to identify those good characteristics in a child. This is especially important for those who misbehave. Sometimes, children and youth seek attention from adults in any form, even when the reinforcement is negative. Highlighting the good behavior in someone will more often lead to repeating the behavior. God loves praise and so does His creation. We are made in the image of God Almighty, and we know from Scripture that He inhabits the praise of His people (Psalms 22:3).

Children, youth, and adults alike enjoy being praised. Praise helps to build our self-esteem and self-worth. I believe this is why you find so many young ladies and men posting pictures of themselves in some very unflattering ways online. Receiving "likes" and "hearts" on social media feeds the desire for praise, which is linked to self-esteem. I also believe that this is why cyberbullying is so impactful and damaging to some of our youth. The negative reinforcement from peers can be embarrassing and devastating to children who are seeking acceptance in this way, especially when they are greeted with ridicule and aggression in such a public way. Having self-esteem is vital to our personal identity. It's an intrinsic need for all mankind and without it our lives may not be as fulfilling. Knowing and understanding our identity in Christ helps us fill this void and need to be pursued, wanted, and loved, even when we do not realize we are broken. Praise God for that!

As I mentioned in the earlier chapters, children are challenged at home with their families, at school, and on social media. I believe this is why the number of children with depression in the United States and abroad is steadily increasing. There is substantial evidence that asserts the correlation of a child's performance in school and the successes or failures they face during their educational years that establishes the groundwork for self-worth and self-esteem. As I pointed out, positive self-worth and self-esteem lead to self-actualization and understanding of purpose. Self-actualization is vital since it is the basis for a person's realization for their maximum potential and possibilities.

Self-actualization leads us to offering wisdom and guidance to those presently with us by serving in our community, being secure in our gift and calling, and positively contributing to society. You may be gifted to teach, cook, minister, decorate, heal, bake, create music or art, encourage, preach, sing, write, dance, etc. You fill in the blank. There are so many gifts that there is room for us all. Discovering your purpose, operating in your gifts, and serving humanity in the capacity that God planned for you from the foundation of the earth extends your lifespan well over 120 years. This is called legacy living.

The late, great Myles Munroe most adequately advised us with this message: "We are all gifted with something that our generation is in need of. It is our responsibility to find out what it is and get it to them!" The enemy works hard to prevent us from accomplishing this goal. Having poor self-esteem could set the child or adult on a course for low expectations, or never trying at all. Not trying is not an option if you are a child of God. God tells us in Deuteronomy 28:13 that we are the head and not the tail, above and not beneath, the lender and not the borrower. These are just a few of the things He promises His children. God placed great potential inside of us all, and it is my heart's desire that you experience that greatness before you leave this earth.

So far, we have learned that self-esteem is directly related to self-actualization and achieving our goals, and that learned helplessness creates motivational, cognitive, and emotional deficits that prevent people from trying.

I would like to offer these nine keys to building self-esteem so that you can overcome the adverse effects of negative thinking about yourself:

- Aim to surround yourself with people who are encouraging, believers, wiser, and uplifting (small group, city groups, or support group).

- Avoid friends or people who gossip, are negative, keep drama, or speak down to you, call you negative names.

- Be an example to friends and loved ones by providing positive words, praise, and compliments when deserved.

- Reevaluate what currently builds your self-esteem and if your physical attributes (butt, breasts, hips) are on the top of that list, seek to replace them with your intrinsic characteristics, such as kindness, a sense of humor, intelligence, and so forth.

- Set realistic goals for yourself. Goals should be specific, measurable, attainable, realistic, and time sensitive (S.M.A.R.T.).

- Use to-do lists and checklists to encourage yourself by accomplishing goals and having control over your day.

- Take a personality assessment to better understand your spiritual gifts and skills unique to you.

- Volunteer and serve your community using your spiritual gifts to help someone less fortunate than yourself.

- Pray for God's words, strength, courage, and wisdom daily to maintain positive thoughts throughout the day.

For your convenience, I have provided these nine steps on an easily downloadable and printable PDF file at AprilTeleeSykes.com. Keep these keys in a place that you are able to refer back to as you work toward creating new, healthier habits. Habits and character tweaks are not something we change overnight, but consistently over time. It takes review and deliberate application in real-life situations. You can begin to build or rebuild your self-worth and self-esteem in doing so.

Like I said before, I know some of you have managed to crawl out of some very dark places. The aftermath has made lasting imprints on your self-identity and self-worth. Experiencing traumatic events, such as verbal, physical, or sexual abuse in your homes, can be traumatic, devastating, and may take some time to reverse the negative effects. However, healing is possible. God's word says that He is able to heal the brokenhearted and bind up their wounds (Psalms 147:3). God wants to mend your brokenness and make you whole again. In another verse, He encourages us with these words:

"My grace is sufficient for you, for my power is made perfect in weakness" (2 Corinthians 12:9, KJV).

It is time to break any chains of mental defeat (strongholds) you've struggled with over the years by purposing yourself to think and behave in the opposite way you are used to. Your past does not have to define your future. Allow God to heal your heart, push past the guilt and the pain, and fill in the brokenness with His supernatural grace. Let today be the end of this vicious cycle! You are victorious in Jesus Christ, and He has overcome the world, so freedom is yours!

CHAPTER 8

GOD IDENTITY

"God is love."
—I John 4:16

Have you ever misjudged someone by making a generalization about who they are, whether positive or negative, only to learn later they were the complete opposite of what you thought? Perhaps you placed parameters on that person's worth or ability with the lowest of expectations upon them. You could even place too high of an expectation on the person or put them into a category of being "untouchable." Perhaps you later came to the realization that there was much more to them after you spent some valuable time getting to know them. Through increased interactions, you may realize that you share similar interests and genuinely enjoy their company when they are around. This person brings excitement and joy into your world with their presence and you may even determine that this person adds value to your life. In fact, now you could not imagine an existence without them. Maybe you marry one of these people or establish a viable business relationship with them.

However, I would like to give you some food for thought. What if you made the mistake of never getting to know them and remained comfortable with a shallow perception of who they really are from a distance? You would miss the opportunity of sharing significant time with this individual and embarking upon a beautiful journey of life or business together. For some of you, that thought might be scary since you have built meaningful relationships with these people. Unfortunately, there are many people who have not the slightest clue of the breadth and beauty of God or His character. This misconception of who God is results in unrealistic expectations of Him, mistruths about what He does or does not do for us, and, sadly, sets the groundwork for an underdeveloped relationship with the Creator.

Many people may assert that there is a God or even believe in the supernatural realm, but never fully explore the depth of that belief. I have often heard skeptics refer to God as "something out there" or "the universe." Christians are not exempt from holding misconceptions about God, either.

I have heard many ministers and Christians speak of "the man upstairs" authoring life's misfortune and heartache to teach people lessons. I cannot count the amount of times I have witnessed people talk about God orchestrating accidents, sickness, or financial woes to get their attention, or that of one of their loved ones. The truth is, many people have a difficult time accepting this fundamental truth, that God is good and wants the best for all of us (mankind).

With all the good that we may experience in this life, there are also many challenges that we face, such as disease, the death of loved ones, hunger, rape, poverty, crime, incarceration, etc. Unfortunately, none of us are exempt from negative situations occurring in this life, which may result in great pain and lasting scars. For many, negative life circumstances make it difficult to believe in or love a God we cannot see. This is especially true when you count God as the one responsible for allowing bad things to happen in the world. Some people operate in a hopeless existence where there seems to be no light at the end of the tunnel. Subsequently, they often develop feelings of shame, doubt, hopelessness, and fear. As believers, we should not wallow in our feelings of hopelessness about the world since we have been assured hope through the promises of God. He promises to be our strength in time of trouble (Psalms 46:1).

In fact, I would like to offer good news for those who have wasted countless years of their life blaming God for unforeseen mishaps and unpleasant circumstances occurring. God is not responsible for the terrible things that happen in this world. Most importantly, He hates to see His creation suffer more than you could ever imagine. I am sure that statement alone will even rock many Christians' theologies. One of God's greatest desires is for His most adored creations to choose Him, build a relationship with Him, and allow Him to teach you who you really are. Like I mentioned before, from the very first book of the Bible in Genesis with Adam to Abraham, then David, to Solomon to Joseph, and right down to Jesus, God reveals tales of men's and women's feats occurring because of their connection to Him. Mankind's progress does not cease to exist or propel forward because they do not choose to follow Him, but you can be certain it is more than likely not God's best for them. So, if God isn't responsible for the bad that happens in the world then who is? Great question, and I am glad you asked. In order to wrap your brain around bad things that occur in this life or even the people who do horrible acts, you must have a basic understanding of spiritual matters. Just as there are good spiritual forces present in this world, there are also evil forces dwelling here as well. As I stated earlier, the Bible delineates how we are not alone in this world and that we have opposing forces we battle all the time.

Again, "We wrestle not with flesh and blood but against principalities, against powers, against the rulers of darkness of this world, against spiritual wickedness in high places" (Ephesians 6:12, KJV). These dark forces or spirits work in concert to create hellacious scenarios in our lives to distract and deter us from obtaining peace, joy, and prosperity in every area of our lives. These forces have been here since the beginning in the garden of Eden (Genesis 3:1). Furthermore, these forces aim to redirect our attention away from God and obtaining eternal salvation. This may seem spooky to some of you but, whether you think about it or not, spiritual beings surround us every day, including the Holy Spirit of God. It always baffles me how some assert their disbelief in something/someone they cannot see, but there is plenty they do not see but know is there. Like I mentioned in an earlier chapter, every day you awake and inhale you should be reminded of how without the element of oxygen, which you do not see, smell, or taste, you would cease to exist. What about germs and microorganisms that we encounter on a daily basis that, if we are not careful, have the potential to cause illness and disease. We do our best to manage these unseen biological factors through good hand hygiene and containment. Just like the air we breathe the unseen spirit of God continues to hover and represent everything good in the world. If you are in need of a quick refresher, just open your Bible to Genesis 1:1–25. One should consider, why it is it so hard for some to believe in the supernatural.

Unfortunately, in every good story you have ever read, heard, or seen there is always a villain or an adversary that presents challenges to the main character. The story of God, the Creator of the universe, also has an archrival, and his name is Lucifer. Lucifer was renamed Satan, which in the Greek means "adversary." He is also referred to as the devil. When broken down, it means He is the manufacturer of pride, jealousy, hatred, and fear, which are spirits that work in complete opposition to the spirit of God. God's spirit is on the opposite end of the spectrum of fear and is characterized as love, humility, kindness, gentleness, and faith. At some point, Lucifer lived in heaven with God, but due to his pride (vanity), selfishness, and desire to be revered as high as God, he was kicked out (Isaiah 14:12–14). Revelation 12:9 recounts the fall of Satan as this: "And the great dragon was cast out, that old serpent, called the Devil, and Satan, which deceives the whole world: he was cast out into the earth, and his angels were cast out with him" (KJV). When you read further in verse 12, you see where the earth is put on notice that Satan has come down to earth; he is angry; jealous of your dominion/authority; and he knows he has limited time to cause havoc and chaos. It was not until after he tricked Eve and Adam in the garden that the enemy gained temporary dominion on the earth by tricking mankind into thinking that we cannot trust what God says (his word) and that our physical existence (opened eyes) is what truly matters. Genesis 3:1–4 describes the initial deception like this:

> Now the serpent was more cunning than any beast of the field which the Lord God had made. And he said to the woman, "Has God indeed said, 'You shall not eat of every tree of the garden'?" And the woman said to the serpent, "We may eat the fruit of the trees of the garden; but of the fruit of the tree which is in the midst of the garden, God has said, 'You shall not eat it, nor shall you touch it, lest you die.'" Then the serpent said to the woman, "You will not surely die. For God knows that in the day you eat of it your eyes will be opened, and you will be like God, knowing good and evil." (NKJV)

When mankind's eyes opened essentially it translates into having a heightened awareness of humanity, a decreased sense of spirituality, and the ability to reason differently from God. Until that point, Adam and Eve believed everything God said and were dependent on Him for every source of inspiration and provision. Ultimately, Eve and, subsequently, Adam experienced a paradigm shift that established a division between mankind and God. This paradigm, or different way of thinking, is sometimes referred to as "the fall of man." The closeness and fellowship that occurred daily in the midst of the garden of Eden was now greeted with a self-reliance, shame, and fear. We now have the ability to think, create, and willfully choose, which makes it easy to consider ourselves as God's equal, therefore, diminishing the need to believe and follow His instructions any longer.

Unfortunately, without God's infinite wisdom, we are like children needing guidance and direction in a huge world that we do not fully understand. The unknown can be extremely frightening and crippling if you do not have a light for guidance. With this awakening (knowledge of good and evil), the enemy (spiritual darkness) is more easily able to use our natural senses to lure us to follow after his earthly kingdom. He is the father of lies and is creative in his tactics, using our perception to forfeit our spiritual rights. Truthfully, the world is beautiful and is full of temptations such as gorgeous men/women, the pursuit of cars, houses, superstars, vacations, and money, which may distract us from Godly principles. God actually gives us a warning about loving the things of the world in 1 John 2:15–17:

> Love not the world, neither the things that are in the world. If any man love the world, the love of the Father is not in him. For all that is in the world, the lust of the eyes, and the pride of life, is not of the Father, but is of the world. And the world passeth away, and the lust thereof, but he that doeth the will of God abideth forever. (KJV)

Often the pursuit of worldly things leads us down a path of self-indulgence, and we then improperly begin to exalt the creation instead of the Creator. Our money, belongings, secular knowledge, and the people we deem celebrity become miniature gods (deities). This is much more easily done than you think. Money has to be one of the most renowned gods mankind looks to for provision. Like our spiritual God offers natural provision, money provides a tangible source of having our basic needs met. Therefore, many will fall into the snare of trusting money over God's lead. You position money as the ruler if you make daily life decisions based on what your bank account says before you consider what God says. Just that fast, you have made your trust in your bank account a deity. God warns us against the love of money and says that it is the root of all evil (1 Timothy 6:10).

Growing up outside of Chicago, I have seen good people get caught up in some very bad things to get money or make a living. Don't get me wrong; having money is not a bad thing, but the LOVE of money can be destructive when you place yourself and others in harm's way to get it. God indeed wants His children to be prosperous and promises that He will not see His seed begging for bread when we are obedient to His word (Deuteronomy 28:1–14 and Psalms 37:25). Obedience to God is securely linked to His blessings and abundance of spiritual and financial blessings. Following God's directives will always lead us down a path of provision. It is important that we trust Him no matter what and not become discouraged when there is a delay. So many times, I remember becoming impatient and scrambling with my own reasoning and seeking for answers outside of the will of God. Each time I've done this my plans fail and I circle around back to where I began.

Unfortunately, delays reveal the level of trust we have in God's ability to provide for us. We serve a jealous God and He desires we seek Him first to supply all of our needs according to His riches in glory (Philippians 4:19). Aside from God being jealous, He knows that creation is incapable of providing the unconditional love and provision that He does (Exodus 34:14). The enemy relishes when man doubts what God says and defaults to his own belief system to accomplish self-directed goals in this life. He understands that questioning God subsequently places us outside of the will of God and worshipping things of this world. We are enslaved to the enemy's ruling when we allow ourselves to be deceived into seeking to engage in activities that make us feel or look good. It may seem harmless to engage in self-gratifying activities, but an ungoverned soul seeking to please itself is contrary to the spirit of God.

God is love, agape love to be exact. Agape comes from the Greek word *agapao*, which is the highest form of love. This type of love does not consider its own self, but the welfare and charity of others. This type of love is unconditional and does not place worth on its subject, but is concerned with giving love, regardless of whether it is reciprocated. Agape love considers itself last and is more concerned with the welfare and state of others. Agape love is not an emotion but is best observed in action. God regards love very highly in the word and He gives His people a mandate to love one another. I mean, it is the very essence of who He is, and who we are as His children (I John 3:1). Moses bestowed the people of God (Israelites) with the Ten Commandments, which was downloaded directly from God. The very first commandment is, "You shall have no other gods before me" and the second is, "You shall not make for yourself an image in the form of anything in heaven above or on the earth beneath or in the waters below" (Exodus 20:3–4, NIV). God was making it clear that the affection of mankind was to be directed toward Him, not the wealth or the demi-gods of Egypt. The other eight commandments provide relational instructions for morality amongst the Israelites. For example, the Ten Commandments, also referred to as the law, was provided under the old covenant, which was given to the people of Israel to assist in governing them as believers in the God of their ancestors. Under the new covenant, Jesus provided a similar command when the Pharisees questioned which law was the greatest to God.

Jesus says that we are to love the Lord our God with all our heart, all our mind, and all of our souls. He also says to love our neighbor as we love ourselves. It is important to differentiate agape love from romantic love (*eros*) and the intimate feeling of love towards a friend (*phileo*) or someone outside of a sexual relationship. Agape love is not an emotion or based on how we feel. Unfortunately, human emotions are fickle and unreliable and should never be in the driver's seat of our "love walk." When emotions are in charge of directing our behaviors versus following after the spirit of God (which is love), we may do and say things that lack sound judgment and we may later regret. Simply put, when you react on impulses to things people do or say and/or are driven by your feelings (good or bad), you are allowing your flesh to rule and place yourself in position to be deceived by God's adversary, Satan. This is one of the fundamental truths revealed in the Word of God. I John 2:15–17 says:

> Do not love the world or the things in the world. If anyone loves the world, the love of the father is not in him. For all that is in the world—the lust of the flesh, the lust of the eyes, and the pride of life—is not of the Father but is of the world. And the world is passing away, and the lust of it; but he who does the will of God abides forever. (NKJV)

As I stated earlier, God is love. He is real love, as the singer Mary J. Blige put it. The love of physical possessions and things of this world are a pseudo-form of love called *lust*. Lust is defined as a strong feeling of sexual desire or an overmastering craving or passion for something that has no lasting effect. Our God is everlasting and reigns forever and ever. Our belongings and creation are temporal, so putting faith in our money, relationships with people, status, and perceived power is fruitless since they are passing away, as the Scripture states. Since the fall of man, the enemy covertly lurks on earth for he is the prince of the power of the air and is actively seeking to deceive people in every manner he can think of, such as sex, selfish ambition, drugs/alcohol, fame, vanity, pleasure, and so forth (Ephesians 2:2).

The enemy uses the things of this world to bait us with the lust of the eyes, lust of the flesh, and the pride of life. God wants us to know the truth about our existence and come into greater understanding of our true identity in Him as spiritual beings. We are more effective in resisting the enemy's deceit when we are aware of the mode of attack as spiritual warfare. We stop blaming natural things, people, and situations for the challenges we face and begin to identify the enemy's tactics. When you know who you are, the power you possess, and the place of victory you fight from, then your enemy has to develop a cleverer strategy or flee altogether. Satan operates in the heavenly realm on earth, which essentially is in the air. The heavenly realm in the Greek is known as *epouranios*, which means the sphere of spiritual activities. *Epouranios* is where both angels and demons dwell and are influencing the things in the natural realm (physical activities). Interestingly, the devil had spent much of his time in heaven, accusing the brethren, and was envious of God's creation.

Heaven and Earth

Let me be clear, Satan hates you because of his fallen position. He is fully aware of the position of authority he lost when Jesus died on the cross. He understands that when you are unsure or unaware of your identity and authority that you will fail to use it, which places him at an advantage to continue to cause chaos in your life. As sons and daughters of God, we have authority to trample over snakes and scorpions in the name of Jesus. That means we have power over all the enemy's devices and, therefore, he is powerless against us when we understand our weaponry. Additionally, Satan has forever been condemned to damnation and has no hope of being redeemed for his deceitfulness and folly. Therefore, he will not be allowed back into heaven with God. Have you heard the adage, "Misery loves company?" This saying accurately sums up the enemy's position. Satan is the king of the "crab effect." If he is going down, you can bet that he is going to take as many people with him as possible. He enjoys causing confusion and spreading lies. His primary goal is to trick and ultimately destroy God's most precious creation: mankind. After the disciples returned from casting out demons, Jesus spoke to them about Satan's fallen position and diminished power in Luke 10:17–19:

> The seventy-two returned with joy and said, "Lord, even the demons submit to us in your name." He replied, "I saw Satan fall like lightning from heaven. I have given you authority to trample on snakes and scorpions and to overcome all the power of the enemy; nothing will harm you." (NIV)

This is good news. As eerie as it may sound to be surrounded by spirits that are working against you in the spiritual realm, we have confidence in Jesus's declaration that we have power over the enemy. We are no longer subject to the accusations of Satan for our sins, since Jesus has provided our ransom and paid our (mankind's) bail for earthly sins, so to speak. God has given His children, through the belief in Jesus Christ, power to reign over the enemy. All we have to do is speak "the right words"—God's word to be exact. We have the ability to trample over snakes and be victorious when opposition tries to discourage or reel us off course (Luke 10:19). The enemy, in the form of a serpent, began this trickery in the garden of Eden with Eve, and he has been scheming to destroy God's precious creation ever since. His greatest trick is to get mankind to believe lies about God and not trust Him at His word (Genesis 3:3–5). If you heard or thought, "God is not real, does not love you, does not hear you, want you, or need you," then you have been deceived. Deceit is the enemy's primary weapon and it began in the garden with Eve. What was the deceit? "Do not believe or trust God!"

The instruction God gave mankind was not to eat from the tree of the knowledge of good and evil. Why would God do this? I'm sure there are several theological theories regarding why He did this, but my best assumption is because it is our worldly knowledge, analytical skills, and trust in our own ability that keep us distant from God and from being dependent on His wisdom and provision. God, in His disappointment with mankind's lack of faith and disobedience in what He said, caused Him to drive us (mankind) out of the garden. He then placed spiritual borders around Eden.

> Then the Lord God said, Behold, the man has become like one of us, knowing good and evil: and now he might stretch out his hand and take also from the tree of life, and eat and live forever. Therefore, the Lord God sent him from the garden of Eden, to cultivate the ground from which he was taken. So he drove the man out; and at the east of the garden of Eden he stationed the cherubim

and the flaming sword which turned every direction to guard the way to the tree of life. (Genesis 3:22–24, KJV)

Many archeologists, surveyors, explorers, and biblical scholars have sought to find the origin of man in Eden. The Bible references four rivers, two of which (Euphrates and Tigris) still exist and flow through modern day Iraq. Although these two rivers exist, there is no true indication of how and where the garden of Eden would have been. It is my belief that Eden was not just a physical place but a spiritual (metaphysical) context. Scripture in Ezekiel 28:13 actually refers to Eden as the garden of God. This explains why no one has truly been able to locate Eden.

Eden is not a physical place but a spiritual one. All of which gives explanation as to why we are more inclined to perceive through the physical lens than our spiritual eye following our consumption from the forbidden tree of the knowledge of good and evil. God protected His heavenly place from wickedness by not allowing us to stay in Eden, where we could have access to eternity with an uncontrolled evil seed implanted in us. An interesting truth is God only instructed Adam to not eat from the tree of the knowledge of good and evil when he was placed in the garden (Genesis 2:15–17). It was not until after Adam sinned that God cursed man (Adam) to return back to the ground from which he was formed and placed the tree of life out of his reach until an appointed time (the Messiah). Then God said to Adam in Genesis 3:17–19:

Because you have heeded to the voice of your wife and have eaten from the tree of which I commanded you, saying, "You shall not eat of it": Cursed is the ground for your sake; In toil you shall eat of it all the days of your life. Both thorns and thistles it shall bring forth for you, and you shall eat the herb of the field. In the sweat of your face you shall eat bread till you return to the ground, for out of it you were taken; for dust you are and to dust you shall return. (NKJV)

Now, we must have food, work, and sometimes struggle to cultivate the land, and then eventually die. This places cruel and unusual punishment in perspective. The loss in the garden of Eden was GREAT. Hard work, turmoil, and death were never God's initial plan. God cursed man at the fall, and the knowledge we thought we gained was reduced to a lowly state of humanity and a natural inclination. Unfortunately, this would be accompanied with fear and symbolic thorns and thistles, which make it difficult to have true understanding of God's creation and this world until the fullness of His word is revealed at the second coming of Jesus. God gave us free will to choose in the garden and, unfortunately, we chose wrong. Some may question, if God is all knowing, then of course He would know that mankind would mess up, so why did He give us free will in the first place? While some might consider free will a flaw in creation, God longed for it to be a poetic love song between man and Himself, with a choice to believe in Him and accept His daily provision. His desire for creation never changed, even with the fall. He still longed to have a relationship with man. In fact, He outlined a plan for redemption from the very beginning that includes reconciliation back into fellowship with Him and for us to live forever with Him in eternity, spiritually (Genesis). That plan was named the messiah, Jesus Christ.

Jesus Christ was our redemption plan and salvation package rolled up into one. Jesus is God, our savior manifested in the flesh. In the old covenant, God was limited in how much time He spent with mankind due to our sinful nature. Initially, our years on this earth in this human vessel extended up to 900 years for some of the earlier believers. However, God found it difficult to be with us because of our sinful tendencies. In Genesis 6:3, He says, "My Spirit will not contend with humans forever, for they are mortal; their days will be a hundred and twenty years" (NIV).

God reduced the lifespan of man to 120 years on earth due to our mortality, sinful nature, and propensity towards wickedness. Paul advises us against the types of sins and behaviors to avoid, as they are in direct conflict with the spirit of God: Murder, jealousy, drunkenness, selfish ambition, hatred, fear, anger, malice, idolatry, and sexual deviations all derive from sin and drive a wedge between man and God. All these things are contrary to the spirit of God, which is love.

God continued to stay nearby and offer His assistance to those who desired to be in relationship with Him (Israelites and their descendants). His temporary fix to fellowship with man included spontaneous appearances and sacred blood sacrifices of animals. The Old Testament describes many scenarios where men and women who believed in the one true living God obtained favor with Him. Believers, such as Noah, Abraham, Moses, Job, King David, King Solomon, Daniel, and Elijah, offered an annual atonement for their sins to God by presenting their best livestock and first fruits as a burnt offering. In exchange for their honor and sacrifice, God provided assistance to overcome adversity and dire situations with His help. God made the impossible possible and delivered miracles no human could conceive of or do alone.

Although these men and women were blessed and experienced unmerited favor with provision, their encounters with the God of the universe was sporadic and intermittent. However, today we are under a new covenant. God is able to manifest Himself and His power through us in an unparalleled way, through the Holy Spirit. He made this possible through His son Jesus Christ's life, death, and resurrection. Jesus dying on the cross was the final sacrifice, which corrected our sin issue once and for all. At the death of Jesus Christ, the veil was torn, and anyone who believed that Jesus died for our sins and was risen from the dead could come boldly to the throne of grace. God could dwell in His creation via the vehicle of the Holy Spirit, and our hearts (mind) would be considered holy ground. God's desire to be with us was so great that He made it possible for Him to abide in us—always.

John 15:4 says this: "Abide in me, and I in you. As the branch cannot bear fruit of itself, except it abide in the vine; no more can ye, except ye abide in me" (KJV). Revelation 3:20 states this: "Behold, I stand at the door, and knock: if any man hear my voice, and open the door, I will come in to him, and sup with him, and he with me" (KJV).

Getting to know God and being in relationship with Him requires actively speaking to Him daily, inviting Him into your jobs, homes, and helping you raise your children. Your desire to be in relationship with Him will draw you to places (church services) where His presence is felt and where others share a similar interest in getting to know Him, as well. This removes the duty out of the relationship and replaces it with desire to be close to your heavenly Father. Whichever way you view it, the statistics serve as proof that we are intrinsically designed to crave a connection to a supreme being or a greater power.

There are others who allow foolish pride and knowledge of worldly physical properties to lead them to reason away this natural propensity toward something greater than themselves. All and all, we are endowed with this desire to understand the ultimate philosophical truth to the questions, "Why am I here, and where did I come from?" We may learn this from reading the Word of God (Holy Bible), which was left for us to first understand God and, subsequently, know ourselves better. John makes it plain when he writes, "In the beginning was the Word, and the Word was with God, and the Word was God. He was with God in the beginning. Through him all things were made; without him nothing was made that has been made" (John 1:1–3, NIV).

This is powerful Scripture, because religions ascribe value to the creation, people, and other life forms. God wants you to understand that He and His word were there before there was ever "a beginning." He is the universe; He embodies it all, and religion is mankind's attempt to revere, understand, and honor His massive divinity. It is so difficult to sum up the magnitude of God that He told Moses to tell the people of Israel, "I AM hath sent me," if the Israelites questioned him about who sent him to deliver them from Egypt (Exodus 3:14, NIV). I love this! Basically, God was saying, I AM everything, point-blank, period. God gives further distinction by saying go to the elders of Israel and tell them the Lord God of their fathers, the God of Abraham, the God of Isaac, and the God of Jacob has sent you.

It is my belief that this is God's way of detailing His résumé of an eternal presence, glory, provision, and unchanging characteristics throughout generations. During those times, word of mouth was how traditions were passed down, and the Israelites had heard the stories about who God was to their ancestors and forefathers. God is all knowing; He is powerful; He is the Alpha and Omega; He is provision (Jehovah Jireh); He is peace (Jehovah Shalom); healing (Jehovah Rapha); He is protection (Jehovah Shammah); He is almighty (El Shaddai); and He is the great "I AM."

The Old Testament authors outline many battles, impossible situations, and clutch moments in which God introduces a new facet of Himself. Each time, a new name would be indicated. We see this first in the story of Abraham and Isaac in Genesis 22:1–19. To summarize the story, Abraham was a man after God's own heart and had struggled with his want for a child with his wife Sarah. After finally obtaining a promise of offspring from whom generations would be birthed, God instructed him to take his beloved child to a mountain top to offer him as a sacrifice. God does not advise him to bring an animal along, which were customarily used for burnt offerings (sacrifices) to atone for sin. Isaac, his son, asked, "Where is the lamb for the burnt offering" (Genesis 22:7, NIV). Abraham replied, "God himself will provide the lamb for the burnt offering" (Genesis 22:8, NIV). It is upon this mountain where Abraham, placing complete trust in God, raised his hand to slay his son when an angel of the Lord appeared to stop him. Abraham looked up and saw a ram stuck in a bush, the more obvious choice for a burnt offering. As a memorial, Abraham named the place at the top of that mountain Jehovah Jireh, meaning "God will provide."

God, the great "I AM," created us first for communion with Him and then with each other. He desires for us to trust Him and desire a relationship with Him over anything else in our lives. Unfortunately, our flesh (the physical properties) leads us astray and we may reflect more of our admiration onto the creation and not the Creator. This is the result of deception and an underdeveloped or unhealthy relationship with our heavenly Father. God warns us in Romans 1:25–27: "Who changed the truth of God into a lie, and worshipped and served the creature more than the Creator, who is blessed for ever. Amen" (KJV). Fear and knowledge of what is experienced in this physical realm (earth) makes it difficult to believe the unseen to the point we choose to ignore it, rationalize away the thought, or settle for a shallow understanding of the spiritual side of our humanity. The longer we do this, the longer we prevent ourselves from living the fullest life we could obtain in this lifetime through the guidance of God via the Holy Spirit.

I'd like to give you some food for thought. Imagine you've just recently relocated to a new city and you don't know a single soul. Eventually, you obtain employment and have coworkers who take on the responsibility of making you feel welcomed to your new company. You learn about your coworkers' ages, marital statuses, and maybe even their children's names. You may consider them to be nice people. In an attempt to include you, your coworkers invite you to a couple of gatherings after work hours, where you share food and dialogue on mutually interesting topics, which are typically work-related at best. At the end of the evening, you go your separate ways and plan not to see each other until the next day at work. You probably can safely assume that your coworkers are now your associates. If you think anything like me, anyone who is placed in the associate box has limited access to you. The parameters of your relationship are relatively small. Although the connection between you and your coworkers may be pleasant, it doesn't pass certain boundaries outside the workplace. If you are new in town, having work relationships with "associates" is probably not enough to satisfy all of your emotional or physical needs. More than likely, you will desire something more meaningful. An associate relationship is significantly different from someone you deem a close friend or family member.

Guess what. Just like you in the new city, God is not really interested in being an associate of yours. He is interested in something more meaningful, something more intimate. He wants to hang out with you outside of church. He wants you to invite Him to the movies, to the family picnics, vacations, to your workplace, and on that new, hot date. Let me explain. Since the beginning of creation, God's aspiration has been for mankind to acquire a close relationship with Him. Truthfully, there are endless benefits gained by being in close relationship to God. It's like being a part of the entourage of the most famous person you can think of. If you're like me, you've watched a few reality shows, including Keeping Up with the Kardashians. One of the things I have noticed has been the sweet perks the people surrounding them experience alongside their close friends or stepsiblings. If Kris, Khloe, or Kim goes on an expensive vacation or dine at a fancy restaurant, the entourage goes as well. Essentially, they are privy to the same lavish lifestyle as the superstar.

Hanging out with the master of the universe gets better and better the closer you are to His intimate circle. Matthew 6:33 writes it like this, "Seek the Kingdom of God above all else, and live righteously, and he will give you everything you need" (NLT). God wants you to desire to be part of His team. In fact, He desires to be more than your friend or team member. He positioned Himself to be "Our Father." Although He longs to be in close familial relationship with us, He will not force the relationship. The caveat to God's design of human beings is that they desire to be in close relationship with HIM by their own volition and will. The Apostle Paul writes in Galatians 4:4–6:

> But when the fullness of the time was come, God sent forth his Son, made of a woman, made under the law, to redeem them that were under the law, that we might receive the adoption of sons (daughters). And because ye are sons, God hath sent forth the Spirit of his Son into your hearts, crying, Abba, Father. (KJV)

This Scripture clearly describes the extent of relation God desires to have with us while we are here on earth. Jesus Christ is the manifestation of the final atonement for sin and freedom from the law so that God could freely fellowship with His creation as He did in the beginning with Adam. Moreover, He has called us His sons and daughters and joint heirs to Jesus Christ. As heirs, we ultimately inherit the kingdom of God, and all rights and privileges from being God's children become ours.

One may question what it means to know God as Abba father. The first thing we need to do is establish what it truly means to be a father. Unfortunately, in today's society, with the overwhelming amount of nontraditional family units, absentee fathers, and broken homes, the perception of a father often becomes muddled. As children of God, we have to be careful not to correlate our negative, personally lived experiences of fatherhood onto the Creator of the universe.

Let us start by having a clear understanding of the definition of father. Merriam-Webster defines the term "father" as a male in relation to his natural child or children, the oldest or most respected member of a society or other body. Additionally, he is the man who gives care and protection to someone or something. The term "father" as a verb is to be the source or the originator of something or someone, or a protector. It is important to note that the word "father" is more than a person, it's an action word. That means you can expect some type of effort or responsibility for your existence to be present on your behalf. God assumes that role in our lives, because He is the originator of us, not because He owes us anything. He is the first and perfect example of what it means to be a father. This is why we cannot limit our expectations of Him based on earthly fatherly experiences.

Imagine yourself in familial relationship with the one who created the term "father." Every good thing about a father that you understand stems from him. He is a father who loves you without condition and is always in pursuit of your heart and affection to the very end. He assumes full responsibility for you, His creation. How awesome is that? He has made a way for us to be fully adopted into His family, with all rights and privileges, through His son Jesus Christ. We do not have to pay ransom or beg for His love. He prods and pursues us continuously.

Now, like any relationship you may encounter, it takes spending time with your heavenly Father to really get to know Him. You have to be willing to free up some space and time in your schedule to know Him intimately. Cool thing about God, Abba father, is He is never too busy to hang out with you. He is sitting there waiting at the throne for you to get into His presence and join in on the heavenly praise party. He promises in His word that He will never leave you or forsake you. It's the ultimate father-child relationship awaiting development.

Your Identity in God

As a very young girl, I was not privy to knowing who my biological father was for most of my youth. I was given conflicting stories about who my dad was for years but, when I was ten, I met him. My mom stopped dating my father soon after getting pregnant because he would not get serious with her. She was seeing someone else off and on during that time as well and allowed him to believe I was his child. She denied she was pregnant to my father, and when she began showing, she told him it was another man's child. Despite not seeing me through development as a baby and young child, my father and I forged a genuine father-daughter relationship. My relationship with my "real" dad didn't grow over night, but over time we began getting to know each other, and eventually our relationship developed into something very solid, strong, and affectionate.

One of the things I remember most about my dad was his collection of pictures of me throughout his apartment. Over the years, the number of pictures grew and were found on the walls, entertainment centers, tables, and nightstands. It didn't matter if I went over to his house once a month or two times a day, I would always look at the pictures. Mostly, I would compare our likenesses by staring back and forth between my pictures and his. Looking at his eyes and hands, I noticed that I could fit mine in them, easily. We have the same nailbeds. I loved my daddy's hands. He and I had so much in common. My love for sports, banana cakes, coconut pie, and my corny jokes all came from him. I would actually sit and do this all the time, with all the pictures—it never got old. I unequivocally knew that man loved me, was proud to be my dad, and wanted to see me succeed. I say this to tell you that father relationships play an important role in understanding ourselves. We find so much of our identities from them.

Our relationship with God should be the same way—where we look at ourselves and view our God and see His likeness and our resemblance in Him. He desires for us to identify ourselves with Him as intimate as family but most importantly the patriarch. God is the head of the family. It is so unfortunate that so many young men and women are missing out on such an integral part of themselves. Trusting God as a father is difficult at the onset due to unhealthy earthly father relationships. Additionally, God's desire to be in relationship with us may be viewed as intimate as being in a marriage.

When a husband and wife become married, they are joined together and they become ONE entity, dependent on each other to accomplish a common goal. In the case of God and man, He unites as one with those who believe in Him to accomplish the work of "love," where love exudes from every crevice of our being and people are better or positively affected because they encountered us.

Human beings were created to LOVE (through relations), just as birds were created to fly. It is against our nature to be isolated and unloving to one another. Hatred is not of God. We are God's hands and feet on this earth. He created us in His image, and He is the direct reflection of love. We are to love our neighbors as ourselves, demonstrate benevolence through random acts of kindness, feed the hungry, care for the poor, watch after the orphaned, visit the jails, be slow to anger and quick to forgive, and, most importantly, love the Lord our God with all our hearts, minds, and souls. We have been called to embody love. In 1 Corinthians 13:4–13, Paul says it like this:

> Charity suffereth long, and is kind, charity envieth not: charity vaunteth not itself, is not puffed up. Doth not behave itself unseemly, seeketh not her own, is not easily provoked, thinketh no evil; Rejoiceth not in iniquity but rejoiceth in the truth; Beareth all things, believeth all things, hopeth all things, endureth all things. Charity never faileth: but whether there be prophecies, they shall fail; whether there be tongues, they shall cease; whether there be knowledge, it shall vanish away. For we know in part and we prophesy in part. But when that which is perfect is come, then that which is in part shall be done away. When I was a child, I spake as a child, I understand as a child, I thought as a child: but when I became a man, I put away childish things. For now we see through a glass, darkly but then face to face: now I know in part; but then shall I know even as also I am known. And now abideth faith, hope, charity, these three; but the greatest of these is charity. (KJV)

Charity is synonymous with the word "love." Now read the verses again, but this time insert the word "love" in place of "charity." You see how love requires the highest level of emotional and spiritual maturity! When we display fickle emotions and love with conditions, we are operating in an immaturity seen in children who are most often concerned with self-gratification. People who operate in love are not concerned with self or what is in it for themselves. Love in this way emphasizes what can I do for others and provides grace for people's shortcomings. I can only imagine how many relationships and marriages could be restored if the people involved learned to love in this way. These Scriptures teach us that love is to be exalted higher than any other spiritual gifts, including the gift of speaking in tongues, prophesying, or healing. Jesus operated in love, and we observe throughout His ministry how He is often moved to compassion before He performed His greatest miracles and healings. Matthew 9:36–38 says:

> When he saw the crowds, he had compassion on them, because they were harassed and helpless, like sheep without a shepherd. Then

saith he unto his disciples, "The harvest truly is plenteous, but the labourers are few; Pray ye therefore the Lord of the harvest, that he will send forth labourers into his harvest." (ESV)

Matthew 10 continues: "And when he had called unto his twelve disciples, he gave them power against unclean spirits, to cast them out, and to heal all manner of sickness and all manner of disease" (KJV).

Jesus's submission to the will of God by healing those afflicted and later dying on the cross for the sins of the world and bestowing us with the gift of the Holy Spirit was a demonstration of PERFECT LOVE! When we accept Jesus Christ as our Lord and Savior and believe that He died for our sins, we take on an identity in the spiritual realm that resembles Christ. We are blessed with the Holy Spirit, who teaches us daily and reminds us of our divinity through Jesus Christ.

In the name of Jesus, our identity is to operate in love, perform miracles, heal the sick, supernaturally know things, be light in darkness, and eradicate the effects of evil and sin for our Father's sake.

Who is the image of the invisible God, the firstborn of every creature: For by him were all things created, that are in heaven, and that are in earth, visible and invisible, whether they be thrones, or dominions, or principalities, or powers: all things were created by him, and for him. (Colossians 1:15–16, KJV)

This Scripture is so powerful since it not only reconciles our relationship with God but also serves notice to all that mankind received its initial identity back to Adam. I imagine this would be similar to losing an ID badge, which allowed you access to all doors, but then it was returned with all privileges (blessings) restored. God had great plans for man when He created us, and spiritual privileges are beyond our comprehension. Thank God for His love which etched out a redemptive plan that was carried out by big brother Jesus.

Now for those of you who have read up to this point but have never considered that your soul (mind, will, and emotions) is in need of salvation from a sinful nature, you have reached the best part of the book. Today, I offer the opportunity to get connected to your heavenly Father in the way He intended from the conception of the world. Paul says that first you must believe in your heart and then confess with your mouth that Jesus died for your sins on the cross and that God raised Him from the grave, then salvation is yours (Romans 10:9). Just repeat these words aloud:

Heavenly Father, in Jesus's name,
I repent of my sins and open my heart to let Jesus in.

Jesus, you are my Lord and Savior.
I believe you died for my sins and you were raised from the dead.

Fill me with your Holy Spirit.
Thank you, Father, for saving me.

In Jesus's name, Amen.

Glory to God! Welcome, my sister and/or brother, to your new adoptive family in Jesus Christ. Yes, it is that simple! Like I told you before, your words are powerful and carry a spiritual authority, so once you confess by saying it and believe it in your heart, it is as you say. You are now saved. Jesus Christ dying on the cross was a pretty big deal, and He paid a pretty hefty price for you to have the privilege to take part in this moment. Now, you may not feel any different physically, or may not be overwhelmed with emotions, but that is okay. Actually, it would be considered normal. Your confession is just the beginning of a life-long journey of continued development and becoming transformed into God's greatest you! We will discuss more about what your life as a Christian should look like in the next chapter, so get ready.

While we are on earth, we will never truly conceptualize the depth or height of how perfect God's love is for us. Without Him and His sweet spirit in us, we are not fully capable of sharing real love as we ought. Therefore, it is of extreme importance and value to get to know Him; learn of His unfailing love for us; and His benevolent benefits. The more we learn of Him, the more we are able to glean an understanding of our spiritual genealogy and purpose. Our identity is deeply engrained in love and humility to serve others as a reflection of our Father, God, who reigns forever and ever.

CHAPTER 9

CHRISTIAN IDENTITY

"Jesus Christ did not come into this world to make bad people good;
he came into this world to make dead people live."
—**Lee Strobel**

According to a 2010 survey by the Pew Research Center, 84 percent of the world population identifies with some type of religion. Religions are wildly varied with their beliefs, rules, and practices. A person's religion may be monotheistic (one God) or polytheistic (many gods). It may be ritualistic or without much structure, depending on the customs taught throughout oral or written traditions. There is only a small percentage of people (11 percent) who do not identify with any religion. Moreover, there are a minute 2.32 percent of people who call themselves atheists. I am uncertain if those 11 percent consider themselves spiritual or not, but these numbers definitely support the truth Paul spoke of, that most of God's creation acknowledges a power greater than themselves. Today, religions have grown tremendously, but across the globe, Christianity is one of the largest religions in the world. Approximately 70.6 percent of Americans identify as Christian. The Christian faith is monotheistic, and Jesus's followers believe in one God. Christianity differs from other religions in that belief in the life, death, and miraculous resurrection of Jesus Christ is the way to secure salvation from sin and eternal death. It is a radical belief for many; however, the historical account of Jesus Christ's life has been researched and proven for centuries by skeptics and believers alike.

America was founded on Christian principles, which is one of the chief reasons why this young country was established in North America in the first place. Many of the first American settlers fled Europe to rid themselves of the government's pressure to follow the Church of England and conform to religious statutes. Many practices pressed upon the people were not biblical principles and were practices stemming from tradition. This was problematic since many of the religious rules pressed upon the people were not founded in spiritual biblical text.

Those who left Europe separated themselves from their former country's religious practices and sought to freely worship God as they chose. Those seeking to worship God freely fled to America. The country flourished and stands today as one of the most influential places in the world. Today, Christianity remains deeply engrained in the foundation of our young country.

Many countries, like America, have strong ties to a religion based on regional and cultural customs. For instance, India has the largest population of Hindus in the world, accounting for approximately 93 percent of those practicing the faith. Some who follow the Hindu faith believe their works on earth are measured and suggest the reincarnated soul is eternal and revisits earth multiple times. A person's deeds in previous lives are reflective of the fortune or misfortune experienced in their current living situation. Therefore, if you experience hardships on earth, then it is probable that your previous life warranted such hardship now. Additionally, your reincarnated soul could be represented in any form of life, including insects and animals. Hinduism is the third-largest and oldest recorded religion and accounts for over 1.1 billion people worldwide. Islam is the second-largest religion with approximately 1.6 billion adherents practicing across the world. Currently, Islam is becoming one of the fastest-growing religions. Islam is practiced a great deal in Middle Eastern countries, such as Iraq, Iran, and Afghanistan. Like Christianity, Islam is monotheistic, and those practicing share the belief in one God as the one true divine deity. Actually, both religions believe in the same sovereign God but differ in the belief in Jesus Christ as divinity.

I believe the reason Christianity is the largest religion in the world is because the Gospel of Jesus Christ is good news. It's a religion of grace and requires less work of the believer. Grace allows the believer to engage freely despite their faults and failures to do everything the righteous way. God's grace cleans our slate by covering our sin with the ultimate sacrifice of Jesus's blood on the cross. The gospel gives us reassurance of God's love and grace for those who believe in Him. We find grace through a savior who did not deserve the punishment given to Him for the cost of sin but bore it all for those who earned it. Jesus took away the work of trying to be perfect when we struggled with sin for centuries without fail. Being dependent on our own works is exhausting, and the grace of God, through Jesus Christ, offers an atonement of sin—once and for all. There is nothing you have to continuously or ritualistically do to prove your worthiness of salvation except have faith that Jesus died for your sins.

One of the most prolific and, arguably, the most disputable philosophies of the New Testament is how one man (Jesus) could bear the weight of sin on His shoulders for everyone on the planet and then put an end to unrighteousness, sin, and death for all mankind once and for all. The only conditions are that we must have faith to believe it is ours and desire to have it. Additionally, that mankind's spiritual relationship with God could mirror the type of relationship Jesus had with God as a son is wonderful. Jesus Christ was our way back into good standing and sweet fellowship with God. Jesus Christ, our second Adam.

Throughout the Old Testament, God has revealed to His people (Israelites) a plan of redemption following the fall of man into sin in the garden of Eden. After the fall, mankind has struggled with a sinful nature and negative thinking, which presented a wedge in relation to a spiritual God. As I mentioned before, God's initial intention was to be in relationship with us, but the relationship was severely strained due to our sinful nature and God's obvious disdain for sin. Jesus Christ was the redemption plan to cure our spiritual issue. The only caveat is that we believe in our hearts and confess with our mouths that he, in fact, died for our sins. The difficult part of this request is to believe, to do away with reason (our carnal knowledge) and listen to a man who was crucified on a cross. It is the greatest love story of all time. A love that is incomprehensible and relentless. God's love pursued us when we did not deserve or desire to be loved in such a way. Jesus demonstrates to all mankind love perfected. Love is more appealing than fear!

The Jewish people perceived Jesus's proclamation of being the Son of God and coming to save the world as blasphemy. It was an especially hard pill to swallow for the descendants of Israel (Jews), who prided themselves on ritualistic worship and obeying God's law to the point of hurting and killing those who didn't. The Apostle Paul was one of those Jews and, prior to his transformation, persecuted and killed some of the early Christians (Galatians 1:13). The way in which the Jewish people worshipped and revered God was passed down for generations. It was their culture, and they would follow tradition to a fault at times.

The Israelites made great attempts to honor God's law and obey His statues, but they always fell short. Annually, the Israelites made burnt offerings and animal sacrifices (which represented their livelihood, provision, and food resources) unto God to purge themselves of sin, but each year, they would have to return (Hebrews 10:1–3). The Israelites were the chosen people of God with a long history of believing and trusting in Him for their provision. The Torah, which is used by practicing Jews today, contains the Old Testament and gives a great emphasis on the first five books of the Bible: Genesis, Exodus, Leviticus, Numbers, and Deuteronomy, which account for the coveted "Law." The Judaic Law governs believers of the Jewish faith and consists of a list of approximately 600 rules they are to follow.

Essentially, Jesus came to disrupt culture and worldly practices that, in the kingdom of God, had little significance. Jesus did not come to establish another religion; mankind created it by defining His followers as such. In turn, we have one of the youngest religions with an array of practices and beliefs. However, Jesus as the messiah and savior for mankind remains the premise of the New Testament.

Christianity is the largest religion in the world. Many sub-religions (denominations) derived since the first church, including the Catholic, Protestant, Eastern Orthodox, Holiness, Baptist, and Pentecostal churches. These different variations may hold slight differences in doctrines and practices of their faiths, but the premise of Jesus's life and death is similar. Let's be clear, Jesus Christ did not come to establish a new religion called Christianity or its subsets created thereafter. This is, yet again, a result of man's reasoning and distinguishing differences of opinion and options. Jesus's ministry has always been about grace, redemption, and worship. Jesus offers an opportunity back to intimately worshiping God and activating our spiritual rights as we once had in the garden of Eden. This is what Jesus was describing and teaching when referencing the kingdom of heaven. Jesus wanted us to know the kingdom of heaven was at hand (Matthew 4:17). The kingdom of heaven is fully operating and in full force if we seek to see it with our spiritual lenses and use it while living on earth.

Unfortunately, there are still many people who walk around with inactive relationships with God, viewing Him as unreachable and only accessible through a minister. As God continues to pour out His spirit and wisdom, more people are moving beyond that notion and embracing spiritual awakening over religion. These awakenings, also called revivals, have occurred sporadically and randomly since the death of Jesus Christ. Revivals are exciting and help believers focus on what's really important, God's presence!

Religion is bondage and relationship with God through the sacrifice of Jesus Christ is freedom. This is why you see an increase of nondenominational churches around the world. We are not separatists but all believers in the Word of God and the sacrifice Jesus Christ made on the cross. It is definitely a great thing for churches to rid themselves of the divisions since the Word of God tells us of the great benefits of the body of Christ being of one accord.

Church-planting organizations, like the Association of Related Churches, have created a model for teaching and equipping churches with tools to grow the body of Christ through structured systems, which ultimately focus on the work of Jesus Christ on the cross. Their largest push is to get the word of redemption and salvation to the lost, serve the communities where churches are placed, and attract more unbelievers to Christ. Our service, sacrifice, kindness, and love functions as an activator of God's power here on earth. Their mission seems very similar to the Apostle Paul when he sought to serve the early churches with guidance through letters outlining Christian conduct and values.

Let's be honest. The message of grace through Christ is good news and sometimes difficult to accept at face value. Paul witnessed to the first churches by providing examples and validating the work of Jesus at the cross as enough to redeem and position us to receive God's spirit indefinitely. It is through fellowship with the Creator of the universe that people find freedom from the snares of sin and find life purpose through the spiritual guidance of God's Holy Spirit. As believers, we house the Holy Spirit, and He resides inside of us. The physical temple was destroyed, and our bodies are now the temple of God when we seek God's kingdom and all His righteousness. It is quite beautiful, actually. Through Jesus Christ, we were bestowed the wonderful gift of the Holy Spirit to walk with us daily. Jesus assures us of this truth in John 14:15–17:

> If you love me, keep my commands. And I will ask the Father, and he will give you another advocate to help you and be with you forever—the Spirit of truth. The world cannot accept him, because it neither sees him nor knows him. But you know him, for he lives with you and will be in you. (NIV)

How blessed are we to say that we are followers of Christ? The Christian faith differs from many other religions in that our belief in having a constant connection to God through a relationship with His Holy Spirit within is essential. However, many Christians fall into ritualistic beliefs and behaviors just as the early church and other faiths did. Unfortunately, loving God from afar is what most people understand. Simply put, God may be sovereign and all-knowing but perceived as unreachable. This is the curse of sin that Jesus sacrificed His life for.

Religion confines us. It is based on rules, customs, ritualistic practices to a divine, supreme deity or deities with pleads and hope for acceptance. The differences are in the belief of knowing the relevance of God Almighty as the head in our lives and, most importantly, relationally connected to Him daily. This type of worship and relationship places us back in the garden. If you are guilty of confining your Christian faith to religious customs and a list of rules, I urge you to shed this tendency. Christianity is greater and more powerful than a set day of Bible study and worship. Begin to welcome the spiritual power that was placed within you daily into every waking moment. When you place God inside a church building, you deny a vital component of your Christian faith. It is time to access and utilize what I like to call a part of our "salvation package." I don't know about you, but I enjoy benefits and I don't like to leave them underutilized.

Yes, we have redemption from sin, but we also have the benefit of the Holy Spirit operating on the inside. I was one of those church members having my encounters with God when I went to church, not realizing there was more of Him to experience. Maybe you are or know the person who lives Sunday to Sunday. Sunday-to-Sunday worshipers spend time with God usually on Sunday mornings within the four walls of a church building.

I truly was only utilizing a small portion of the benefits God provides when we accept Jesus Christ as our personal Lord and Savior. I really did not have any idea that God was accessible all the time and that my blood-covered sin was not so great that He could not hear my prayers.

If you have been employed anywhere worthwhile, then you know about benefit packages. Benefits are offered by employers in addition to your pay and are meant to provide greater ease in your work-life balance. Employees have a choice to use these benefits or not. In the secular world, I understood the values in those additional benefits. Therefore, I elected to use them all. Why would I not elect for health and dental coverage and wait to pay full price at the hospital in the event of a medical emergency? Why would I work my full-time weekly shift and not go on a paid vacation when I've accrued time to take off? That would be silly, right? Our spiritual benefit package is no different. We can elect to use it or not, but it would be silly not to.

However, there I was, a young woman not using my spiritual package. As a young woman who had been going to church since the seventh grade, I didn't have a clue about the benefits offered as a Christian. Don't be like me. If you are old enough to understand grace, you are old enough to understand an intimate spiritual relationship with the Creator and tap into a part of your spiritual benefit package, a package designed to make your spiritual-natural balance easier while living on earth. We don't have to wait until we die and go to heaven to experience God's heavenly kingdom on earth (Matthew 6:10).

The younger you are when utilizing this salvation package, the better. It's better since true intimacy with God (Holy Spirit) will help shape decisions in your life that place you further away from the snare of the enemy. The enemy is always lurking, but with God's help through the Holy Spirit you will be able to spot His devices a mile away.

As the demands of everyday living make our schedules increasingly full, it's of extreme value to have an active relationship with God outside of church. Our lifestyles are so demanding that many people struggle with time management for family, spouses, and God. This includes finding time to attend a church service on a regular basis. Unfortunately, some place going to church on the back burner. There is a growing number of Americans who say that going to church every weekend seems like too much to ask. Approximately 51 percent of Americans say that they attend church at least once a month or more. The other 49 percent say they rarely go to church and believe that there are too many other competing factors, such as hectic work schedules and life circumstances, that prevent them from going. Unfortunately, not attending regular church services is more popular for young adults as they find other meaningful activities outside of religion to participate in on the weekends and throughout the week.

Let me offer you some helpful news, being in relationship with God does not call for you to attend church every weekend, twice a month, or only on Easter. Church service should be happening all the time, inside and around you. Jesus provides a way for us to be in continuous attendance and our bodies become the living temple of God. You are literally walking around as the church. 1 Corinthians 6:19–20 reads:

> What? know ye not that your body is the temple of the Holy Ghost which is in you, which ye have of God, and ye are not your own? For ye are bought with a price: therefore glorify God in your body, and in your spirit, which are God's. (KJV)

This is great news, since sometimes the pressure to get to church to see God is more religious than relational for many believers. I think it's fair to say that religiously attending church out of fear and obligation is not impressive to the heavenly Father. Actually, this way of worship limits you from experiencing God in your daily life, whether in work, child rearing, recreational activities, hospital rooms, or jail cells. Christian marriages, homes, and work environments should feel quite different and outsiders should sense it before they are ever told who is or who is not a believer.

God and His angels in heaven rejoice when we invite Jesus to hang out with us every day and in all situations. God has angels on assignment, and they harken to accomplish His will on earth when we speak His word and are in constant communication with Him. God is air, and air is everywhere. Therefore, He is not confined to the walls of a physical sanctuary or building. Why do we put Him there? The angels wait patiently in the spiritual realm on assignment to assist us in accomplishing God's will on earth (Psalms 103:20). Why would you wait to employ angels on Sundays and during a church service? Please don't get me wrong, attending church is a great thing and the power of God has moved in great and mighty ways in the sanctuary. The Word of God advises us that, when two or three people gather together of one accord to praise and worship Him, He is there with them and will give us anything we ask for (Matthew 18:19–20).

The more time you spend getting to know Jesus and His goodness, the more you will be drawn to places where the spirit of God dwells and is heavy in the midst. This more often is in the congregation of your sisters and brothers in Christ at church. Yes, you got it—you'll want to attend church out of reverence and relationship instead of obligation. Fellowship could also be done in a small group, marital union, Bible study, gathering around a laptop, or at a dinner function. You will grow into a place where you forgo some of the other things you perceive as important when you realize that He who is within you is greater than any external situation could offer. You will not want to forsake the assembly of the saints because the experience of God's presence is the most freeing and liberating experience your soul could have on this earth. Chains are broken in His presence; sicknesses are healed in His presence; addiction is overcome in His presence; and people are set free from mental bondage in His presence. Praise God for His spirit bequeathed to us through the death and life of His son Jesus.

Jesus Identity

To truly understand the Christian faith, we must first examine and understand the life of Jesus Christ. Without the life and death of Jesus Christ, there would not be a Christian. The first followers of Christ were dubbed with the term Christian years after His death since many were in hiding and met in smaller groups resembling His meetings with the disciples. Their meetings and groups were simple, discussing the miraculous life and death of Jesus. Additionally, they talked about His instructions to His followers before He died, which was to go and become fishers of men and make disciples of them. He also advises them that His believers will do similar and even greater works than He did once He returns to the Father (John 14:12). Jesus left a legacy behind when He left the earth. His followers, while He was alive, gave account to all they witnessed and experienced. He left those who knew Him in awe because of the many observations of miraculous healings of the sick, feeding the multitude, raising the dead, and casting out demons. As miraculous as His short life was, it was His death that made the greatest impact and changed the trajectory for men and women who believe forever. Jesus Christ came to fulfill a prophecy of a savior to come and redeem the world from sin. Following a miraculous conception to a virgin named Mary, Jesus experienced hardship and difficult times dating back as early as His birth.

Jesus was born during troubling times, and the ruler of Rome, Caesar, decreed a census for all of Rome. His stepfather, Joseph, who was of the bloodline of David, returned to Bethlehem to register the family. Joseph and Jesus's virgin mother, Mary, sought lodging for a suitable place for their son to be born but were found without. There were not any rooms left in the inn since so many people had travelled to Bethlehem for the census. Jesus was essentially born where farm animals are housed (Luke 2:1–20)—a stable—in conditions ill fit for a king and the redeemer of the world. Jesus, conceived by divinity, experienced His birth in a lowly manger in conditions resembling poverty. Flat out, Jesus was born poor and was able to share in understanding this hardship. His conception and birth are precursors to the supernatural miracles he'd accomplish but also the tribulations and difficulties He would endure. At the time of His birth, circumcision, and dedication, many people prophesied to His parents who Jesus was and what He would accomplish in His life.

The Messiah came to redeem all nations from sin; to be a light of revelation to the gentiles who served other gods; and glory to the people of Israel. The prophecy of the Messiah was fulfilled through Jesus Christ paying the price for our sins by dying on the cross as a living sacrifice. Jesus's sacrifice was an outward demonstration of perfected love. Love is sacrifice and that's why Jesus emphasized service in His ministry (Luke 22:27). Additionally, Jesus was born into a royal family. Mary was betrothed to Joseph, who was in the lineage of King David. This places Jesus in the lineage of royalty and believers are the beneficiaries. Everyone who sees and believes in His life as a sacrifice for our sins becomes a joint heir to Him and, therefore, is reestablished as a son or daughter of God. Galatians 3:26 reads: "We are all sons and daughters of God through faith in Christ Jesus for all of you who were baptized into Christ have clothed yourselves with Christ" (NIV). That is great news. There is neither Jew nor Greek, slave nor free, male nor female, for you are all one in Christ Jesus. If you belong to Christ, then you are Abraham's seed, and heirs of the throne according to the promise bestowed upon Abraham.

Today the story of Jesus Christ's life and death serenades like beautiful love song that captivates many, but it was not the case immediately after His death. In fact, many followers of Christ endured persecution and death for ministering in His name. Many Jews thought that the man crucified on the cross was blasphemous towards God and He and His followers were abominations. In fact, eleven of the twelve disciples suffered brutal deaths by crucifixion and execution following the death of Christ. The Roman Empire was enraged at the idea of people proclaiming that Jesus of Nazareth was indeed divine and had been resurrected from the dead. The government went through great lengths to rid the area of those preaching and spreading this information to others. Those who were devout Jews and placed the Judaic law in high reverence considered this message of Christ blasphemous. Among those was Saul of Tarsus, later called Paul the Apostle. The Greek word *Christianos* means "followers of Christ."

As believers in Christ, there are two major statutes that we were instructed to abide by in this life that supersede all other commandments. The first is to love the Lord our God with all our hearts and with all of our minds. The second is to love our neighbor as ourselves. Paul sums up the entire law in a single command in Galatians 5:14: "Love your neighbor as yourself" (NIV). As you read further in verses 16–21, he gives us instruction on how to accomplish this daunting task:

So I say, walk by the Spirit, and you will not gratify the desires of the flesh. For the flesh desires what is contrary to the Spirit, and the Spirit what is contrary to the flesh. They are in conflict with each other, so that you do not do whatever you want. But if you are led by the Spirit you are not under the law. The acts of the flesh are obvious: sexual immorality, impurity and debauchery; idolatry and witchcraft; hatred, discord, jealousy, fits of rage, selfish ambition, dissensions, factions and envy; drunkenness, orgies, and the like. I warn you, those who live like this will not inherit the kingdom of God. (NIV)

If you can take hold of this revelation, then you will be able to more effectively live as Christ did while He sojourned through this earth. We are incapable of loving our neighbor as ourselves, being slow to anger and quick to love and administer grace to those who demonstrate negative behaviors that hurt us in our own strength; however, we can do all things through Christ who strengthens us (Philippians 4:13). It takes God's strength to provide people with the grace that is required to operate in the fruits of the spirit daily. John 14:21–23 describes it this way: "He who has My commandments and keeps them, it is he who loves Me. And he who loves Me will be loved by My Father, and I will love him and manifest myself to him" (NKJV).

I believe Judas questioned Jesus by asking, "Lord, how is it that You will manifest Yourself to us, and not to the world" (John 14:22, NKJV). Jesus answered and said to him, "If anyone loves Me, he will keep My word; and My Father will love him and We will come to him and make Our home with him" (John 14:23, NKJV). Jesus is letting His followers know that being in a relationship with Him places you in direct relationship with God. Now, He will not only come to you, but He will come and make His home inside of you. Like I mentioned before, it is not until Jesus came onto the scene that we were able to reclaim what was stolen from us in the garden of Eden— daily communion with God as He did with Adam in the cool of the day (Genesis 3:8).

There are four fundamental precepts we should follow to stay in close communion with our heavenly Father. We learn these by observing the life of Jesus Christ. Jesus provides the following guidance for us to implement kingdom living to help us fulfill our God-given purpose in life:

- Jesus stole away quiet time for prayer and fellowship with God.
- Jesus found Himself in Scriptures before He began His ministry or life purpose.
- Jesus surrounded Himself with Godly counsel and people wiser than Himself to glean knowledge and advice.
- Jesus gave His life as a sacrifice doing good for others while He lived and then again in His death.

Just like Jesus Christ, we discover our spiritual gifts and life purposes by reading the Word of God and stealing away in prayer. Prayer and speaking in our heavenly language (speaking in tongues) is how we communicate with

God through the spiritual realm. As with other natural relationships, communication with God is a two-way street and requires us to listen as well. Effective prayer is more than us rambling a list of requests toward Him. Our prayers, desires, thoughts, and requests may go forth, but then we must learn to wait for God to answer us with instruction and guidance.

Listening requires quiet time away from distractions of the television, our phones, and even our loved ones. There is no set formula for stealing away to a peaceful place, but it is essential that we do. Some people designate certain times of the day, like in the early morning or prayer closets/places, to reduce the likelihood of distractions. Everybody's day is different, so you choose what works best for your current situation and make the sacred time a priority. Jesus spent much time talking and praying to God before He ministered to the multitudes, performed miracles, healed the sick, and ultimately fulfilled His life's purpose on the cross. God gives us instructions in our worship and prayer time with Him.

I have found it helpful to keep a journal nearby when I spend quiet time with God since I want to jot down what He tells me. God downloads instructions on our hearts and they serve as wisdom to guide us through life. "Thy word is a lamp unto my feet and a light unto my path" (Psalms 119:105, KJV). Getting quiet, praying, and reading the Word of God is essential for guidance as it was with Jesus. It's reassuring to know that God does not expect us to do anything that Jesus did not while He was here on earth. Jesus is our big brother and serves as the best example. Additionally, we have to personally read the Word of God and supplemental readings for greater understanding of what God is communicating to us through His divine Scripture. I cannot stress this point enough. Scriptures provide us with truth about matters in this life and wisdom from the ages. There is no greater history book than the Bible, so allow it to lead you and provide insight on human behaviors and ways to avoid future pitfalls.

Outside of spending time with God and reading his word, we have to be careful about who we allow into our personal space and with whom we choose to spend our time. Jesus spent time with the scribes, rabbis, and teachers who were more familiar with the Word of God before He branched off on His own. We can easily do this by finding a good church to attend and sitting under quality leadership or spending time with a mentor. I am grateful for the leaders that I have gleaned guidance from along the way, with a special thanks to Bishop George Davis of Impact Church.

We can also find and join a local small-town or city group to support what we learn in our ministry. Be prayerful about your decision to attend a church and expect God to answer you. It is important to evaluate who is feeding you spiritually and not to just go with the flow or where it is familiar and comfortable. I have heard and seen many people going to churches their parents introduced them to as kids for the sake of tradition and routine. This is not wise and may leave you spiritually immature throughout adulthood. We should always be growing spiritually. If you look around and see that your life choices, attitude, and behaviors resemble those of someone who is not attending church at all, then it may be time to assess why. Please, ask God where He wants you to be and be obedient if and when He tells you to move.

Other ways we are guided by Godly counsel is by reading books from authors who are experts on a particular topic in the Word of God. Authors like Gary Chapman, T. D. Jakes, George Davis, Joyce Meyer, Jimmy Evans, and Myles Munroe, just to name a few, have written great books over the years on topics spanning from finances, love, Holy Spirit, grace, depression, and leadership. I remember the impact of reading my bishop's book *Passing the Tests of Life*. It sparked a desire to want to know more about the Bible and what God had to say about life. Hence, I began reading the Bible more than ever before. I was astounded to find that God had a lot to say about several areas in my life, including my attitude, loving people, fears, and gratefulness. It is important to make sure the author references the Bible so that you are not led astray by someone's personal belief system, which may completely contradict God's holy word. All in all, make learning about God a must and be wise in your book choices. Remember, the author's words serve as counsel, so you want it to be wise, and there is nothing wiser than being fed Godly principles. We should always be interested in learning and growing, since God warns us that people are destroyed from lack of knowledge (Hosea 4:6).

There are two ways to learn. One way gives you a pigeon's view of where you are, only to learn at eye level as you step forward. Pigeons don't fly very high and, therefore, their vision is limited to the environment within their visual field. The second way gives you an eagle's vantage point to learn years beyond the span of your vision and physical perspective. Vantage point provides grace, wisdom, and an ability to avoid trouble before it happens. It allows for you to choose directions and pathways that get you to a destination faster and quicker than someone haphazardly walking into roadblocks. Choices we make are often influenced by what we see, so the eagle's point of view is the ultimate view. Choose the wisdom of others; choose a spiritual vantage point; choose a life that places you well ahead of your peers and into a life of blessings that your hands won't have room to hold!

Lastly, Jesus came to serve humanity by doing good, and those who believe in His life and resurrection are called to do the same. Mark 10:44–45 says, "And whosoever of you will be the chiefest, shall be servant of all. For even the Son of man came not to be ministered unto, but to minister, and to give his life for ransom for many" (KJV). As Christians, we are called to be more than fan club members. We are to participate in our leg of the race by taking the baton from those who ran before us. The book *Not a Fan* by Kyle Idleman really emphasizes this idea.

I'll offer this story to further illustrate my point: Once, I attended a live taping of a television game show. Before the taping began, the production team was strategic in placing certain people in particular areas of the studio who could potentially get more camera time. Those in certain sections surrounding the stage were verbally prepped about their role of being really enthusiastic and animated. Before the show's host stepped on the stage, a less famous person stepped on the stage with a microphone and, for twenty minutes, he told the audience that we were not mere spectators, but that production was relying on our responses to make the show lively. Our natural responses and clapping were to become exaggerated and thunderous. We were not in the comfort of our living rooms, and so the producers needed to direct our behavior. Sitting still without interjecting our feedback was not acceptable in this setting and rehearsal was required. Unfortunately, like in our living rooms, this non-participatory position is where many Christians settle into at church, relying on the worship team and/or minister to stir them. Today, I will put on my hype man shoes and encourage you that we need you actively participating on the team in order for the production of saving souls and for miracles to flow to others. This is exciting news!

There were two valuable lessons that I took from my experience of that live taping. First, the obvious was that there is a lot that goes on behind the scenes to make a simple televised game show exciting and worth watching. The second is that everybody has a part in production, not just those who are in front of the camera or on the front pew in the church. Those behind the scenes and backstage play a very important role in supporting the vision of the leader. We are equally and uniquely important to the body of Christ and winning souls. I Corinthians 12:12 says: "For as the body is one, and hath many members, and all the members of that one body, being many, are one body: so also is Christ" (KJV). Romans 12:6–8 says:

> Having then gifts differing according to the grace that is given to us, whether prophecy, let us prophesy according to the proportion of faith; Or ministry, let us wait on our ministering: or he that teacheth, on teaching; or he that exhorteth (encourage), on exhortation (encouraging): he that giveth, let him do it with simplicity; he that ruleth, with diligence: he that sheweth mercy with cheerfulness. (KJV)

This is not an all-inclusive list of the roles we may play in the body of Christ, so do not become discouraged if you do not identify with any of the offices stated above. This is Paul's way of illustrating the point (by way of the Holy Spirit) the diversity in divine purpose everyone possesses. In fact, I want to share another very similar Scripture with you in I Corinthians 12:15: "Now if the foot should say, 'Because I am not a hand, I do not belong to the body,' it would not for that reason stop being part of the body" (NIV).

Wouldn't the foot still belong to the body? Or suppose an eye says, "I'm not an eye, and so I'm not part of the body." Wouldn't the eye still belong to the body? If the body were only a nose, we couldn't see a thing. If the body were only an eye, we couldn't smell a thing. But God has put all parts of our body together in the way that He decides is best. Each body part, whether it's the heart or the ear, plays a significant role in the function of the body. Understanding your role or function in life is essential so that you may operate in your role more effectively. Some of us are fortunate to come into the realization of that purpose (identity) then strive to identify with a niche to become a vital component of society at some point in our lives. There are those who discover it in early adulthood, others who do so later in life, and some never do. The important thing is that you find your role.

Unfortunately, there are many others who have a more challenging time getting the fullness of understanding their true identity and purpose in society and struggle to find meaning throughout their entire lives. Many will die without witnessing the full manifestation of their gifts, settling into a life beneath their potential. I do not want that for you, and I am sure that's not what you want, either, which is hopefully the reason you are reading this book in the first place. Maybe your struggle to realize and walk in your potential is due to circumstances outside of your control, such as misguidance from parents, modern-day slavery, being an orphan, or physical or sexual abuse. Often these situations result in mistrust, poverty, and/or simply a lack of knowledge, which shrinks thinking and stunts the ability to dream beyond what is seen. Now, we surely cannot change our past and the hurtful things that may have happened to us in our youth, but we can change the way we think about it. Every day, we make a decision to be victims or victors to the circumstances we encountered.

Joyce Meyer is a prominent minister who frequently shares her experience of sexual abuse as a young child at the hands of her father. For many years before her ministry flourished, she harbored ill feelings towards her father and was victim to the negative emotions of guilt and shame this heinous act caused her. With God's help, she found the grace to forgive her father and eventually free herself into becoming the woman God called her to be. Dedicated to spreading the word and love of God, Joyce has written countless books, spoken all over the world through television evangelism and personal engagements, and has established many outreach initiatives that reach across the globe to serve the poor, abused, and hurting souls of countless people.

Forgiveness is one of the most freeing things we can do as humans. It allows us to shift our thoughts and our energy from negativity towards more positive ambitions. Joyce Meyer was able to do just that. No longer bound by the negative emotions and wounds her childhood experience left her, she has become one of the world's largest and most influential ministers of our time. Her life is a testament that, no matter the hurt, we are able to overcome challenging circumstances we are faced with. Through the grace and strength of God, we can turn our lives into a beautiful tapestry of experiences that transcend human reasoning and help others come to understand the power love has over sin!

The key to ruling over your personal domain (family, finances, and work) is to strengthen the element of yourself that is made in the likeness of God—your spirit. It takes a strong person to forgive, and God equips us with His strength to do that and so much more through His Holy Spirit. It is not always easy to do, especially when your spiritual man is weak, and the voice of God is faint in your life. You have to build, sculpt, and work out your spiritual man as you do your physical body. What I have come to learn about working out and, more specifically, body sculpting is that it takes discipline, dedication, routine, time and effort. Body sculpting to have a physique like singer Beyoncé or actor Channing Tatum takes commitment. If you are overweight and desire to lose weight, you will have to make some significant changes with your eating habits and activity to obtain a leaner physique, such as working out, weightlifting, eating smaller portions, and choosing healthier food options. You cannot expect to lose weight through little activity and overindulging in fatty or large portions of food.

Strengthening and sculpting your spiritual man after the likeness of God is no different. It takes discipline and dedication. We create habits, which help us build characteristics that resemble our heavenly Father. We do this by going to church, praying, reading the Bible, listening to worship music, and surrounding ourselves with people who share a similar interest in spending time with God. Most importantly, we are obedient to what He tells us. However, there is good news. God does not intend for us to build up our spiritual man with our own strength. In fact, God says in 2 Corinthians 12:9: "My grace is sufficient for thee: for my strength is made perfect in weakness" (KJV). Therefore, unlike our physical gym workouts in the flesh, where our results are dependent on how much weight we lift or how many miles we run, our spiritual man becomes stronger the more we rely on the power of God. Jesus refers to God as the "true vine," which is the ultimate source of life. He calls us to abide in Him, and He will abide in us, as a branch cannot and will not bear fruit alone. We obtain spiritual power to do what our flesh proposes to do through reading His word, praying in the spirit, and developing the fruits of the spirit.

The fruits of the spirit are contrary to the flesh and they are love, joy, peace, longsuffering (patience), kindness, goodness, faithfulness, meekness, and self-control (Galatians 5:22). This is actually one of my favorite Scriptures to reflect on and keep me focused on the character of a believer. I realize that I am not capable of demonstrating these fruits in my own mindfulness and will power. I understand that God is the source of life, and my connection to Him is how to cultivate the fruits of the spirit which helps each one of us be loving, generous, and caring when we, in ourselves (fleshly desires), would rather do something else. God has provided us with the gift of not having to rely on our own strength to obtain rest from anxiety or develop the fruits of the spirit.

As believers, our biggest work is to strive to not rely on our own thinking and ability. This is what Scripture means when it says we are to labor to rest and rest upon the power of God (Hebrews 4:9–11). Through the death and resurrection of Jesus Christ, He has given us the Holy Spirit to help and teach us all things (John 14:26). Your spirit is what was created in God's image, not your flesh. Your spirit desires to be considered more than your reliance on natural abilities and mental reasoning. God wants us to do spiritual checks before we make daily mundane decisions. Yes, the Holy Spirit wants you to consult with Him on driving directions, household purchases, what trips to go on, and when and when not to say something. Jesus says in John 14:26: "But the Advocate, the Holy Spirit, whom the Father will send in my name, will teach you all things and will remind of everything I have said to you" (NIV).

Under the new covenant, following the death of Jesus Christ, we are able to check with the Holy Spirit, which now resides within us. Isn't that awesome? This is one of the greatest underutilized gifts that the body of Christ has in its possession. I will admit that I thought operating in the Holy Spirit was spooky and a bit strange at first. Growing up, I would observe older women catch the "Holy Ghost" and dance out of control around the church. They would fall out on the floor, and some would speak in weird languages that I did not understand. It was all too weird, and I remember saying to myself, "I do not want the Holy Ghost!" If you know me, then you know I like being in control of what I am doing, so dancing and behaving uncontrollably just seemed absurd. Maybe you can attest to having this same belief. Or, even better, were shunned for it in the church where you worshipped. If I had the slightest clue as to the breadth and depth of the help provided by the Holy Spirit, I would have thought and spoken differently about my desire for the Advocate's help.

The Holy Spirit's help and guidance is foreshadowed several times in the Old Testament. If you recall the Scripture from Psalms, several hundred years before Jesus's birth, King David prophesied how God will visit with the son of man. David writes in Psalms 8:4: "What is man that you are mindful of him, and the son of man that you visit him?" David knew the gift we were able to obtain in our lifetime, and he approached God almost in a jealous manner. I can hear David now: "Why do they get to be with you all the time?" King David knew how blessed he was from occasional sporadic appearances from God Almighty. Christians are blessed to live during a period where God does more than visit us from time to time. His Spirit dwells inside of us. Ain't that good news?

In closing this chapter, I want to encourage Christians to realize that retraining our thinking to consider spiritual affairs over the flesh is a continuous task. We have to move out of the acute stage of the spiritual hospital so that we can begin spiritual rehab, like in an outpatient setting, where doing our individual home exercise program includes independently reading the Word of God and supplemental resources to strengthen our learning. It also includes attending church and small groups, which produce a healthy spiritual capacity to impact the world around us. I am reminded of Scripture in Romans 12:2 that is very near and dear to my heart: "Be not conformed to this world: but be ye transformed by the renewing of your mind, that ye may prove what is that good, and acceptable, and perfect, will of God" (KJV). If you or God aren't shaping your thoughts, then the world very well may be.

We will never be able to fully grow up as Christians if we do not seek God's help in transforming our thinking about our carnality. Carnal mindedness is operating in your flesh and assimilating to a worldly perspective for daily living. As believers, we are called to reflect the image of Christ in everything we do. We should talk like Him, pray like Him, desire like Him, seek God's will like Him, and, most importantly, LOVE like Him. We have a higher calling that exceeds the casual conversation with others as we lightheartedly identify ourselves as Christians. The lost and unsaved should see it before you say it. This is definitely not always easy and is a continuous process. Ministers and preachers cannot fulfill the great commission alone. We were all called to be the hands and feet of God. Jesus has commissioned us all with duty to spread the message of salvation and reconciliation to others.

Christians have to wake up, stop being self-seeking, and stand on their post so that Jesus's mission of saving souls is accomplished. We cannot afford to remain as infants in the spiritual kingdom, requiring pastors and clergy to spoon-feed us the Word of God. So many Christians remain on the milk and are considered infants in the kingdom of God (1 Corinthians 3:1–2). I love Paul for addressing the church of Corinth to provide reproof and correction to Christians content with living worldly and never growing up in the Spirit. Emotionally and physically hurting people are relying on you and me to get over the self and be the answer to their prayers. Many who identify as Christian are content with pastors and ministers operating in their spiritual gifts but conveniently excluding themselves, neglecting to assume responsibility for their part in winning souls.

Please visit AprilTeleeSykes.com to complete your very own personal spiritual assessment and begin the journey of leading a more purposeful and meaningful life as a Christian. Every single one of us has been called to be fishers of men and witnesses about our savior Jesus Christ. Therefore, Christians should be mindful of our interactions with others and how we may be perceived. Does our daily walk serve as witness for our Savior, who is able to provide our basic needs, or do we complain about our surmounting bills that are due? Does our attitude reflect the grace, love, and mercy shown to us, or do we snap back with anger and disgust when someone offends us? Do our souls radiate a joy, calm, and peace that passes all understanding, or are we full of fear and anxiety shaped by life's constant uncertainties? Truly, encounters with Christians should be a little different or peculiar from those in the world.

Personal Reflection

I meet a lot of people in my line of work and have encountered many folks in my spare time, and one thing is for certain: I have more often been able to identify those who spend time with God before they ever utter a word about their spiritual belief systems. It's in their smile, their service, their conversation, willingness to help, and radiating light that makes the room brighter by them just being there. It is not weird or spooky. It is just God manifesting Himself in His sons and daughters. With the help of the Holy Spirit, Christians' natural inclinations, behaviors, and emotional responses begin to differ from those in the world. Our lives should start to reflect the image of our Creator. One bit of Scripture that is extremely transformative regarding the application of the living word comes from James 1:21–25, which says:

> Wherefore lay apart all filthiness and superfluity of naughtiness, and receive with meekness the engrafted word, which is able to save your souls. But be ye doers of the word, and not hearers only, deceiving your own selves. For if any be a hearer of the word, and not a doer, he is like unto a man beholding his natural face in a glass: For he beholdeth himself and goeth his way and forgetteth what manner of man he was. But whoso looseth into the perfect law of liberty, and continueth therein, he being not a forgetful hearer, but a doer of the work, this man shall be blessed in his deed. (KJV)

God calls us to not only to be hearers of the word but doers. He is not interested in merely our attendance numbers at church. Going to church every Sunday is not indicative of your level of faith and it is surely not the barometer for acquired spiritual power Jesus promised His followers. It is not our attendance but our fruit, which positively impacts the kingdom of God and wins souls. It is our following of the Word of God that gives us liberty and freedom from our mental baggage. It is our desire to possess the power Jesus bestowed to us when He died on the cross, which empowers us to break chains, heal sickness, perform miracles, find rest from worry, and live a prosperous life here on earth.

I love the metaphor that God uses of the mirror as it relates to hearing and having an understanding of the word. It is not until we read the word and apply it to our lives that we see ourselves as we ought to. We see ourselves walking in victory and overcoming the world as Jesus did. If we come to church Sunday after Sunday to listen to the minister preach a good word, then walk out the church doors and continue viewing life through a worldly lens without application, we allow space for the enemy to invade our lives with deceit and destruction.

Moreover, we are like a person who turns away from a mirror and forgets their face. Our truest identity is not reflected in the earthly experiences we have collected throughout our lifetime, but through the Word of God. In the end, our mirrors should reflect less of ourselves and more of the image of Jesus. We are called to be the light of the world, and a city seen on a hill must be seen. God is glorified when we let our light shine (Matthew 5:14–16). We should make people wonder about our unrelenting favor, joy, and peace as Christians. The world should see something different in us and desire it for themselves. The world is looking for an answer, and God has placed it in you. If you are the only Jesus people will see, make Him shine bright!

CHAPTER 10

WORSHIP IDENTITY

"Let everything that has breath praise the Lord."
—Psalm 150:6

Humanity was created for worship and meant to imitate heaven on earth. Simply put, our life on earth should resemble the spiritual realm (angels) with our constant praise and adoration of our Creator. Revelation 4:8 says that the angels sing about His throne all night and day singing, "Holy, holy, holy."

There is a natural pull toward worship, because God put it there. He placed it inside each one of us in the beginning when He blew His breath of life into our nostrils. We were created to worship. The very first relationship that ever existed was the one between God and Adam. Before Eve, it was just God and Adam in Eden. Adam spent all his time in communion with God and tended to the purpose God spoke over him with caring for every living thing in the garden. Daily communion with the Creator was the most natural thing for Adam, and he walked in obedience tending to the world God allowed him stewardship over.

When Eve was created, she worshiped and reverenced God alongside her husband until she was deceived into disobedience. Her sin stemmed from a suggestion and thought that she could be like God with knowing good and evil (Genesis 3:5–6). Coincidently, Adam and Eve's disobedience to God's command catapults us into a sinful nature and subsequent separation from our relationship with Him. Sin (disobedience) caused us to view the world through a different set of lenses. We traded our spiritual lenses for a pair of natural lenses that are dimly focused to the spiritual world. We then shifted our attention from God onto our intrinsic and extrinsic values and desires outside of God and His will for us.

Essentially, when our vision changed, so did our thoughts and desires about what is and is not good. We desired what we saw, heard, and felt over what God needed from us—our worship—through our obedience. Instead, we began to exalt ourselves as gods with our reasoning and explanations, ultimately looking inwardly and also outwardly for ways to satisfy our need for worship. Our inward looking resulted in self-righteousness and pride, while our outward looking resulted in idolatry and lust by worshiping things, places, and people found in the universe. Both extrinsic and intrinsic views resulted in a disconnection from our heavenly Father.

One may ponder, if God placed worship inside of us, how could man so easily fall into worship outside of Him? This mistake is easy to make, considering what we are made of. God was clear about the value of His creation at its conception with this statement in Geneses: "It was good." He was impressed with the stars, sun, animals, trees, oceans, rivers, insects, and, of course, mankind. You and I were not excluded from that proclamation. Everything God created was good and made from an abundance of love that we will never quite understand while in our physical bodies. He created man to engage with Him, enjoy His creation, and glorify Him for making this wonderful world for us. Humanity is attracted to God's creation because of its beauty. I believe this is why mankind so easily sits and stands in admiration to musical artists and athletes in awe of their creativity and prowess in their music and sport. We are made from beauty and there is beauty in all that was created in the universe. We seek opportunities to be near His waterfalls, mountains, rain forest, beaches, and sand dunes on vacations because nature reflects His beauty.

As I mentioned before, sin caused a separation between God and mankind, making it difficult for man to understand the fullness of his/her spiritual Creator and to place proper honor where it belonged. Paul says it this way in Romans 1:19–20: "Because that which may be known of God is manifest in them; for God hath shewed it unto them. For the invisible things of him from the creation of the world are clearly seen, being understood by the things that are made, even his eternal power and Godhead: so that they are not without excuse" (KJV).

It clearly states, that all of creation on a subconscious level is aware of the power and spirit of the almighty God. Throughout history, man's pursuit for a greater understanding of His existence and the meaning of life has led each seeker down a multitude of paths toward spirituality and worship. God created His people to worship Him and give Him glory at all times (Isaiah 43:7). Our God is to be glorified because He created it all. He holds every star, every galaxy, every planet, the sun, the moon, the heavens, most importantly you and me in His hands. The word glory means to have high renown, won notable achievement, magnificence, great beauty, and great praise. His presence, magnificence, beauty, and notable achievement is seen throughout His creation.

Many of us search out this metaphysical understanding of ourselves and look for signs of something greater or bigger than ourselves. This is the reason there are so many different religions. Since the beginning of time, the need to worship has led mankind toward several spiritual pursuits of deities (mini gods). Throughout history, we have observed people worshipping everything from the moon, stars, trees, water, earth, gold, precious stones, wealth, animals, people, and so forth to better understand their human existence and to assert meaningful purpose in their lives. No doubt, God's creation is marvelous and a splendor to behold. However, the glory was never intended for creation, but for the Creator of it. All of the glory belongs to Him, forever and forever! God is seeking for His creation to give Him glory for all He created. I believe this is one of the very reasons why God distinguished the Israelites as His chosen people in the Old Testament of the Bible.

The Israelites were committed to worshiping the God of their forefathers, Jehovah. When other nations were worshiping other things and gods in the world, they were generally faithful. I say "generally" because there were times when they fell short of their fidelity to Him. As I stated earlier, most traditions, such as religion, originate from the cultures and families we are born into. Being born Jewish connects one to a faith in Jehovah God instead of other deities and gods. In the Old Testament, one reads and sees how the Israelites were known to be God's chosen people since the traditions within their families' belief systems were a devoted trust in the God of their forefathers, Jehovah and Yahweh. This was inherited. Their forefathers passed down their belief systems through countless stories of Jehovah, providing and showing Himself through the miraculous. Over time, Jehovah acquired subtitles for His name by the Israelites, such as Jehovah Nissi, God, who is our banner and fights for us; Jehovah Rapha, God, who heals us; Jehovah Shalom, God of our peace; and El Shaddai, God Almighty. These titles and names for God were established at different times when God revealed a new facet of Himself to His believers through deliverance and provision.

Generations had lived and died throughout the years, but God would continually show Himself to each generation in these different ways. In the story of Moses, God provided this final settlement of what the Israelites should call Him: "I AM!" God should be called "our everything." God is everything all wrapped into one. His creation set out to place Him in supreme position to be honored, glorified, and praised by those He created (Revelation 4:11). Unfortunately, that has not always been the case, and throughout history, man has struggled in doing so. In the ancient times, those outside of the Israel or Jewish culture, such as the Canaanites and Phoenicians, worshiped many gods and/or deities. So much so that God used His servant Moses to provide this precept to His people, "I am the Lord your God, who brought you out of Egypt, out of the land of slavery. You shall have no other gods before me" (Exodus 20:2–3, NIV).

This warning came about when people worshipped gods of silver, gold, wood, and other things found in creation as they sought provision. Other gods were named, such as Mot, the god of death; Baal, the god of rain; and Anat, a goddess of war, just to name a few. Today, cultures, like those in West Africa, worship their dead ancestors, offering sacrifices in return for spiritual guidance and supernatural provision. In biblical times, the god Baal-Hadad was reverenced for rain and storms. People would burn offerings of livestock, crops, and, at times, their very own children for supernatural outcomes. In times of drought or when crops were scarce, the people sought the divine lordship of Baal to bail them out, so to speak. If you were to examine the cultures of those times, you would understand why worshiping Baal was so popular among other nations.

Unlike our experience here in Western civilization, the prosperity and provision of the people derived from the production of crops, herding animals, and human offspring. Agriculture still exists but is muted in the backdrop of the modern American food industry, which is the mass production of food funneling from livestock produced on concentrated animal feeding operations and produce from factory farms to massive grocery store chains, stoves, microwaves, and fast-food restaurants. There was no such thing as driving up to McDonald's or eating at your local pizzeria for nourishment when you were hungry. Everything you ate or could sell was dependent on what you could produce from the land. I realize this is much different from what many of us are accustomed to, especially if you were born in the twenty-first century. If there were a drought, it would have a major impact on food resources, finances, and the overall livelihood of the nation.

Sometimes, people looked to the mini gods in hopes of greater returns of food. Baal was the deity representative of rain, which was directly linked to their ability to produce crops or food. Graven carved images were created to represent the mini god, and sacrifices were made at altars to demonstrate devotion and allegiance with a desire for supernatural results to occur within their agriculture. Sacrifices of burnt offerings of their vegetation, livestock, and even human life would be made as a display of surrender and complete reliance on the god providing.

Although the Israelites were God's chosen people, there were many times when they worshipped gods like Baal, as well, being heavily influenced by other cultures. It was during those times when God would raise up a prophet to distinguish the difference between Himself and those lesser gods. He did it with Moses when Pharaoh's magicians threw down their staffs and they became snakes as proof of divine power, Moses threw down his staff and it became a python and ate them. In the story of the prophet Elijah, there was a drought and famine throughout the land. God used Elijah to show the people that He was greater than Baal and that He could provide the rain that they were in desperate need of. Elijah was so confident in his God (Jehovah) that, with a renowned shortage of rain or water in their region, he boldly threw it down on the ground (a wasteful act). He then prayed God strike fire upon the ground, which was saturated with water.

It is one thing for fire to emerge from land that is dry, but it is another thing for fire to be created from something wet. The two elements do not mix but rather eliminate each other. This story is so beautiful because, before one drop of rain hit the ground, He allowed Elijah to hear it first. He then bragged to the people that it was coming. To those who know little about spiritual affairs, they would think he was crazy to speak claim of something not visible and praise God about something that had not occurred yet. Nevertheless, it was in Elijah's praise that the rain manifested, and the land was prosperous again. Those who worshipped and called on Baal to deliver were disappointed that their god did not deliver and, subsequently, were forced to acknowledge Elijah's God instead (I Kings 18:36–39). God does this over and over in biblical history and continues to demonstrate His supreme divinity even today. He cannot be contended with.

Many people may choose spiritual deities and worship outside of God, but He reigns supreme forever and ever. God's word will not return null and void, so once He says it, you can bank on it! What did He say? There are approximately 3,000 promises listed in the Holy Bible for His believers. The word says that He promises to never leave or forsake you when you believe. He promises that He has never seen His seed begging for bread. Promise after promise, He provided and delivered to those who believed in Him. He promises to be our peace and our healer. When difficult times occur, take

God's word to the bank! You praise Him for His history of divine intervention. You praise Him for His word and promises. You praise Him for being the almighty El Shaddai. During the time of Elijah, there was the nation of Israel and the gentiles. Everyone else, whose culture or family lineage may have believed in other gods (polytheism) was considered Gentile.

The Israelites were discouraged against marrying or acquainting with persons outside of the Jewish faith because of this very reason. By marrying outside of the Jewish faith, you placed yourself and family at risk for worshiping mini gods. Jewish people referred to the gentiles as "dogs" or "wild cur." You may be asking, but why call them a dog? Quite frankly, calling someone a dog seems pretty harsh. This was especially true and not expected to come from the mouth of Jesus. However, there He was, comparing a Canaanite woman to dogs (Matthew 15:21–28). Let's consider the characteristics of a dog. Dogs are loyal, sometimes to a fault, and worship whatever master is feeding them at the time. Dogs lick the face and lay at the feet of their masters. They follow behind anyone they perceive will provide a meal or other life necessities. Gentiles, such as the Canaanites, Moabites, and Hittites, worshiped and sacrificed burnt offerings and some of their most prized possessions to mini gods in exchange for provision, children, rain, and other life necessities, posturing themselves at the feet of these secular deities seeking hope and restoration. Their worship of other gods is why they were sometimes called "dogs."

When the Canaanite woman approached Jesus to heal her daughter, Jesus had a fame that preceded Him at this point in His ministry. He was known for healing, casting out unclean spirits, and doing well amongst the people. She was relentless in her efforts to get His attention. He used her belief and faith as a teachable moment and an opportunity to further explain His ministry by saying, "It is not right to take the children's bread and toss it to the dogs" (Matthew 15:26, NIV). Up to this point, His miraculous acts were utilized to bless those within the Jewish culture who were called the children of God. Those outside of the Jewish culture did not believe in or have faith in Yahweh, a monotheistic God. Therefore, it was not considered proper to use time and resources for persons who were not God's children.

The gentile woman's faith and belief that Jesus could heal her daughter from the unclean spirits demonstrated the posture of her heart and her understanding that Jesus was the Messiah. She had taken a stance in her heart that she wanted to experience something different, something real, and more tangible than what she experienced in her culture. The posture of heart could be observed by her pleas and cries to Jesus indicative that her source of help would not come from the mini gods she and her ancestors served, but from the one sent by the one true God.

Jesus granted the lady her wish and healed her daughter from the demon possession. At this pivotal turn of events, Jesus showed his disciples and followers that access to God and His blessings will now be open and available to all of those who believe and not just the Israelites (a chosen people). He was sent for mankind's redemption and reconciliation back to God in the garden of Eden. Jesus is how God's promise to Abraham of making his descendants as numerous as the stars comes to fruition (Genesis 22:17). It is through the belief in Jesus Christ as the Messiah, that all have access to the provisions and many blessings of Yahweh.

Believing is as simple as a choice of your heart and confession with your mouth! I believe this is why Scripture says that, if we only have faith the size of a mustard seed, we would be able to move mountains. "Faith is the substance of things hoped for and the evidence of things not seen" (Hebrews 11:1, KJV). Faith is a thought and a belief that can radically alter our life decisions and circumstances. Generally, when we believe something and talk enough about it, we will move in the direction of those thoughts and words. Henceforth, no matter what family you were born into or culture you were raised in, you are now granted the opportunity to choose to believe or not to believe in Jesus Christ. The tough part is examining your heart (mind), what is influencing your spiritual beliefs, and what you have established as a god or the most important thing in your life. Are you willing to dethrone the gods or religions presented to you as a youth? Are you willing to say that Jehovah God, not money or your parents' money, is where you look to for provision?

Take a moment, right now, to examine what things you have placed in the worship seat in your life. What is it that owns all of your attention and adoration? Is it money, designer clothes, career, the trendiest devices, the opinion of others, or family (spouse/children)? Does the attention and adoration you give to these things relieve or cause more stress and anxiety in your life? How do these things compare to your belief and fellowship with God? Is more of your time spent pursuing these things? Does your pursuit of material and financial gain leave you feeling stressed and tired? In contrast, how do you feel during and after a spiritual encounter with God? Is it accompanied with more peace and less stress? God did not intend for us to have anxiety, stress, and worry. In fact, He instructs us to cast our cares on Him because He cares for us (1 Peter 5:7). It's interesting that God places rest as a priority for Himself after creation by resting on the seventh day (Genesis 2:2). Why would the Creator of the universe place such emphasis on resting and putting down the plow for an entire day? The plow is just a synonym for the work we engage in daily. God, in His infinite wisdom, modeled rest to His creation so that we would turn from our daily toiling and tend to the matters of creation. He desired that we take the time of rest to reflect on the gift of life and worship the Creator of it all. Scripture actually encourages us to rest from our works and worry and place our cares onto our Creator. Obedience to God's word is directly related to our rest (Hebrews 4:1–11).

Obedience requires total surrender to God's leading and allowing His guidance to make provision and fill the gaps of our lack. Many people, especially in more developed countries like the United States, have a difficult time carving out time for rest because we are so busy being in control over our destinies and life outcomes. In doing so, we place so much undue stress on ourselves that we never enter into God's available rest (Hebrews 4:5). Never resting, barely sleeping, relying on external aids to allow for temporary relief from our worries of the world. Once you established in your heart and mind that you truly want God to be your source, you are ready to experience the supernatural in your life. Age does not matter in the kingdom of God. God has done great and miraculous things through youth before and He can do it again.

He did it with David and the giant Goliath; Caleb in spying out the land; Daniel in the lion's den; Joseph with his interpretation of dreams; and Jesus with His miracles, healings, and ultimate sacrifice of His life to save souls. Jesus was only twelve years old when He found Himself in the Scriptures. Jesus was reading and studying with the teachers and scribes in the synagogues when He discovered His purpose at a very early age. Who told you that you are too young? Who told you that you were too old? Let's not forget Abraham and Sarah. Where did that thought come from? It is time to free yourself from ageism, personal, economic, and cultural limitations. When you have examined your heart and have faith in Jesus Christ, you may receive salvation from sins.

Sin separates us from worshiping God with all our heart and keeps us from experiencing a relationship with our Creator. Through Jesus's death and resurrection, we all may choose to be saved or not saved from sin's fear, shame, and sting of eternal death. It does not matter if we were raised in Japan, India, Brazil, the United States, or the Philippines. Salvation availability to all is the message of reconciliation and is "the good news!" Religion was never God's intent, but relationship. Relationship is the primary purpose of reconciliation. God provides us with a book of divinely inspired literature called the Holy Bible so that we may have a greater understanding of Him and our purpose through Him. Of the world population, roughly 54 percent consider the Holy Bible a sacred text. Today, the Holy Bible has many translations, including the Greek and Hebrew, which contain both the Old and New Testaments. The New Testament is one of the oldest manuscripts, with over 5,000 copies demonstrating its validity and reliability across centuries and nations. God's intentions for the Bible was not to provide us with a bound book of rules and regulations out of fear. Obligation to serve God out of fear and rigorous works of good steers us toward religion, not relationship. One of the best things about relationship is our experience of intimacy. A good relationship is defined by the ability to communicate, share, adore, grow, and trust. Our relationship with our heavenly Father is no different. In fact, Christians should aim to have such a relationship with God in this way.

Communication

Let's first discuss communication. Communication is the foundation of any sound and healthy relationship. We depend on communication to express our desires, dreams, plans, fears, and failures to friends and loved ones. Effective communication requires an open and genuine exchange of ideals and feelings for growth to occur. One of the most understated dialogues and communication styles occurs between man and God. Communicating with God is vital to our success in this life and it definitely facilitates growth in any relationship. We communicate with God through prayer, supplication, journaling, and when we speak in our spiritual tongue. Most Christians understand prayer as the way believers talk to God. We, in all of our good senses, lay out a list of all the things we need from God and want His help to accomplish. This lopsided, one-way communication suits many just fine as they present their wish lists to God with hopes of Him delivering on those wishes eventually one day. Many of those people are like I once was, when the thought of God actually speaking back was unfathomable. One day, while listening to my pastor give testimony about a promise God made to him and delivered on, I asked, "How does he know God told him that? Why does God talk to him and not me?" These two questions were pivotal in my steps toward clarity and finally experiencing for myself how God communicates to His people.

God speaks to us through the Holy Spirit, our advocate, and through the living Word of God found in the Bible. The more we lean in to hear Him, the clearer God's voice becomes. God desires that we communicate with Him and not talk at Him. He wants to share things with us, things about our future, character, purpose, directions, and instructions for dealing with life. He speaks through His spirit-inspired word, the Holy Bible, through confirmations spoken through other people, and through a soft, still voice inside of us. This still voice may be interpreted as your subconscious but it's there. God grants His children with a calm and unexplainable knowing beyond our natural comprehension. It is discernment for the best way to handle a situation or to understand information beyond our knowledge. With this information, His beloved children are able to have a rest and peace that surpasses all understanding.

God does not tell us anything that will contradict what is written in his spiritually inspired word. Listening and communing with God daily is pleasing to Him. We worship God when we seek His advice and input with managing our daily lives. Placing His leadership and Lordship over our plans is one of the greatest ways we honor Him. He relishes in our obedience and our desire to accomplish His will for our lives. His will for our lives is better than what we think we want and need. It diminishes the fear and anxiety that plagues our thoughts and causes sleepless nights. Whether we know it or not, we need God's will manifested in our lives. His plans and will for our lives include prosperity, blessings, divine counsel, and confidence in His expected end. A life in eternity places us beyond the boundaries of our physical shells and into the kingdom of heaven. We can only do this when we put down the megaphone with a laundry list of requests and actively listen to what God wants to communicate to us.

Trust

Every relationship will crumble and die without the foundational component of trust. If communication is the foundation, then trust is a pillar, which holds it up. Trust in a relationship is non-negotiable and its absence significantly impacts and shapes the perspectives of those involved. Every human requires trust to feel safe and to thrive in a relationship. Our dreams, desires, secrets, and fears are safely shared in the individual we trust. We welcome our loved one's input on the intimate details of our lives. This could be mother, father, sister, spouse, or coworker. We have faith that their guidance and insight will sharpen and develop us into the people we hope to be. We rest well at night knowing we are secure with them at our side. At times, when they are absent, we find comfort in knowing they will return and remain faithful while away.

This is true no matter the type of relationship. Many close friends of mine live in entirely different states. However, I can count on them no matter the circumstance and through some of the most difficult times. My friends and I may not talk or see each other every day, but I find them to be trustworthy when it matters. This relationship is not one-sided, either, since I am confident that my friends' trust is a covenant. Trust is a solemn promise; trust is integrity; and trust is built on truth, not lies. When we fail to trust our loved ones or prove to be untrustworthy, we open the door for the enemy to come in and insert ideas that result in fear, anxiety, and anger. These types of emotions are dangerous, since they are often accompanied by a negative action.

Adam and Eve's sin in the garden was due to lack of trust. They allowed doubt to creep in and they mistrusted God's intent and motives for parameters. Unfortunately, their mistrust led them down a path of disobedience and spiritual death. We have a valuable lesson in examining the initial sin in the garden. Mistrust results in fear, shame, emotional pain, and hiding. Mistrust means no faith and leads to infidelity—trusting other gods and deities. God desires our fidelity and for us to trust in Him solely. We have been redeemed back into a healthy relationship with God through Jesus Christ. Jesus's blood covers us, and God turns the blind eye as if our mistrust in Him never happened. Today, we can choose to rely on our heavenly Father for our provision. We can choose to trust His instructions and prompting in managing our daily lives. We can choose to walk by faith and not by sight. Our faith is pleasing to Him and allows Him room to pleasantly surprise us with His miraculous ways of coming through. Choose to trust God above everything!

Growth

There's a highly recognized Scripture which states, "Iron sharpens iron." The Scripture simply denotes the interdependence on two like-minded individuals' reliance on each other to facilitate growth in each other's lives. The sharpening of iron is needed in order to obtain optimal outcomes in romantic and family relationships, finances, job opportunities, and health. We rely on God and His word to sharpen us to the point of supreme effectiveness in every area of our lives. We should rely on His infinite wisdom and guidance to lead us toward promotion in the eyes of man. God should be in the center of every situation and circumstance we encounter because, with Him, we are better. Connection to our Creator facilitates our personal growth because we have the greatest understanding of our supernatural access. We then rely on His omnipotence to step in and fill in the gaps on our behalf when we fall short or display inadequacies in certain areas.

God encourages us to know that when we are weak, He is strong. God's help should take the pressure and weight off our shoulders for a need to do it all. Our relationship with God serves as our "trump" card in any given situation. Our association with Him places us at an advantage and our opposition to the devil at a disadvantage. God's role is for us to look, feel, and act better because we know Him. We gain full access to all the supernatural privileges because we have an "in" with the greatest superstar of all times. God provides us an example and model through Jesus Christ for us to get this done. Jesus relied on the heavenly Father and stayed in communion with Him daily to accomplish the miraculous. Our role is to stay connected to the father and enjoy the privileges of being a part of the entourage. Being connected to the best entourage takes our Wimpy Kid moments and supernaturally morphs them into Incredible Hulk moments with an abnormal growth spurt.

Praise and Adoration

We all know how a genuine compliment could place us on cloud nine for a good two days, or even a week. Praise and compliments are ego boosters. You would be hard-pressed to find someone who has not been flattered even a little bit upon receiving one. Our father in heaven created us in His image and He loves when His creation presents their praise and worship to Him. Our praise and worship serve as a compliment to the Creator of the universe and He smiles over us when we give Him attention. There's Scripture that says, God sings over us when we exalt His name (Zephaniah 3:17). Our praise demonstrates our faith and understanding of His supremacy over our simple earthly matters. Our praise reflects our knowledge of His ability to perform what we cannot. We see, throughout Scripture, how praise and adoration is one of the greatest ways in which mankind has experienced an undeniable encounter with the Creator.

One story in particular that highlights the significance of praise is found in the book of Acts. Paul and Silas were thrown in jail for casting out an unclean spirit from a female fortune-teller slave. This was upsetting to her masters since they made income from her predictions. While in jail, Paul and Silas were not found whining and complaining about the injustice they endured but instead were heard by the other prisoners praying and singing hymns to the most high God. Their praise changed the atmosphere and produced a violent earthquake. The prison doors were opened, and the shackles fell from all prisoners (Acts 16:16–26). Paul and Silas's praise freed them from the prison walls and their physical shackles, but it also softened the hearts of those witnessing the miracle, including the jailer (Acts 16:27–34). Following this miraculous event, the jailer and his entire household became believers in God through Paul's witness of Jesus Christ.

This is important to note because people are watching to see how we will react to difficult circumstances and situations. Our positive outlook and approach could lead someone to Christ. Praise invites all of heaven into the earthly realm and the miraculous occurs and those who are bound (mentally and physically) are set free. God's presence is accompanied with angels who, in concert, praise Him alongside us. God's angels hearken to His voice to perform what He commands of them. They, in turn, lend themselves as our defensive line to accomplish impossible feats.

I love sports, especially football and basketball. One of the greatest components of solid basketball and football teams in winning over their opponents is a great defense. Defense prevents the opposing team from scoring and allows for the offense to make big plays. As I said before, we are in a spiritual war over darkness. Many fight a losing battle without any understanding of their spiritual attack.

Understand, we have a choice to fight this spiritual war alone, or to allow God to extend His mighty hand and heavenly defensive team to assist us in our daily wins. God shows up in some of the most miraculous ways when His people gather on one accord and have the same mind to worship Him. I have witnessed the power of God move mightily in my worship experience, which extends past going to an actual church building or sanctuary. The sanctuary is within you, and the resurrection of Christ has allowed for us to be the temple of God (I Corinthians 3:16).

God promised us His Holy Spirit and He delivered to His believers on the day of Pentecost. Therefore, we can praise God everywhere we are. We can praise Him in our house, in our car, on our jobs, in a public bathroom, or at the gym. I'll let you in on a little secret. We free ourselves from the mental bondage of anxiety and depression when we focus on praising God though good and bad times. Paul tells us in Philippians 4:6–7 that we are to "Be careful for nothing; but every thing by prayer and supplication with thanksgiving let our requests be known to God. And the peace of God, which passeth all understanding, shall keep your hearts and minds through Christ Jesus" (KJV).

Praise takes the focus off our inadequacies but onto the strength and power of our Lord and Savior. God is able to deliver us from any earthly situation, including poverty, relationship problems, financial troubles, estranged family, and sickness. The Book of Psalms comes from the Hebrew word *tehillim*, which translates to "praise." Psalms is filled with songs of thanksgiving, hymns, prayers, and cries from psalmists like Solomon, Asaph (chief musician of David), and King David, who was a great warrior of God. These men, like you and I, experienced turbulence during their lifetimes but, through all their trials and tribulations, they were able to see the hand of God intervene on their behalf numerous times. In difficult times, they would cry out to God; in times requiring patience, they would sing hymns of His unmerited goodness; and in times of victory, they sang songs of thanksgiving. The psalmist gives us assurance that, even when we are not feeling or doing our best, God continues to be worthy of praise and is able to see us through. Psalms 150:1–6 encourages us with these words:

> Praise God in the sanctuary; praise him in his mighty heavens. Praise him for his acts of power: praise him for his surpassing greatness. Praise him with the sounding of the trumpet, praise him with the harp and lyre, praise him with timbrel and dancing, praise him with the strings and pipe, praise him with the clash of cymbals, praise him with the resounding cymbals. Let everything that has breath praise the Lord. (NIV)

Worship and praise come fairly easily to me since I serve in the music ministry at my church. Actually, I have served in similar capacities since I was a kid, so I naturally enjoy it. Maybe some of you find it difficult to vocalize and demonstrate your gratitude because of lack of confidence in your singing ability. It's not about your ability to sing all the notes correctly.

It's about the positive words and adoration that you are singing about your God. Like everything else in life, it becomes easier with practice and repetition. Stop rehearsing the negative thoughts aloud and start singing about His goodness. Tell God about your love for Him and your gratefulness for His ultimate sacrifice of His son, Jesus Christ.

Interestingly enough, praise is one of our greatest weapons! Praise confuses the enemy and causes them to turn on each other. He did it with Joshua when the walls came tumbling down, following seven rounds of marching and ending with a great shout of praise. Praise says that I see beyond my natural circumstances and I know victory is on the other side of my tribulation. Praise says that you understand that spiritual principles trump worldly situations. Praise releases what is bound in heaven onto earth. Praise shifts our thinking from our earthly problems and places value to the Creator of the universe who is able to intervene. Praise opposes our negative words and allows us to demonstrate gratefulness to our Creator. Praise puts our thoughts on the things that are above and on the one who is able to positively influence the situations we face. Praise is the most effective way to defeat the enemy. Praise says I trust God and believe Him over everything and anything else.

We are in spiritual warfare with dark forces that want us to doubt God's ability. God has equipped us with weapons of mass destruction in the spiritual realm. It is in our praise! It's time to unleash your greatest weapon and go into battle. Speak well of His name. Speak His truth over the world's truth. Start singing songs that edify Him. Begin dancing and playing songs that glorify His name. Choose psalms and songs that speak of His goodness and tender mercy. Recite lyrics that tell stories of His unfailing and unrelenting love for us and the sacrifice of His son Jesus who died on the cross for us. Praise Him because He deserves it!

CHAPTER 11

WARRIOR IDENTITY

*"Let today be the day you give up who you've been
for who you can become."*
—Hal Elrod

It does not matter who you are; big, little, or small, if you intend to have any real success in this life, you must fight and persevere for it. The spiritual battlefield is not for the faint of heart and requires a warrior's mentality and spirit. Isaiah 40:31 says, "But they that wait on the Lord shall renew their strength; they shall mount up with wings like eagles; they shall run, and not be weary; and they shall walk, and not faint" (KJV). Psalms 27:14 says, "Wait on the Lord: be of good courage, and he shall strengthen thine heart" (KJV).

No doubt, managing life circumstances can be quite frightening at times and requires a great deal of courage. Battling physical and mental illness, dealing with the loss of a loved one or the aftermath of divorce, being a victim of rape or incest, and not having enough financial resources are more than challenging circumstances. In this world, sin is ever present and, due to difficult and opposing circumstances, people, and undue hardships, we often battle mental, emotional, and physical wars daily. These battles are both inwardly and outwardly manufactured. They are mostly formed out of fear, hatred, bitterness, resentment, envy, malice, unforgiveness, disbelief, greed, covetousness, and sexual lusts. Understanding spiritual warfare helps us identify the real enemy, build mental toughness, and, most importantly, prepare us to put on our inherent spiritual armor. God's spiritual armor is a necessity since we wrestle with spiritual giants who won't rest easy until we forfeit our life and purpose. Again, "For we wrestle not against flesh and blood but against principalities, against powers, against the rulers of the darkness of this world, against spiritual wickedness in high places" (Ephesians 6:12, KJV).

As believers, we have great news in that we are not fighting alone! Once you believe in your soul's redemption through Jesus Christ, you are locked and loaded to contend against the enemy.

Growing up, I loved playing video games such as *Street Fighter*, *Mortal Kombat*, and *Tekken*. I realize I am probably dating myself a bit, but I am trying to make a point. One of the coolest features of those video games was the fighter choices. In *Mortal Kombat*, each fighter had a profile and a special skill set used to oppose their enemies. The fighter Scorpion could supernaturally turn into a snake and poison his enemy with venom by removing his mask. The fighter Sub-Zero blew ice and froze his enemy for at least three seconds to unleash a fury of combo moves on his opponent. Fighter Liu Kang could suspend himself in the air long enough to bicycle kick his opponent in the face for a good fifty feet. My personal favorite was Raiden. Raiden had gray hair and possessed features of an older man. I am sure these features were in place to indicate a level of his wisdom. Raiden was great because of his vantage point and position during fights. Raiden would strike his opponents out of their arm's or foot's reach. He stood several feet away from his opposition and then flew towards them to knock them down, similar to an eagle. He also used his telepathic powers to reposition himself in a different direction than anticipated. He essentially blindsided his enemies with brute force by anticipating their moves.

As believers, we have to tap into our spiritual gifts and realize we are not alone on the spiritual battlefield. We too have special skill sets that our Creator endowed us with to fight our enemy. When we choose to listen, we can see our enemy coming a mile away and unleash our spiritual fury and authority. The enemy will not know what hit him! It is important to know that, no matter the circumstances, you are uniquely created as a spiritual being with a supernatural genetic makeup. At your core still remains what God initially designed. You were made in His image and likeness, with creativity, divine vision, extraordinary wisdom, and His *dunamis* power. The word *dunamis* in the Greek means to possess a strength and inner power that is not dependent on external or personal, physical ability (Ephesians 6:10). It is God's desire that you take hold of this *dunamis* power to defeat His archrival while we sojourn this earth.

Tapping into this power source allows us to walk out the very vision He had for us from the foundation of the earth—a vision of dominion over everything under the heavens and the supernatural ability to create lives beyond our wildest imaginations. Your identity is uniquely connected to that vision, and from it your daily motives and actions are derived. You are no longer an ordinary individual accepting every experience that occurs to you without retaliation. You possess a supernatural power to push through any adversity and stand tall against difficult life circumstances. What you believe about yourself is key and will ultimately manifest outwardly through what you do or don't do. What God has planned for you is so powerful and impactful that the enemy and his evil spiritual forces seek ways to destroy your vision before it begins. He uses your family members, coworkers, friends, spouse, customers in the grocery line, classmates, folks in traffic, and lack of resources to get through to you and your emotions. Essentially, our wayward emotions lead to incorrect thinking and the behaviors that follow. If the devil can get you thinking incorrectly, he has an ideal opportunity to kill, steal, and destroy your joy, peace, identity, or purpose (John 10:10).

I do not intend to scare but to serve notice that there are, indeed, demonic forces that we battle daily. These spiritual forces are not presented as spooky, scary ghosts, but are found in human interactions, environmental barriers, life circumstances, cravings of the flesh, and our negative thoughts. Revelation 12:9 describes how God cast down Satan, the deceiver of the world, and his demons from heaven to earth. Satan operates in the spiritual realm, causing physical havoc here on earth. He makes accusations against you based on circumstances he creates through other people and our negative thinking about it. In one Scripture, Paul describes Satan as the prince of the power of the air. He says, "As for you, you were dead in your transgressions and sins, in which you used to live when you followed the ways of this world and of the ruler of the kingdom of the air, the spirit who is now at work in those who are disobedient. All of us also lived among them at one time" (Ephesians 2:1–3, NIV).

Falling into disobedience is easily done. As soon as we entertain a thought outside of God's will and His living word then we are sinning and operating in disobedience. You see this subtle type of sin illustrated following Jesus's revelation to Peter that He is going to die on the cross. Peter forbids Jesus to entertain such thoughts and tells Jesus that He is not going to die. Peter's response was genuine and with love. Peter's words seemed appropriate and what I'd expect a true friend to say but not to Jesus. In fact, Jesus rebukes Peter and says, "Get behind me, Satan!" (Matthew 16:23, NIV).

My initial thought was, "Wow, that seems harsh," and I questioned if Jesus was overreacting. However, I later realized that He was not overreacting. In fact, He was teaching us a lesson about understanding the power of Peter's words. Peter's response was contrary to the will of God and, therefore, words from Satan. Peter's words, if pondered long enough, could have activated doubt and fear in Jesus's heart and possibly cause Him to forfeit His divine purpose to save the world. I cannot stress enough the values of watching your words, what you are listening to, and are visually entertaining yourself with. The prince of the air and his evil forces are lurking and waiting for you to say the wrong thing and express your disbelief in the Creator.

However, there is good news for those who believe in the death and resurrection of Jesus Christ. Jesus snatched back our authority from the ruler of the air and, now in the name of Jesus, we are able to fight and defeat the enemy just as Jesus did. You must learn to play offense by putting on the whole armor of God so that you can stand against the devil's schemes (Ephesians 6:11). Your biggest offensive play is reading the Word of God and understanding how to speak during your daily spiritual fights. A valuable defense is having the shield of faith so that you can extinguish the fiery darts the enemy flings at you. Those fiery darts come in the disguise of someone's hurtful words or actions that spark negative thinking, pride, fear, and/or self-doubt. Believers in Christ are equipped with faith by hearing the Word of God (Romans 10:17). Faith stands in opposition to fear, self-doubt, pride, and negative thinking when life's circumstances contradict what God says. Life changes all the time and having faith in God helps you maintain a state of peace when chaos is swirling about.

Not only to we hear the Word of God, we also speak God's word aloud so that our inner man has a witness. The more we hear our voice speaking God's positive words of affirmation, the more easily we can drown out the lies, fear, and chaos the enemy wants us to believe. This is the way we can stop meditating and rehearsing the negative narratives we often replay about ourselves to ourselves. God is the master of the universe, and His preeminence remains uncontended. Focusing on God's defeat record sets your thinking in alignment with absolute truth, which trumps any negative feelings or thoughts you have about your own skills and abilities. You have to believe and maintain your faith in God, no matter what things may look or feel like to you with your natural eye.

Remember to fear not, for the Lord your God shall fight for you (Deuteronomy 3:22). Your world could be in shambles as we speak and seem unrepairable, but God is able to redeem the time. You may even be thinking your sin is too great for God to ever forgive you. I am here to tell you that you are wrong. Regardless of what you have done or what someone else negatively thinks about you. God is faithful to forgive you and has the final say about your salvation. Paul says there is no difference between you or a person who is righteous-minded. "For all have sinned, and come short of the glory of God" (Romans 3:23, KJV). Isn't that reassuring? When you know God's character, you know that there is no respect of person for those who believe in the justification of our sins through the atonement of Jesus Christ. Through Jesus Christ, you and I are justified from all our faults. Unfortunately, our salvation from sin is not where it ends. As I mentioned earlier, our lives have to be transformed by the renewing of our minds (Romans 12:2). Easier said than done, right?

Giants

Our justification of sin through Jesus Christ does not mean we are exempt from life's challenges and worldly temptations. These challenges and temptations sometimes feel overwhelming and present themselves as giants in our lives. Our inner spiritual man may be redeemed but our outward man is still having a natural experience. As I mentioned before, when Adam and Eve ate the fruit (information) from the tree of the knowledge of good and evil, mankind took on a sinful nature (humanness). In our humanness (natural being), we instinctively have a tendency to be more aware of our flesh, first and foremost, and are easily tempted into sin. Self-control, discipline, and overcoming the emotion of fear are some of the greatest obstacles to obtaining success in this life. Managing fleshly temptations and fear in your own strength may be difficult and sometimes seem impossible. At least it has been that way for me. I believe that learning to control our thoughts, impulses and fleshly urges is one of the greatest keys to winning in this life. Giants can be intimidating and often their appearance causes us to forfeit before we even enter the battle. Just like the Israelites, we must defeat the fear and temptation resulting from our negative thinking before entering into the promises of God.

The Old Testament is filled with examples of physical giants the people of God faced. Although many of the giants were large in stature and physically strong, God's people eventually conquered them with the help of

Jehovah. Oftentimes, God would use the most unlikely people and the most unqualified individual to accomplish his will and to defeat the enemy in battle (1 Samuel 16:7). The Bible stories presented are meant to build up believers' faith in God's ability to assist His creation in troubling and difficult circumstances. It also serves as validation that separating ourselves from Him results in us losing battles.

One popular example is in the story of young David and his miraculous slaying of the giant Goliath with a simple sling shot. Another story involves the Israelites and Caleb exploring the Promised Land. The Israelites had finally crossed over into the Promised Land after spending forty years walking in circles in the wilderness. The land was beautiful and rich but there was one problem: it was already occupied by giants and the Israelites would need to slay them in order to possess it. In Numbers 13 you read the story of the report the men came back with after Moses instructed them to explore the land. The Israelites viewed themselves as grasshoppers and were confident that the giants also viewed them as such. As grasshoppers they wouldn't be able to defeat the enemy to inherit their land. Their negative view of themselves was reflected in their words and had potential to stop them from moving forward into a new area in life. This life is described as a land flowing with milk and honey and grapes requiring two men to carry.

It's interesting to think that this negative perception of themselves would have left them in the wilderness if Caleb and Joshua hadn't stepped up and declared that they are overcomers and are able to possess the land (Numbers 13:20). These examples highlight the significance of not comparing ourselves to others because it can negatively shape our thinking. Fear, although often an illusion, appears in our lives as a terrifying force to prevent us from moving forward. Therefore, one of the biggest giants we face in life is fear.

Fear Giant

Prior to being tricked by the serpent in the garden of Eden, Adam and Eve roamed the garden freely without clothes and in close fellowship with God. They were able to eat from all trees in the garden, including the tree of the knowledge of good and evil. They were living and dwelling in the garden, but their desire was to be in the spirit. It wasn't until they ate from the forbidden tree that they realized they were naked and separated themselves from God. It was not until they had an understanding of their nakedness that they were ashamed of it. Additionally, they demonstrated their first sign of human emotion. An emotion the enemy uses to distract mankind from moving forward and obtaining the blessings of God. He uses an emotion that we've observed since that dreadful moment in the garden of Eden: "FEAR!" Genesis 3:7–10 reads like this:

> Then the eyes of both of them were opened, and they realized they were naked; so they sewed fig leaves together and made coverings for themselves. Then the man and his wife heard the sound of the Lord God among the trees of the garden. But the Lord God called to the man, "Where are you?" He answered, "I heard you in the garden, and I was afraid because I was naked; so I hid." (NIV)

It's important to ponder what is going on here. Fear and shame caused them to hide themselves and run away from God in the garden. I found it interesting that after they realized that they were naked, they immediately remedied the issue by piecing together fig leaves for garments. Adam and Eve did what mankind continues to do now when we decide to live a sinful existence: we attempt to hide and cover it up so that no one sees our fallen state. We disconnect ourselves from God or people who may remind us of what sin we are trying to cover up. We are comfortable hanging in places with others who are also hiding and will not remind us of who we were. Although Adam and Eve were now wearing clothes, they still ran away from God in fear. This shows that it was never about them being naked. Essentially, they had become aware of their flesh, but they had disconnected from their inner spirit man. Their disobedience was the sin and their coverings were like filthy rags in His presence.

Fear is the greatest separator of mankind and God. Fear is not of God and has Satan written all over it. "For God does not give us the spirit of fear, but of power and of love and of a sound mind" (2 Timothy 1:7, NKJV). It is no coincidence that the Word of God contains 365 Scriptures, which advise God's people to "fear not." Fear and faith are polar opposites of each other, and the word says, without faith it is impossible to please God. Interestingly, we have 365 days in the year and 365 Scriptures we can ponder daily to build up our faith and promote transformation of the mind. The enemy is certainly busy, but God is continuously showing us through His word that the enemy is defeated, and no amount of shame or embarrassment could keep Him from loving us. We no longer have to hide out of fear, and we can enter into His presence with our filthy rags when we believe we are forgiven. God understands man in his fallen state and sent Jesus to demonstrate this truth.

In fact, Jesus spent much of His time preaching and teaching to the sinners and to the tax collectors because God was providing a way for us to fix the sin issue once and for all. The Pharisees, teachers, and Sadducees (religious people) despised this part of Jesus's ministry because they were so greatly concerned with trying to be righteous and placing judgment on others who were not doing the same. They attempted to stringently follow rules of the law (Old Testament) and continuously failed at doing so. Just like Adam and Eve in the garden with their sewn fig leaves, they worked hard to fix the sin issue but failed. Jesus experienced much hate and rebuke for hanging with known sinners, but He was too busy tending to God's business to heed to the murmurs and complaints of His religious haters. Jesus often spoke in parables to minister about the kingdom of God to illustrate God's heart for the lost through the story of the Prodigal Son in Luke 15:11–24. It reads:

> There was a man who had two sons. The younger one said to his father, "Father give me my share of the estate." So he divided his property between them.

> Not long after that, the younger got together all he had, set off for a distant country and squandered his wealth in wild living. After he had spent everything, there was a severe famine in that whole country, and he began to be in need. So he went and hired himself

out to a citizen of that country, who sent him to his fields to feed pigs. He longed to fill his stomach with the pods that the pigs were eating but no one gave him anything.

When he came to his senses, he said "How many of my father's hired servants have food to spare, and here I am starving to death! I will set out and go back to my father and say to him: Father, I have sinned against heaven and against you. I am no longer worthy to be called your son; make me like one of your hired servants." So he got up and went to his father.

But while he was still a long way off, his father saw him and was filled with compassion for him; he ran to his son, threw his arms around him and kissed him.

The son said to him, "Father, I have sinned against heaven and against you. I am no longer worthy to be called your son."

But the father said to his servants, "Quick! Bring the best robe and put it on him. Put a ring on his finger and sandals on his feet. Bring the fattened calf and kill it. Let's have a feast and celebrate. For this son of mine was dead and is alive again; he was lost and is found." So they began to celebrate. (NIV)

It does not matter how far away you have gotten from your spiritual father or the sin you have committed. He is always seeking to find His lost sheep, sweeping to find His lost coin, or waiting with open arms to welcome home His lost son. He will leave the ninety-nine sheep to locate the one (Luke 15:4). God is constantly beckoning and encouraging us to reconnect with Him spiritually. We are His beloved, His children, and He is concerned about us. God desperately wants us to repent (turn) and commune with Him in His heavenly realm.

One of the other things that fear does is cause us to use our words unwisely. When we are afraid, we say things and subsequently do things that places a target on our backs for the enemy to attack. As I stated earlier, fear is the opposite of faith and when we speak out of the emotion of fear, we often manifest that belief outwardly. Just the same as if we speak out of faith, we see the physical manifestations of those words as well. Jesus says to the Pharisees in Matthew 12:30–31, "This is war, and there is no neutral ground. If you're not on my side, you're the enemy; if you are not helping, you're making things worse. There's nothing done or said that can't be forgiven" (MSG).

When you read a little further in verses 34–37, Jesus tells them, "It's your heart, not the dictionary, that gives meaning to your words. A good person produces good deeds and words season after season. An evil person is blight on the orchard. Let me tell you something: Every one of these careless words is going to come back to haunt you. There will be a time of reckoning. Words are powerful; take them seriously. Words can be your salvation. Words can be your damnation" (MSG). Jesus desired that we understand the value of our words so that we begin to use them in a beneficial way. We are at war and understanding how to use our words wisely is a great offensive play as spiritual warriors.

Flesh Giant

Learning to distinguish between our flesh, soul, and spirit is a must to be truly successful in this. Our body, spirit, and souls are not the same and we have to determine which one we will allow to take the lead. Man (mankind/human) is a three-dimensional being. We have our physical bodies or flesh, our soul, and then our spirit.

Naturally, our flesh seeks to take precedence over our spiritual nature since we see, hear, feel, smell, and taste with it every day. Our daily perception of this world is often through the lens of our physical bodies, our flesh. The moment we take our first breath, our sensations are bombarded with data about the world around us, whether it is cold, hot, loud, quiet, loving, or distant. Our flesh desires feelings of pleasure, euphoria, and comfort. It seeks things that feel, smell, taste, and look good. Our flesh does not want to be inconvenienced and would be content with self-gratifying and pleasure-seeking activities all day. Unfortunately, activities driven by our feelings and emotions are not always accompanied with pleasurable results and effects.

Paul says in Romans 7:14–15 that the flesh desires what is contrary to the spirit, and the spirit what is contrary to the flesh. They are in conflict with each other, so you are not able to do whatever you want to do. I like the Amplified Bible translation, which reads like this:

> We know that the Law is spiritual; but I am a creature of the flesh [worldly, self-reliant—carnal and unspiritual], sold into slavery to sin [and serving under its control]. For I do not understand my own actions [I am baffled and bewildered by them]. I do not practice what I want to do, but I am doing the very thing I hate [and yielding to my human nature, my worldliness—my sinful capacity]. (AMP)

Another Scripture, found in Galatians 5:16–21, illustrates the point of allowing the Holy Spirit to transform our inner man to look more like Christ through the developing the fruits of the spirit. In fact, I encourage you to take a moment to pick up your Bible and read these verses in their fullness before you proceed. This will help you better understand this ever-present conflict within us.

Like Paul, I have found myself in many situations where I may know the right thing to do, but struggle to execute what is right. I battle my heightened emotions of lust, pride, anger, fear, disgust, and disappointment when opportunities arise. I find it difficult to not rely on my intellect, reason, and past experiences to problem-solve, handling life's challenges when they arise. I have lost several internal fights on different occasions due to my sinful nature.

I have many examples of allowing my flesh to rule. I've acted out of pride when I felt my intellect was being challenged or I was spoken to condescendingly. I've also talked over someone to prove my point. Other times, I didn't say anything at all, while I stewed with a scornful look on my face that said, "You better not say another word to me!" While driving in my car to work, I've yelled in frustration and waved my hand in a dismissive manner at the person who cut me off without using their signal. I might not have stuck up my middle finger, but my wagging pointer finger gave them the curse of the century. I left the scene and replayed the events all the way home, becoming angrier at the audacity of the person. Before I knew it, I created an environment for a bad day.

In my singleness, I have succumbed to my feelings of loneliness and engaged in the sinful act of sexually "knowing" someone I was not married to. It may have been wrong, but at the time—it felt so right. Unfortunately, I carried emotional scars attached to the failed relationships that lay in the balance of those lustful moments. I know what the word says about anger and sexual lust, but yet my flesh screams the opposite. Controlling my mouth has also proven to be challenging. I grew up in a home where quick witted retorts were common so "clapping back" sometimes comes too easy.

Additionally, over the years I've constructed a defense mechanism for controlling getting my feelings hurt, so, I'm locked and loaded to check someone if I feel slighted or threatened. In the moment, I might feel vindicated, but the anger and frustration typically linger long past the incident and leave me emotionally drained the more I ponder on or talk about it. Unfortunately, the initial acts of sin are not always unpleasant to our bodies or souls. Often, they may be pleasurable and enjoyable! Our bodies, minds, wills, and emotions begin to crave things that have consequences we have reasoned away with poor judgment. Sex is beautiful and it was created by God to be that way, so it does feel good; however, when we act outside of a covenant, it creates a potential list of emotional, psychological, and physical problems that are sometimes difficult to reverse, like sexually transmitted diseases or an unplanned pregnancy, like mine.

Just like sex, drugs and alcohol often come in a pleasurable package. I understand the urge and temptation very well. I am sure you have seen or known someone who struggles with drug addiction or alcoholism and thought, "Why won't they just stop? Their teeth are falling out, for goodness sake," or "They cannot keep a job!" I'm sure they didn't intend to get strung out on drugs and lose everything they care about at the outset, but the initial feeling of getting high or numbing pain was worth chasing it a few more times until it became something their body craved and physically (chemical imbalance) could not do without. Although drugs are not mentioned directly in the Bible, there are several references to maintaining a sober mind in the word, especially as it relates to alcoholism. The Living Word gives us several warnings against drunkenness and the need to steer away from overindulgence of that particular vice.

One Scripture in particular explains the effects of alcohol on a person's productivity and state of mind, which are less than stable. King Solomon in Proverbs 23:29 poses these questions: "Who hath woe? Who hath sorrow? Who hath contentions? Who hath babbling? Who hath wounds without cause? Who hath redness of eyes?" (KJV). He then replies in verse 30 with this answer: "They that tarry long at the wine; they that go to seek mixed wine" (KJV). He offers wisdom afterwards in verses 31–33, advising believers with these words: "Look not upon the wine when it is red, when it giveth his colour in the cup, when it moveth itself aright. At the last it biteth like a serpent, and stingeth like an adder. Thine eyes shall behold strange women and thine heart shall utter perverse things" (KJV).

Drugs and alcohol reduce our inhibitions, which makes us susceptible to the enemy's attack through negative feelings, negative thinking, negative speaking, and, ultimately, negatively doing (or not doing). Sexism feels good in the moment but afterwards often leaves us with feelings of shame and disgust. It did for me. What initially seems fun and exciting is generally accompanied by inconvenient and unpleasant consequences. Financial strain, poverty, addiction, depression, imprisonment, and disease or no fun.

Do not be deceived. Your life's purpose is so valuable and is not worth the temporal lust and pleasure we experience in indulgence in fornication, adultery, drugs, etc. Many of the consequences we experience on earth are formed into mental strongholds, obstacles and giants we face in our daily lives. The consequence of sin and disobedience creates hardships and sometimes unnecessary challenges God would desire us to avoid. Unfortunately, giants are unrelenting, and they taunt us daily. And so we must be vigilant and purposeful in stripping their power and hold over us. Truly, there are only two paths in the end: allow the giants to slay us by stealing our identity, joy, peace, and purpose or we defeat them by embracing our spiritual identity with the help of God in Jesus's name.

There are many things that separate us from deepening our relationship with God. Primarily, it is our reasoning, wayward thinking, and disobedience that keep us away. Our fleshly desires and worldly affections will never compare to what's available to us in our father's house. As Christians, we have to understand the body, soul (mind), and spirit triad that encompasses our existence so that we can effectively train the triad with the spirit man as the lead. Renewing your mind through reading and saying God's word, praising Him for His sufficient grace, and seeking Him daily is essential to spirit-led living. It is truly the best way to conquer the giants we face in this world and live under God's supernatural grace of strength and countless blessings.

In concluding this book, I would like to reiterate this important fact. You were created for greatness and a divine calling that far exceeds your wildest dreams and imagination. The greatest way for you to discover who you are, determine your unique purpose for this planet, and get your life back on track is through the redemptive blood of Jesus Christ. People from all social and cultural backgrounds seek to find significance in this life and make sense of their existence, often settling for religion and adhering to a list of rules out of obligation.

Prayerfully, you no longer have a desire to settle into religious customs and ritualistic behaviors to satisfy your internal question of why you exist. God created you for something great and he's ready to show you what that great thing is if you allow Him to take the lead. God desires to be in relationship and to team up with you to make life easier. Jesus requests this from us in Matthew 11:28–30: "Come to me, all you who are weary and burdened, and I will give you rest. Take my yoke upon you and learn from me, for I am gentle and humble in heart, and you will find rest for your souls. For my yoke is easy and my burden is light" (NIV).

Please, allow God to do the work alongside you to help ease the burden of successfully navigating through life. Some of you reading may have already found success at tapping into your natural, God-given talents or feel like you are on the brink of beginning to do so now that you have read this book. If so, that is wonderful news! Others of you may lie somewhere in the middle with a vague understanding of what gifts you possess and how you could ever apply those talents to something tangible in this lifetime. If you are that person, continue to seek God through prayer, reading, and active listening. God will answer you and deliver on His promise to use you and connect with you if you are receptive. Moreover, if you have not done so already, please complete the online spiritual gift assessment by visiting AprilTeleeSykes.com. Understanding the area(s) in which you are naturally gifted may be beneficial to helping you navigate the purpose God created you for.

In addition to engaging in prayer and spiritual assessments, I encourage you to get active in your local church(es) and community events. Let your interests be a guide in deciding where and how you serve the local church and community. Know this: there is plenty of work but few laborers (Luke 10:2). Unfortunately, even for those with an understanding of their God-given talents and how to establish a pathway to success, it is fruitless when crowded with fear, pride, doubt, and worry. Therefore, relationship with God and seeking His presence is more valuable than using your spiritual gifts and talents for capital gain. Scripture in Jeremiah 10:23 says, "I know that the way of man is not in himself; it is not in man to direct his own steps" (NKJV).

You see this happen all the time, especially in the entertainment world, where people possess great musical, theatrical, or athletic prowess. Just tune in to an episode of *Unsung* or the cable channel E! to observe how the person who looks to have it all struggles with issues of identity and self-worth. Some entertainers, business moguls, and athletes have these awesome careers with millions of fans and admirers, but, somehow, their careers and/or even their lives are abruptly shamefully ended due to substance abuse, mental anguish, or some other misfortune. From the outside looking in, it appears they have it all and you may wonder, "Why on earth would they squander away such a beautiful opportunity or the ideal life away?" You may even ask yourself, as you scratch your head, "What am I missing here?" The answer is not what you are missing but who they are missing.

Relationship with God is the missing piece of the puzzle. No matter what life you create, it will never be fully complete until that missing link is connected and reestablished to God's heavenly kingdom on earth. The weapons of spiritual warfare are not carnal (flesh) but mighty through God for the pulling down of strongholds (mental hang-ups) and spiritual wickedness in high places (2 Corinthians 10:4). God helps us clean up our stinky thinking with His truth and abolish the lies spoken to us by the enemy. Do not be deceived into believing that because you may go to church, your puzzle piece is magically found, and you are exempt from warfare. Remember, spiritual relationship is the goal not church attendance. There's no amount of money and weekly church attendance that can assist you with winning a spiritual fight. It is vain and empty without a solid relationship of trust, obedience, and reliance.

Like I mentioned earlier, I had been going to church since the second grade and did not realize my spiritual inheritance until I was thirty-five years old. Don't be like me; the sooner you become spiritually mature, the greater your outcomes will be. My life has been greatly enhanced since I've learned to allow God to help lead my daily steps. God has given us the recipe for success with His written word on how to truly win and be successful in this life. I am not without my challenges, but I truly sense God's hand and strength in my weakness. Throughout Scripture, God illustrates this point at varying times in our lives as we learn to rely on our faith in God and turn to Him for direction and guidance to overcome life's challenges.

He showed us first with Noah, then with Abraham, Moses, Daniel, Ruth, David, Paul, and a host of others, how relationship and trust in God produces great results in this life (Hebrews 12). Most importantly, He gifted us with the witness of our Lord and Savior, Jesus Christ, who provided the ideal demonstration of what being in a familial relationship with God produces. John 3:16 says, "For God so loved the world, that he gave his only begotten Son, that whosoever believeth in him should not perish but have everlasting life" (KJV). Jesus is the way, the truth, and the life (John 14:6). He is the life that man was not able to partake of following our disobedience and fall into sin in the garden of Eden. When God kicked Adam and Eve out the garden, they no longer had access to the tree of life, and mankind struggled throughout their lives to find atonement from their sins through their own efforts of annual animal sacrifices and other possessions. We now live under the covenant of grace and Jesus serves as the ultimate sacrifice.

We are now reconciled with God to experience deeper intimacy with Him through the gift of the Holy Spirit sent as a helper following Jesus's death. Hebrews 4:16 says, "Let us then approach God's throne of grace with confidence, so that we may receive mercy and find grace to help us in our time of need" (NIV). Jesus's blood serves as a buffer for our sins and offers mankind access to God and His unfailing grace every day not only on Sunday. God designed for us all to reflect His very own image as spiritual beings (Genesis 1:26). Jesus Christ provides the way and channel back to a spiritual relationship with our heavenly Father once and for all. No more need for religious and ritualistic acts to prove our worthiness. No more covering our shame and guilt when we enter into His presence. We enter into His presence boldly, as lions! We are confident that He forgives us of our sins when we believe and confess His word over our lives. God loves you, wants you, and desires you no matter the sin. That is the Good News!

God has so much He wants to get to us if we learn to operate in His spiritual nature and resist the desire to succumb to our personal belief systems and the challenges we face in the natural realm. Our father is rich in goodness, and to experience His presence is euphoric. There's not one negative label we can internalize inside our heads and identify with that He is not able to erase. Everything we are is demolished, restored, or amplified into greatness when we allow God to come in and tell us who we really are. Yes, our past provides the groundwork for our individual personalities, but, without a makeover in Christ, our personality lacks true flavor. The character of Jesus

Christ becomes our seasoning, our salt, the accent. This is why we are able to be salt and light in the world (Matthew 5:13). Our natural being stands out a little more when we add Jesus's super to our natural (supernatural). Without the Holy Spirit guiding us daily, we risk our perspectives and behaviors being deeply influenced by worldly ideals. Essentially, we begin to blend in and look like everyone else. Our shine is dimmed when we resemble those operating under a worldview perspective.

Although those in the world may appear content and put together outwardly, they seek light as well and are drawn to the difference inside of us. Many people are hurting and seeking answers for peace in all the wrong places, such as drugs, money, dating relationships, status, and careers. With so many people looking for the answer, show them the solution. Show them God's solution. Show them LOVE. Love drowns out fear. This is a difficult task when we blend in with the crowd, looking and sounding like everyone else around with our negative complaining and murmuring about things we don't like or fear. God needs you to stand out! No matter the level of darkness our culture experiences, our speck of light offers an exit and a pathway into something more beautiful than the world can offer. Light offers a dying world peace! Peace calms storms, peace calms an unsettled soul, peace resolves depression, and peace provides assurance that, although we have endured for a night, joy comes in the morning.

He has a great work lying dormant inside of you. Get ready for when He begins to share His thoughts about you with plans to prosper you, to give you hope and a future (Jeremiah 29:11). The feelings of guilt, shame, defeat, and pride are shattered in His presence and the lies from the enemy are exposed. The person you thought you were is now history. Transformation is inevitable when you have a true encounter with God. Our transformation becomes intensified the more time we spend with God and allow Him to be the reigning voice in our lives. God encounters are transformative, and Scripture gives us many accounts of God dismantling a trajectory misaligned with His purpose and giving the person a new name and vision. He did it to Saul on the road to Damascus when He changed his name to Paul. He did it to Abram when He changed his name to Abraham, meaning "father of many nations":

> When Abram was ninety-nine years old, the Lord appeared to him and said, "I am God Almighty; walk before me faithfully and be blameless. Then I will make my covenant between me and you and will greatly increase your numbers."

> Abram fell facedown, and God said to him, "As for me, this is my covenant with you: You will be the father of many nations. No longer will you be called Abram; your name will be Abraham, for I have made you a father of many nations." (Genesis 17:1–5, NIV)

God will change your name! In fact, He needs to change your name. Who we were in our past is not as relevant as where God wants to take us. You are a fearfully and wonderfully made; you are prosperous; you are beautiful; you are a fighter; you are a warrior; and you are victorious! I can testify to the transformative power of the Word of God. It transformed me. It is the Word of God that makes an adulterous husband return home to his wife and family, the prostitute say never again will my body be sold for money, the drug dealer and gang banger put down his gun, the addict flush their product down the toilet, the alcoholic pour their drink down the drain, and the sinner man find his way back home to his heavenly Father.

No doubt, a hurting and anxious world needs to hear your story to be inspired by your testimony of salvation and redemption. Remember that God's redemptive plan puts us in right standing with Him as a relational friend and child. This redemptive plan remains in place, no matter what sin you may have committed or may commit in the future. Your heart is what He desires, and He will teach you His ways to help you overcome the spiritual attacks, mental baggage, and hurdles that prevent you from enjoying a beautiful relationship with Him.

He desires for you to be a partaker of His kingdom and join in His army of believers to defeat our adversaries. We defeat the enemy and his divisive schemes to destroy us when we know the TRUTH, learn to trust God over everything else, and when we fully understand our identity in Him! Elevate your relationship with Jesus Christ and your Creator so that He can continuously reveal your purpose and identity to you. Jesus has already won the battle and, therefore, we are standing on the winning side in all circumstances against the enemy. Walk in your inherent victory and dominion over this world, brothers and sisters. It is yours for the taking. May you continue to grow into everything God ordained for you from the foundation of this earth.

Peace and blessings!